NOT AN ORCHID...

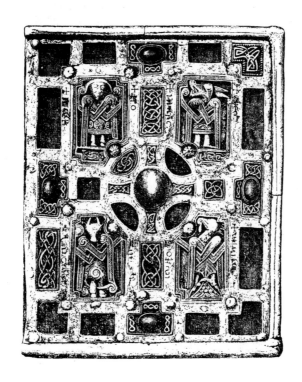

Hugh Dan MacLennan
Kessock Communications
1995

Design, origination and layout by Hiscan Ltd,
Inverness, Scotland.

Printed by Highland Printers,
Inverness.

Published by Kessock Communications,
North Kessock, Inverness.

A catalogue record for this book is
obtainable from the British Library.

ISBN 0 9526195 0 4

Chuidich Comhairle nan leabhraichean am foillsichear le cosgaisean an leabhair seo

Fhuaras taic bho na buidhnean a leanas cuideachd ann a bhith a' foillseachadh an leabhair seo:

Comunn na Gàidhlig

Comadaidh Gàidhlig Chomhairle Sgìreil an Eilein Sgiathanaich

Comadaidh Telebhisein Gàidhlig (CTG)

Comunn Gàidhlig Inbhirnis

Pròiseict Nàiseanta nan Ealan Gàidhlig (NGAP)

Urras NicUaig

The publisher gratefully acknowledges financial assistance from the following:

Comunn na Gàidhlig

The Gaelic Books Council

Gaelic Committee, Skye and Lochalsh District Council

Gaelic Society of Inverness

Gaelic Television Committee

Governors of Catherine McCaig's Trust

National Gaelic Arts Project

FOR

KATHLEEN

DO CHONNRADH NA GAEDHEILGE

A Chonnradh chaoin, a Chonnradh chòir,
Rinn obair mhòr gan òr gan cabhair,
Glacaidh an cios a dlighim daoibh,
Guidhim, glacaidh go caoimh mo leabhar.

A chàirde clèibh is iomadh là
D'oibrigheamar go breàgh le chèile,
Gan clampar, agus fòs gan èad,
'S dà mhèad àr dteas, gan puinn di-chèille.

Chuireabhar sùil 'san bhfear bhi dall,
Thugabhar cluas don fhear bhi bodhar,
Glacaidh an cios do bheirim daoibh,
- Guidhim, glacaidh go caoimh mo leabhar.

[A Literary History of Ireland - Douglas Hyde]

*"Cumaidh sinn suas an cluidh-iomain,
Cluidh is grinn' a tha fo'n ghrèin".*

There is for every nation a history, which does not respond to the trumpet call of battle, which does not limit its interests to the conflict of dynasties. This - the history of intellectual growth and artistic achievement - of less romantic than the popular panorama of kings and queens, finds its material in imperishable masterpieces, and reveals to the student something at once more vital and picturesque than the quarrels of rival parliaments. Nor is it in any sense uncscientific to shift the point of view from politics to literature. It is but a fashion of history which insists that a nation lives only for her warriors, a fashion which might long since have been ousted by the commonplace reflection that, in spite of history, the poets are the true masters of the earth. If all record of a nation's progress were blotted out, and its literature were yet left us, might not we recover the outlines of lost history?

[A Literary History of Ireland - Douglas Hyde]

*"We will keep up the shinty play,
the finest game under the sun"*

ACKNOWLEDGEMENTS

Lean gu dlùth ri cliù bhur sinnsire

Completing the formal list of acknowledgements for an undertaking such as this is almost as daunting a task as producing the book itself.

My appreciation of the financial contributions made to the production by various organisations is recorded elsewhere. Suffice to say here that I am extremely grateful for their assistance. *Not an Orchid* would never have seen the light of day without them.

It is unfair perhaps to single out individuals, but I owe a great debt to the following for their advice and material which was most gratefully received: first and foremost my good friend Brendan Harvey, Belfast and his wife Anna for their unfailing advice, assistance and hospitality; Gordon Gilchrist, Ayr; special thanks to Jack Richmond, Newtonmore for permission to use material from his unique archive of the game and also for his advice; Hugh Barron, Inverness once again for his outstanding scholarship, attention to detail and patience in proofing the whole book virtually single-handedly; John Willie Campbell, Gorthleck for access to his own unique collection of records of the game; Murdo MacDonald, Archivist, Argyll and Bute District Council; Coll MacDougall of Oban; The School of Scottish Studies; Lorna Pike, Dictionary of the Scottish Language; Miss Marion Campbell of Kilberry; Fred MacAulay, Inverness; Martin MacDonald, Inverness; Neil Matheson and Willie MacDonald for their piping expertise; Aberdeen University shinty club; and many others.

From distant shores I received great help from Dr Cliff Cumming of Deakin University, Geelong, Victoria, Australia, and Professor John Reid of St Mary's University in Halifax, Nova Scotia. I trust that by their efforts the international horizons of shinty and hurling have been pushed ever further afield. As will be apparent from the following pages however, there is no sense here of breaking new territory. We were merely following in the footsteps of our fathers.

I am indebted also to the proprietors, editors and staff of various newspapers who have assisted in this project with their usual courtesy and understanding, and who also gave permission for material to be used: *The Inverness Courier; West Highland Free Press; The Oban Times; Badenoch and Strathspey Herald*. I should also thank the Shinty Yearbook comittee for their help and permission to quote freely from that most valuable source.

No anthology can be produced without the assistance of library staff. Their expertise and patience continues to amaze me. I am particularly grateful to the following: the National Library of Scotland which is one of this nation's greatest assets; The Mitchell Library, Glasgow, particularly the Glasgow Room; Aberdeen University and most of all the Special Collections staff; Belfast City Library, Inverness Library, and in particular the staff in the Reference Section.

The collection would not be what it is without the outstanding contribution of four people in visual terms: Simon Fraser of Inverness for his fabulous illustrations which were specially commissioned in most instances and also his contribution

Glenmorangie CAMANACHD CUP Final 1994 - 4 JUNE - BUGHT PARK
Fort William 1 Kyles Athletic 3

The year was 1994,
The Kyles went North again,
To win the ancient Shinty Cup,
From the wild Lochaber men.

The papers said - 'Forget it lads',
Hugh Dan was to the fore,
The Cup is going Fort Williams way,
T'will be a handsome score.

But the lads of Kyles weren't listening,
They hadn't read the script,
Hugh Dan and all his minions,
Were sadly cast adrift.

The game began with pressure,
From Fort William strong and fit,
But the lads in blue ne'er wilted,
As they dealt with every hit.

Then Kyles began to settle,
The ball flew up the park,
And Tommy, Dan and Kenny,
In the centre made their mark.

T'was Lochaber's turn to suffer,
And suffer soon they did,
Our wingèd footed Peter,
Left MacMillan good as dead.

How we cheered our gallant heroes,
Both at Inverness and home,
As the dream of shinty glory,
Dawned upon us - everyone.

The boys in blue went pressing on,
To help increase the score,
And tho' the Fort tried all they knew,
They were shaken to the core.

A slip from Tommy on the wing,
Sent Peter running free,
MacMillan stopped him with his stick,
The ref blew up - 'a penalty' quo' he,

A silence fell amongst us all,
As Corky lined it up,
A Nic|olson wouldn't let us down,
In the final of the cup.

Argyllshire cheers then rent the sky,
Two goals were just the ticket,
Hugh Dan and all his doubting crew,
Were on a sticky wicket.

When half-time came we were informed,
Of what the Fort would do,
They'd use the wind, their skilful men,
Would make the Kyles feel blue.

For just a while, they did assault,
Our goal with feint and sally,
But Kenny, Andy, Fraser and the halfs,
Stood firm 'gainst every rally.

At last a goal went in our net,
Hugh Dan was in his glory,
A matter of time he told us now,
Till the Fort concludes the story.

But alas! for him he reckoned not,
Midst all his ifs and buts,
It's called tradition in the game,
In the Kyles we call its guts.

So the gallant twelve just buckled to,
With the help of Norm and Andy,
But the endless sweeping Northern tide,
Failed to shake Big Andy.

Two men stood out in all the storm,
Red Ron and Dan MacRae,
The spirit of the men from Kyles,
Was sure to win the day.

As time passed by the boys in blue,
Kept up the breakneck pace,
Until again our flyer Pete,
Won yet another race.

Once more the ball was
blasted home,
The score was three to one,
Hugh Dan agreed the game
was lost,
The Fort's cup hopes were
done.

The whistle went, the game
was o'er,
The boys in triumph stood,
As David raised the cup aloft,
Our hearts with pride overflowed.

Of all the men who played that day,
On the Bught's green grassy sward,
Big Andy's medal was the crown,
T'was Kyles supreme award.

So as we join to celebrate,
This team that was terrific,
From North to South from East to West,
The Toast is - 'KYLES ATHLETIC'.

(with thanks to HRM)

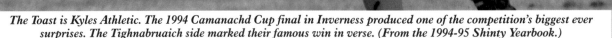

The Toast is Kyles Athletic. The 1994 Camanachd Cup final in Inverness produced one of the competition's biggest ever surprises. The Tighnabruaich side marked their famous win in verse. (From the 1994-95 Shinty Yearbook.)

Derrynane Abbey, Waterville, Co. Kerry, by John Foggarty, engraved by R. Havell, London. (1831). This aquatint with hand-colouring shows the ancestral home of Daniel O'Connell, with The Liberator depicted hat-in-hand in the foreground. With thanks to the National Library of Ireland. (From Treasures from the National Library of Ireland, edited by Noel Kissane, The Boyne Valley Honey Company, 1994.)

through ilustrations taken from *Sgàthach - the warrior queen*; Chris Tyler for his brilliant contribution to shinty lore over the years through his cartoons. The new ones he produced for the Orchid at the drop of the hat were, as ever, humorous in the extreme and full of character. Ewen Weatherspoon performed minor miracles copying old photographs and other material; and the redoutable Gordon Gillespie who often came to my assistance when I needed to capture the sense of drama and action that only shinty and hurling can provide. My thanks also to Trevor Martin, Inverness, for the front cover picture.

I am obviously also in the debt of many other photographers and illustrators too numerous to thank individually. I have not been able to contact them all prior to publication. I trust they will accept my indulgence as a failing on my part and a tribute to their own work.

Likewise it has not been possible to elict a response from a number of other authors, publishers and other agencies whose work is reproduced here. I trust no-one will take offence in the circumstances. All contributions have been graciously and faithfully acknowledged and included without alteration.

I would like to thank David Beck of the Inverness Courier for his assitance via his computer skills which kept me functioning at a crucial stage of the project and finally the staff at Hiscan, Inverness, who performed their usual miracles on the text with a patience and fortitude which seems to know no bounds. My thanks to Steve Conner, Aileen Snody and Iain Campbell in particular. This was not their first book on shinty. They probably fear that it will not be their last.

This volume was a hugely ambitious project for me personally to undertake given its nature and the circumstances under which I labour daily. I should also thank my friends, family and colleagues, particulary at the BBC in Inverness for their infinite patience in trying circumstances. There were times when the BBC studios must have appeared to be no more than a *poste restante* office for contributions being sent from far and wide. My periods of prolonged disappearance and and insistence on talking about nothing else apart from "The Book" are now, I trust, fully explained. My thanks too to the staff of Comunn na Gàidhlig for their assistance, particularly with photocopying.

I must finally thank my wife Kathleen for her continued support. When we first met, I was producing my first major production on shinty. She got more than she bargained for when she married me. Her diligence on the computer has been invaluable and I have no hesitation in dedicating the finished product to her.

My apologies to anyone I may have missed out, but every contribution to this book, no matter how small, was greatly appreciated.

All those named above are, of course, absolved from any of the blame for sins of ommission and commission perpetrated between these covers. Responsibility for these and any errors of fact which may have crept in despite my best efforts rest with me alone as editor.

Hugh D. MacLennan
September, 1995

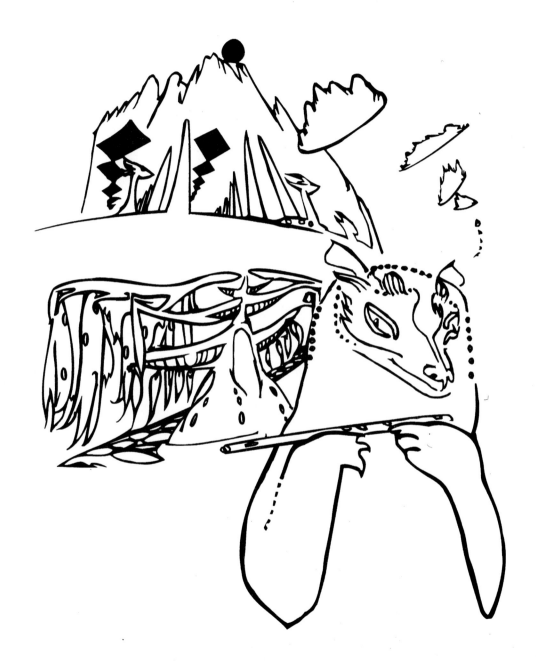

The Littlejohn Album, frontspiece. With grateful thanks to Aberdeen University shinty club. The illustrated album accompanying the Littlejohn Vase, is one of shinty's most beautiful artefacts. The imposing trophy is played for annually by the university shinty teams. A copy of the album is held by the Gaelic Society of Inverness in their collection in Inverness library. The original is held by Aberdeen University.

The Campbell scroll, presented by Kingussie Camanachd club to their Honorary Secretary John Campbell, who became the first Secretary of the Camanachd Association.

ROIMH-RÀDH

Gur binn a sheinneas glòir nan caman!

Dhèirich an leabhar seo a rùn a bha gam bhuaireadh bho chionn fhada - barrachd a dhèanamh gus an litreachas, an ceòl agus na h-òrain a tha an luib na camanachd a sgaoileadh chun mhòr-shluaigh, ann an dreach a bhiodh an dà chuid iomchaidh agus goireasach.

Cha ghabh aon leabhar sgrìobhadh a tha a' mìneachadh dè th'anns a' chamanachd agus dè seòrsa saoghal anns am bheil (agus anns an robh) an gèam a' tighinn beò.

Ach an seo tha mi air oidhirp a dhèanamh air saoghal na camanachd - gu sònraichte ann an Alba agus ann an Eireann - a mhìneachadh dhan mhòr-chuid. Chan e cruinneachadh a th'ann dhen h-uile càil a chaidh a sgrìobhadh riamh mu chamanachd - ach ann an dòigh cha mhòr nach e. Tha mi air stuth dhen h-uile gnè a tharraing a diofar raointean de dh'eachdraidh nan Gàidheal. Agus mar a dh'aithnicheas sibh, tha an saoghal sin gu math nas fharsainge na dìreach criochan Alba agus Eireann.

Bu chòir dhomh cuideachd a chur nar n'aire gu bheil mi air an t-seann litreachadh a ghlèidheal 'sa'chumantas - anns an t-seadh nach do rinn mi ach fìor bheag de sgioblachadh air gin de na pìosan a tha mi a' foillseachadh an seo.

Air a h-uile oisean ann an saoghal na Gàidhlig tha cunnartan an luib litreachadh agus gnàthasan-cainnte. Cha deach mi am bogadh cus an sin. Cha b'e leisge sam bith a bu choireach ach sdòcha dìth-misneachd, ach bha mi cuideachd son dìlseachd a nochdadh do gach ùghdar is bàrd a chaidh romham. Siad na faclan aca fhèin a th'air na duileagan a leannas, mar sgriobh is mar a lìbhrig iad fhèin iad sna làithean a dh'fhalbh. Carson a rachainn-sa a dheanamh oidhirp sam bith piseach a thoirt air stuth a tha cho eireachdail agus cho prìseil?

INTRODUCTION

The inspiration for this collection arrived, as these things tend to, in a way which can, at best, be described as roundabout and slightly mysterious. I am indebted principally to Professor Allan Macinnes of the Department of Economic History, Aberdeen University. Had he not persuaded me in slightly dubious circumstances to finally take the plunge and return once again to the status of student, the Orchid might never have flowered. I am indebted to him for his advice, persuasion and continuing commitment. As the finest shinty player ever to don the colours of St Andrews University, it is fitting that he should play a part in the final production.

I am also indebted to another anthlogy, George Bruce and Frank Rennie's *The land out there* (Aberdeen University Press, 1991) for no small measure of inspiration. I had always wanted to write the "complete" and definitve work on shinty. That is, as I discovered at a very early stage in my career as a fledgling author, an impossible ideal.

The land out there, however, comes close to providing an ideal at which to aim. I am happy to admit that I have modelled this collection on it in many ways and I would highly recommend it to anyone wanting to know more about the natural forces, "humours and contrary opinions" which make us what we are - Gaels and Scots, people of the land, with sport as one of our all-embracing and most crucial influences.

Not and Orchid is in many ways similar to *The land out there*. They have much in common, but they are at the same time very different. They are both, in their own ways, about people. Without the people - in the Orchid's case the many players and heroes who have graced Gaelic life - from Cù Chulainn to Somhairle MacIllEain and many more - neither collection could have been produced.

I should say that in terms of the minefield that is Gaelic spelling and orthography, I have retained the original in all the articles, poems etc quoted. I have been faithful to all the originals in that they have been reproduced in their pristine form. That was not from any laziness on my part, but from a wish to present all the material in its truest and most original manifestation.

I have also not, as a rule, provided translations of the Gaelic material. There are two reasons for this: firstly the crucially limiting factor of space; and secondly the fact that to reproduce many of them in translation would lose much of the original effect and quality. They were, after all, Gaelic first and foremost and it is not for me to tamper with them in any respect, other than to offer them to as wide an audience as possible, while remaining faithful to the orginal.

Sweeter than anything the smack of the caman on a flying ball!

Celebrations! Fort William shinty club won the Camanachd Association Challenge Trophy for the first time in 1992 at Old Anniesland in Glasgow. This stunning picture capturing their celebrations was taken by Coll MacDougall, shinty correspondent of The Times, who had split his trousers and remained in the stand, almost accidentally capturing this unique shot.

Ewen Weatherspoon's evocative representation of shinty as an organised sport, celebrating the centenary of the game's ruling body, the Camanachd Association, in 1993.

CONTENTS

SCHINNIE/SHINNIE/SHINY/SHINYE, N,

(schinnie,)/shinnie/ shiny/ shinye, n,

[Obscure. Cf. Gaelic sinteag a skip, a pace, later Scots shinty (1769) the game, (1773) the stick, 18th century English shinney (1794) the stick.] A game played with a stick curved at one end like a hockey stick and used for striking a ball; also, the stick itself. [With respectt to the Kirk-yeard, that ther be no playing at golf, carrict, shinnie (Liber Coll. Glasgow, p. lxviii shinny], in the High Kirk, or Kirjk-yard, or Blackfriar Kirk- yeard, either Sunday or week day; 1589 Glasgow Kirk S. 16 Oct. in Wodrow Life of Mr David Weems 14 in Biog. Coll. II (Maitland Club 1845).] The bairnes of France have the exercise of the tap, the pery, the cleking, and (instead of our gouf, which they know not) they have shinyes; 1665-7 Lauder Journal, 125, He did transub Himself to ball; the Parliament to club, Which will him holl when right teased at ane blow Or els Sir Patrick will be the shinnie goe; c 1690 Bk. Pasquils 181.

[Dictionary of the Older Scottish Tongue, (ongoing), University of Edinburgh.]

Dave Anderson of Kingussie with Ali MacKintosh of Glenurquhart in hot pursuit in the 1988 Glenmorangie Camanachd Cup Final.

FOR THE UNINITIATED

"Camanachd is not an orchid; nor is it a new biological eccentricity, nor the latest freak of pathological nomenclature. It is a recreation. In Scotland there are three games which can best claim to be native to the soil - golf, curling and shinty and the greatest of these is shinty, whereof the Gaelic name is camanachd...."

[From The Globe, 1893.]

From Bede's Life of St Cuthbert. The Saint was "too fond of games" as a boy.

Shinty - or camanachd as it is traditionally known in the Gaelic-speaking West Highlands - is an ancient game. Introduced to North-West Scotland along with Christianity and the Gaelic language nearly two thousand years ago by Irish missionaries (St Columba is said to have arrived on these shores as a result of some shenanigans at an Irish hurling match), the game can safely lay claim to being Scotland's national sport.

There is no doubt that shinty was popular at various stages virtually nation-wide. It is to be found from the wind-swept rocks of St Kilda to the more hospitable and gentler plains of the Borders. Indeed, it is claimed that golf was born out of shinty players practising, alone or in pairs, the art of driving the ball with the caman, or stick

The game is also to be found on a much wider plain - the world-wide stage with exiles taking shinty to the furthest flung corners of the globe - from South America to the war-ravaged wastes of Europe through two world wars, to the two dozen camain issued to the battalions of the Lovat Scouts during the Boer War, to the Maritime region of Canada, where the game was re-introduced in 1991 by a party of players from the Kingussie and Skye clubs.

The Exiles' spectacle: The Club of True Highlanders playing shinty on Blackheath common in London, in the early nineteenth century.

Shinty, as with many other aspects of Highland heritage and the Gaelic language in particular has been frequently threatened, both by Statute and under the influence of other movements in society. That the game has survived the combined assaults of Royal edicts against popular and "uncontrollable" games, as well as the Sabbatarianism which followed the Reformation and outlawed the playing of sports on the day of rest, not to mention the rapid erosion of the Highland way of life as described by historians such as Jim Hunter and Roger Hutchinson in his excellent history of the game Camanachd!, (Mainstream, 1989) is a tribute to the people involved in the setting up of the organisation which drew this "intriguing web of wayward strands" together one hundred years ago - the Camanachd Association, shinty's ruling body.

A series of hugely interesting and memorable exhibitions matches 100 years ago were the immediate catalyst leading to the formation of the Association which has seen the game develop from a series of loosely organised (and sometimes barely organised) clubs and structures, into an efficiently run and progressive organisation (although it has had its moments of farce and crisis!) with some forty clubs competing on a regular basis; commanding national media attention and significant sums of sponsorship, both from commercial organisations such as The Glenmorangie Distillery Company, who became involved in the sport in the 1970s, multi national fish-farmers Marine Harvest who sponsor the national leagues, and local authorities such as Highland Regional Council who have made significant investments in funds to enable clubs to improve their facilities.

Shinty in its organised form has come a long way since it fought to survive in the glens of the Highlands and much further afield, in public parks as far from its main heartland as Wimbledon, Manchester, Cottonopolis and even in Grampian Region where the Aberdeen North of Spey Club appears to have been one of the earliest formed, in the 1840s.

The Highlands of Scotland were, and still are, the heartland of shinty, though there was feverish activity in shinty terms on both sides of the border, in a fantasy world of Celtic twilight.

camamhil, see camomhail.
caman, -ain, pl. -ain [& camanan,] Club for playing shinty, hurley, or golf. Not a cricket-bat, as given in some dictionaries, as *cam an* must have a curve in it. 2(DU) see cam. ag, 4.
——achd. *s.f.* Shinty, hurley, golf.

Camán, -áin, pl. id., m., a bend ; a stick with a crooked head ; a hurley for ball-playing ; c. baíre, id. (B.).

shinty *shin'ti*, shinny *shin'i*, ns. a game like hockey, of Scottish origin, played by teams of 12: the slim curved club (the caman, also shin'ty-stick) or leather-covered cork ball (or substitute) used therein. [Perh. from Gael. *sinteag*, a bound, pace.]

iomain, *pr.pt.* ag iomain, *v.a.* Urge, drive slowly as cattle. 2 Toss, whirl, roll. 3 Conduct. 4** Drive anything forward on the ground, kick forward, as a football. 5 Play as at shinty, football, or any driving game. Iomainidh iad, *they shall drive* ; 'gan i, 'sa chath, *driving them backward in battle* ; am bheil thu dol a dh' iomain ? *are you going to play!* ciod e an iomain ? *what game !* ; a dh' i. ohaman, am ball iomain, or am ball iomanach, *shinty*.
iomain, -e & -each, -ean, *s. f.* Driving, act of driving or urging. 2 Drove of black cattle. 3 Tossing, act of tossing. 4 Whirling, rolling. 5‡‡ Crowd. 6** Drove of sheep. 7**Sounder of swine. Ag i—, *pr.pt.* of iomain. Gach i. leatha féin, *each drove by itself* ; a' leantuinn nan iomaine, *following the droves* ; lorg-iomain or slat-iomain, *an ox-goad* ; is leòir a tha thu a' gabhail iomain, *you are being driven back badly.*
iomain-cuain, *a.* Driven by the storm.

It was usual in the Highlands, however, to have the principal games of shinty at New Year or Old New Year. In these contests, often between two districts or parishes, there was no limit to the numbers taking part with players arriving and departing at will, and often play continued from the forenoon until darkness fell.

In many districts, the game died out however towards the middle of last century, but tended to continue in places such as Badenoch, Lochaber and Strathglass where interest never waned and the annual "cluidh-ball" was kept up, even into the present century.

The modern, organised form of shinty therefore is only to be found from the mid to later 19th century. By this time there had been a considerable drift of Highlanders into the towns and cities of the south and clubs began to be formed as a means of retaining territorial identity, as well as for social reasons.

By the end of the century, greater mobility, mainly due to improved means of transport, helped to make shinty more popular and gradually games began to be organised between clubs located at considerable distances apart. Gradually the local rivalries began to be replaced with a more competitive, ambitious atmosphere.

The earliest mention of an organised club (an exception, as it was in existence in the first half of the 19th century), seems to be that in the *Inverness Courier* of January 11, 1849, where it is reported that the members of the North of Spey Shinty Club, Aberdeen met on the links on January 1st "for conducting the long established Celtic game". The players were divided into two sides and hail keepers (goal keepers) appointed.

Their coats were then taken off and the ball thrown up, the play continuing for nearly two hours. Those wearing "red signals" were the winners. In the afternoon, led by a piper, the whole company proceeded to the North of Scotland Hotel for a repast, after which Mr Sutherland, who was chairman, complimented the club on the orderly manner in which the contest was played. The various shinty reports in the *Highlander* newspaper between 1874 and 1881 indicate that the earliest clubs were outwith the Highlands in Edinburgh, Glasgow, London and even in Manchester and Bolton. An account is also given of a game in Birmingham in connection with the Celtic Society in that city in December, 1878.

The oldest club then in existence was the one in Edinburgh "Cuideachd Chamanachd Dhun-Eideann". On January 1st 1874, the annual game was held in the Queen's Park, the day being as boisterous as on the occasion of the clubs' first match with the 93rd Regiment (The Sutherland Highlanders) two years before.

It was a club rule to play on New Year's day, however bad the weather. The players began to assemble at noon and the time was called at 3pm. The Chief, MacDonnell of Morar, was present along with honorary members including Sheriff Nicolson and D. MacKenzie, Advocate. "A great and enthusiastic crowd thronged the park".

Shinty is being dragged, often kicking and screaming, into the 21st century. Developments such as Team Sport Scotland's initiatives sees shinty once again making inroads into many of the urban areas where, 100 years ago, it was played with gusto.

Skye Camanachd versus Newtonmore in the 1990 Glenmorangie Camanachd Cup Final.

Shinty is at a cross-roads, or perhaps more accurately stuck on a roundabout. The game's dilemma is whether to promote the ancient sport of the Gael as a modern, vibrant sport, or to preserve it as a quaint aspect of Highland culture. It is all too often in many areas, dependent on the efforts of a small number of hugely dedicated individuals. Its state continues to be fragile at best.

It has, after all survived the ravages of two World Wars and the many economic disasters which have beset the Highlands - decisions taken by executives of multi-national oil companies in the US, or Admirals of their navy to sail for home. The falling birth-rate and school closures are other historical afflictions to have assailed the sport.

It should not, however, be beyond the wit and wisdom of the administrators who have inherited the responsibility of running what is regarded, quite rightly in my view, by its participants as the greatest game in the world. For life-force and continuing success however, the game must continue to aspire to skill and spectacle at the highest level. If these remain as the guiding inspiration of its administrators and truly amateur participants, then shinty will maintain the traditions which were founded many thousands of years ago and have stood the test of time. It will also remain one of Scotland's truly national assets.

Ronald Ross (left) shinty's national of player the year, 1995.

THE SOCIAL BACKGROUND OF CELTIC LIFE

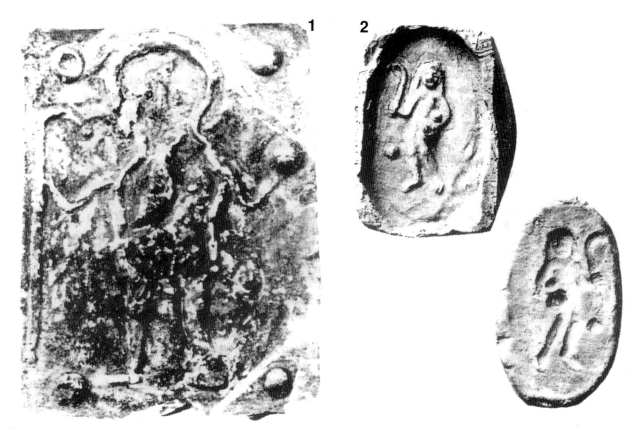

Figures with carved sticks and balls:
1 part of a ritual crown, Hockwold-cum-Wilton, Norfolk, England; 2 pottery mould, Kettering, Northamptonshire, England.

Some sorts of boards were very popular, and no doubt helped to pass the long evenings. Field games were also encouraged; like rugby football in the public schools of today, the sons and foster-sons of the nobility were taught to play at an early age. The hero Cù Chulainn excelled at such games. A nice description of his sports equipment is given in the *Tàin*. Just as Culwch, in the *Mabinogion*, sets out to find his cousin Arthur's Court and establish himself there, so in the *Tàin*, Cù Chulainn sets out, against his mother's will, to find Macha and become a member of the King's household; for the King, Conochobar, is his mother's brother:

The boy went forth and took his playthings. He took his hurley stick of bronze and his silver ball; he took his little javelin for casting and his toy spear with its end sharpened by fire; and he began to shorten the journey by playing with them. He would strike his ball with the stick, and drive it a long way from him. Then with a second stroke he would throw his stick so that he might drive it a distance no less than the first. He would throw up his javelin and would cast his spear, and would make a playful rush after them. Then he would catch his hurley stick and his ball and his javelin; and before the end of his spear had reached the ground he would catch its tip aloft in the air.

So, juggling in this carefree fashion, the hero-to-be makes his way to his uncle's Court to seek his fortune and cement his fate. When he comes to Emain Macha the little boys of the Court are playing hurley; he outrages them by not observing the prohibition that it is taboo for anyone who comes on to their playing-field without first securing their protection. They all attack him, but he makes short work of them - 150 boys, in fact. Fergus is playing chess with the King while the game is in progress. The chess-board is named Cendchaem, 'smooth head', as are the weapons of the great heroes and gods accredited with supernatural powers and qualities.

A game like hurley - probably closely similar to the modern caman played in the Scottish Highlands, for example, and somewhat akin to hockey - was very popular in the earliest tales. Cù Chulainn will not follow his uncle to Culann's fort until he has finished playing this game:

Conchobor went to the playing-field and saw something that astonished him: thrice 50 boys at one end of the field and a single boy at the other end, and the single boy winning victory in taking the goal and hurling from the thrice 50 youths. When they played a hole-game - a game that was played on the green at Emain - and when it was their turn to cast the ball and his to defend, he would catch the thrice 50 balls outside the hole, and none would get past him into the hole. When it was their turn to keep goals and his to hurl, he would put the thrice 50 balls unerringly into the hole.

This team game was known as bàire; the goal was a hole dug in the ground. Two figures from Romano-British contexts seem to be playing, or equipped to play, a game like hurley or hockey. One, from Kettering, and now in the British Museum, occurs on a clay mould from a Romano-British kiln. The figure is naked, and carries a stick like a hockey stick and a ball and probably a head; he is addressing a second ball. The other figure, also in the British Museum, appears on a plaque from a ritual crown or diadem found at Hockwold-cum-Wilton, Norfolk. He holds a stick like a hockey-stick in front of him in his right hand, and raises a ball in his left hand. Four balls decorate the corners of the plaque. He too is naked.

[A. Ross, The Pagan Celts, pages 79-80.]

NUAIR A BHA CÙ CHULAINN NA BHALACH

Nuair a bha Cù Chulainn na bhalach agus e ag iomain air slèibhtean na h-Eireann, s beag a bha fhios aige gum biodh buidheann de cheud neach eadar luchd-ciùil, dannsairean agus cluicheadairean na camanachd a'tighinn le plèin a dh'Inbhirnis son dà gheam eadar-nàiseanta.

Chan e a-mhàin sin ach bha, airson a'cheud turus riamh, buidheann de chluicheadairean òga fo aois dà bhliadhn' deug a Baile Ath Chliath, a thàinig a chluich an aghaidh sgioba de dh'òigridh a chinn a tuath.

Cha b'ann an diugh neo an dè a thòisich ceangalan spòrs thairis air a'Chuan Eireannach. Gu dearbh nach ann an luib troimhe-chèile aig gèam camanachd a chaidh naomh Colum Cille a chath a mach a Eireann mìle is coig ceud bliadhna air ais.

Sin eachdraidh na cùise, ach se an rud air nach eil cus dhaoine ag amas, nach e rud ùr sam bith a th'ann riochdairean an dà ghèaim a bhith a'tighinn còmhla. Ach chan eil ach ceud bliadhna bhon thòisich na ceangalan eachdraidheil a'tighinn beò gu ìre mhòir sam bith.

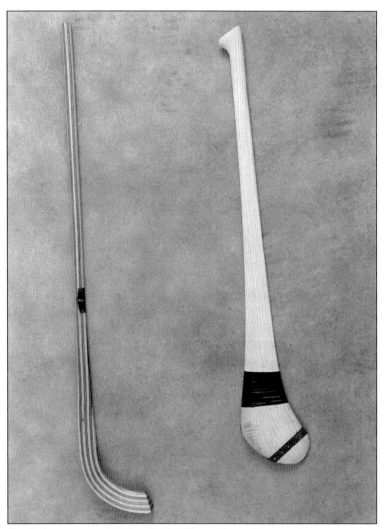

An dà chaman mar a tha iad an diugh - Albannach agus Eireannach.

Sann ann an ochd ceud deug, ceithir fichead sa seachd deug a chaidh na ceangalan a chur air stèidh bhunaiteach, a thàinig gu ìre ann an 1993 le ceud neach a'tighinn air plèin a dh'Inbhirnis son geam eadar-nàiseanta aig àrd-ìre.

Sa bhliadhna sin, chluich sgioba camanachd Chòmhdhail an aghaidh Baile Ath Chliath aig Parkhead ann an Glaschu. Rinn Còmhdhail a'chùis a h-aon deug gu dha. Agus ann an Lunainn, aig Pàirc Stamford Bridge, far am bheil sgioba ball-coise Chelsea a'cluich san latha th'ann, bha sgioba camanachd Lunainn agus sgioba a Eireann co-ionnan, 4-4. Chaidh Còmhdhail a Bhail' Ath Chliath dà mhios an deidh sin, ach cha deach gèam a chluich eadar Albannaich agus Eireannaich a rithist airson deich bliadhna fichead.

Sann sa bhliadhna naoi ceud deug, fichead sa ceithir a bheòthaich èibhleagan nan ceangal a bha Colum Cille gun fhiosda dha fhèin air cur thuige. Chaidh cuireadh a thoirt do sgioba a Alba a dhol a null gu Aonachd Tailteann. Agus a measg nan laoch a Alba a chluich air beulaibh ceithir mile deug Eireannach, nach robh sdòcha buileach a'tuigsinn dè bha iad a'faicinn, bha seòid a Earra-Ghaidheal - Clann IcNeacail, agus Sgiathanach, Cailean MacCalmain. Agus an rèiteire - Iain "Kaid" MacIlleain.

Agus dè thachair? Bhuinnig Alba dha gu h-aon. Se cnag na cuise ged tha nach do bhuinnig sgioba a Alba riamh bhon latha sin aig priomh ìre nan cluicheadair. Carson? Mas freagair sinn sin, 's dh'fhioch sùil a thoirt air staid a'ghèaim Eireannaich san latha th'ann. Tha ceud cluiheadair Eireannach ri camanachd son a h-uile fear ann an Alba. Aig a'phriomh gheaim aca ann an 1993, bha tri fichead sa ceithir mìle gu leth neach an làthair. Agus thug an geam a steach còrr is muillion not.

Agus sann le leithid sin de dh'airgead a tha Comunn Luthchleas Gael (An GAA) air tòiseachadh a'leasachadh a'phàirc aca ann am Baile Ath Chliath aig cosgais còrr is millean not. Agus nuair a bhios a'phàirc ùr deiseil, bithidh suidheachain innte airson trì fichead sa ceithir mìle neach.

Ciamar a rèisd a chaidh aig na h-Eireannaich air tighinn chun na h-ìre sin taobh staigh ceithir fichead bliadhna, agus camanachd na h-Alba fhathast a'sporghail san dorchadas, le dìreach dà fhichead buidheann?

Innsidh an GAA dhut gu bheil còrr is seachd mìle, da cheud, is leth cheud buidheann òigridh a'cluich geamanan Gàidhlig. S ao-coltach an dà ghèam ma tha, agus a-nis air ais chun na ceist - carson?

Tha am freagairt, saoilidh mi, ann an co-dhunadh a rinn Comunn na Camanachd fhèin trì fichead bliadhna air ais. Dìreach nuair a bha na ceangalan ag ath-bheòthachadh a rithist, chaidh innse do dh'àrd urrachan a'ghèaim, nach robh còir aca a bhith a'daingneachadh nan ceangal ri muinntir na h-Eireann. Chaidh an GAA a chomharrachadh mar bhuidhinn a bha an aghaidh Breatainn. Thàinig am fios a nuas bho gu h-àrd agus gu math àrd tha e ri thuigsinn - nach bu chòir a chòrr gniothaich a ghabhail ri Eireann. Agus ghèill Comunn na Camanachd. Co-dhunadh cho luideach, 's dòcha, sa rinn iad riamh. Agus bha daor cheannach aca air.

Cha robh a chòrr guth gu bhith air gu faisg air fichead bliadhna air ais. San eadar-ama, chaidh camanachd na h-Eireann air feadh an t-saoghail, agus chaidh an gèam a chur air bun-stèidh cho laidir ri spòrs nàiseanta sam bith.

Agus bha Comunn na Camanachd fhathast a' sporghail san dorchadas agus criochan a'ghèaim a sìor theannachadh. Ach fichead bliadhna air ais, chaidh na h-èibhlean ath-bheòthachadh aig ìre eadar-nàiseanta a rithist. Se an rud a fhuair muinntir na h-Alba a mach nach cumadh iad ceann a mhaide ri na h-Eireannaich ged tha, agus nach b'fhioch iad a bhith ris.

Ach chaidh na geamanan ath-bheòthachadh a rithist aig ìre aois bliadhna thar fhichead ann an 1988, agus coig bliadhna an deidh sin, bha de mhisneachd aig muinntir Alba na chuireadh iad geam aig àrd-ìre eadar-nàiseanta air dòigh a rithist.

Agus mar a tha fhios againn a nis, rinn Alba a'chùis. Ged a b'fhada a bha an latha ri thighinn, s math a b'fhioch e feitheamh!

[Uisdean MacIllInnein: Leabhar Bliadhna na Camanachd, 1993.]

Tiodhlag Chomunn na Camanachd dha'n GAA-1984.

SNÀMH DÀ EUN

The third opening: Finn MacCool was a legendary hero of Ireland. Though not mentally robust, he was a man of superb physique and development. Each of his thighs was as thick as a horse's belly, narrowing to a calf as thick as the belly of a foal. Three fifties of fosterlings could engage with handball against the wideness of his backside, which was large enough to halt the march of men through a mountain-pass.

[Flann O'Brien, Snàmh dà eun, At Swim Two Birds, Penguin Classic edition, page 9.]

"*We'll have a game of shinty*, was the first thing she said, next time I saw her, then she picked up a caman, with its bent end of hard flat edges, that she had hooked in to her belt, and a hard wooden ball from a pocket in the front of her dress. I thought, *this is a waste of time. I'm supposed to be here to learn the arts of war, and she's going to play a game.* But I didn't say anything to her - after all we didn't have teams, so how could we play a game like shinty? Then she gave a shriek of a whistle that mearly tore the inside of my ear out! And suddenly we were surrounded by sturdy men with camans in their hands. *Choose your team*, she said. *I'll be watching how you play. A good player will make a good warrior.*

Sgàthach threw her caman to me, then before I had caught it, she threw the wooden ball, as hard as she could, at me. I was so angry with her for wasting my time with this silly game, that I swung my caman at the ball with all my might, striking it so hard that it hit the hillside behind her castle like a bullet and churned its way through the belly of the rock, leaving a tail of flaming hot dust behind it. Later, I heard it came out the other side of the hill with such force that it killed three shepherds and a miller grinding his corn before curving into the sea in a great cloud of steam. Aoife, the queen of the other side was so angry she declared war on Sgàthach. I don't know though. Aoife liked to fight. Sgàthach was brave, but she thought fighting was silly, unless you had a really good reason to fight.

I *do* know that I was nearly in a fight - a really *big* fight, with all the other warriors. They were *furious*. They surrounded me with their camans like raised swords - and suddenly they became swords. Just as that circle of steel was about to slice down out of the sky and cut me to pieces, Sgàthach shouted *Stop*! Then she turned to me and said *You! Unless you are prepared to control your temper, and act as if you are part of the team, then there is nothing I can teach you.*

[Sgàthach the Warrior Queen, by Aonghas MacNeacail. Illustrated by Simon Fraser.]

TÀIN BÒ CUAILGNE: THE CATTLE RAID OF COOLEY

Chan eil sgeulachd a-measg nan seann sgeulachdan Eireannach sdòcha cho ainmeal neo cho eireachdail ri Tàin Bò Cuailgne. Chaidh na sgeulachdan an cruinneachadh agus an sgriobhadh an toiseach le na manaich san 12mh agus 14mh linn. Tha na sgeulachdan fhèin - sgeulachdan Ulaidh - a' dol air ais chun treas linn. Sann a seo a tha sinn a' faighinn a mach mar fhuair Cù Chulainn ainm.

In this tale of The Cattle Raid of Cooley, centerpiece of the eighth century Ulster cycle of heroic tales, the brave young Hound of Culann earns his name. Medieval monks recorded these Celtic tales in their manuscripts after centuries of an oral tradition. Fragments of the texts can be found in the Book of the Dun Cow compiled at the monastery of Clonmacnoise in the 12th century, the Yellow Book of Lecan compiled in the late 14th century, and the Book of Leinster. Translated by J. J. Campbell.

The following year the smith Culann invited Conor to a banquet, and asked him to bring only a few of his companions, as he had neither the space nor the means for a grand entertainment. Conor accepted, and, before he set out, he went as was his custom to see and say farewell to the boys of the corps.

He watched them at four games. In the first, Setanta kept goal against all the three fifties, and they could not score; yet when they all kept goal together he scored against them as he wished. In the second, Setanta guarded the hole, and though each of the hundred and fifty balls came to the edge of the hole, not one did he let in; yet when they all guarded together he had no difficulty in getting the ball past them into the hole. The third game was the tearing-off of mantles: Setanta tore all the hundred and fifty mantles off in a trice; they could not as much as touch his brooch. In the fourth game they wrestled, and with all the corps against him Setanta stood firm on his feet, yet when he turned to the attack he left not one standing.

Conor said to Fergus, who stood with him:

"If that lad's deeds when he is full-grown are in keeping with his deeds today, we are a lucky land to have him."

"Is there any reason to believe," said Fergus, "that his prowess, alone of all, will not increase with the years?"

But Conor said: "Let him come with us to Culann's feast. He is worthy."

"I cannot go just yet," said Setanta.

The king was surprised that the boy did not at once leave everything for the opportunity of going to a banquet with the select royal party.

"Why so?" he asked.

"Because the boys are not finished playing," said Setanta, "and I cannot leave until the games are finished."

"We cannot wait so long," said Conor.

"You need not wait. I shall follow you."

"You do not know the way."

"I shall follow the tracks of your chariots."

That was agreed. And Conor's party arrived at Culann's house, where they were welcomed to the feast which was ready laid for them. Culann said to Conor when the company were settling to the feast:

"Before we begin, tell me, is this all the company? There is none to follow?"

"None," said Conor: "all are here." He had already forgotten about Setanta.

"The reason I ask," said Culann, "is that I have a magnificent hound, which is my watchdog, and only myself can handle him or exact obedience from him; and none dare approach the neighbourhood when I loose him to guard the house. And I should like to loose him now before we begin."

"You may loose the hound," said Conor. The hound was loosed, and he made a circuit of the place and sat down with his head on his paws, a huge, fearsome guard.

Meanwhile the six-year-old boy had left his fellows of the boy-corps of Emain Macha, and was on his way to the house of Culann, the smith. He had no arms of defence, but passed the time of the journey with his hurling stick and ball. The hound bayed a fearsome challenge as he came to the house, but the boy continued his play until the hound sprang at him. Then he hurled the ball so that with terrific force it went right down the hound's throat, past the great open jaws and teeth, and as the hound reared back with the force of the blow and the pain, he grasped it by the hind legs and smashed its head to pulp on the stones of the yard.

At the sound of the hound's baying Conor had leaped to his feet remembering the boy. They all rushed out, certain Setanta was being torn by the hound, and were overjoyed to see him alive—all except Culann, who was filled with sorrow as he gazed on the hound.

"It was an unlucky day I made a banquet for Conor," he said. He turned to the boy. "You are welcome, boy, for your father's and mother's sake but not for your own. You have slain the only guard and protector of my house and my substance, of my flocks and my herds."

"Do not grieve," said the boy. "I shall see you are none the worse for what has happened."

"How can that be?" asked Culann, looking at the six-year-old boy.

"If there is a whelp of that dog's siring in all Ireland," said Setanta, "I shall rear and train it until it is able to guard and protect you as well as its sire; and until then I myself will guard your house and your property, even as your hound did."

"That is fair," said Conor.

"And you will be Cù Chulainn, the Hound of Culann, in the meantime," said Cathbhad the druid. "And that shall be your name, Cuchulainn."

"Indeed, I prefer my own name, Setanta, son of Sualtam," said the boy.

"But the name Cù Chulainn will be on the lips of all the men of Ireland and the world, and their mouths will be full of its praise," said the druid.

"For that I would accept any name," said the boy; and from that time he was known as Cù chulainn.

[The Irish. A Treasury of Art and Literature, 1993, pages 27-28.]

CÙ CHULAINN ÒG: YOUNG CÙ CHULAINN

For this boy was reared in the house of his father and mother at Airgdigh in Magh Muirtheimhne, and the stories of the youths of Eamhain were told to him. For this is how Conchubhar spends his time of kingship since he assumed sovereignty: as soon as he arises, settling the cares and business of the province, thereafter dividing the day into three, the first third of the day spent watching the youths playing games and hurling, the second third spent in playing *brannamh* and *ficheall* (board-games) and the last third spent

in consuming food and drink. until sleep comes on them all, while minstrels and musicians are meanwhile lulling him to sleep. "Though I am banished from him, I swear," said Fearghas, "that there is not in Ireland or Scotland a warrior the counterpart of Conchubhar."

The stories about the youths and boys in Eamhain were told to that lad, and the little lad asked his mother if he might go to the playing-field at Eamhain.

"It is too soon for you, my son," said his mother, "until there go with you a champion of the champions of Ulster or some of the attendants of Conchubhar to ensure your safety and protection from the youths."

"I think it too long (to wait) for that, mother," said the little boy, "and I shall not wait for it, but show me in what place lies Emhain."

"Far away from you is the spot where it lies," said his mother. "Sliabh Fuaid is between you and Emhain."

"I shall make a guess at it then," said he.

The boy went forth and took his play-things. He took his hurley stick of bronze (*a chaman crè-umha*) and his silver ball; he took his little javelin for casting and his toy spear with its end sharpened by fire, and he began to shorten the journey (by playing) with them. He would strike his ball with the stick (caman) and drive it a long way from him. Then with a second stroke he would throw his stick so that he might drive it a distance no less than the first. He would throw his javelin and he would cast his spear and would make a playful rush after them. Then he would catch his hurley-stick and his ball and his javelin, and before the end of his spear had reached the ground he would catch its tip aloft in the air.

He went to the place of assembly in Eamhain where the youths were. There were thrice fifty youths led by Follamhain Mac Conchubhar at their games on the greens of Emhain. The little boy went on to the playing-field into their midst and caught the ball between his legs when they cast it nor did he let it go higher than the top of his knee nor lower than his ankle, and he pressed it and held it close between his two legs, and not one of the youths managed to get a grasp or a stroke or a blow or a shot at it. And he carried the ball away from them over the goal.

Then they all gazed at him. They wondered and marvelled.

"Well, boys," said Follamhain mac Conchubhar, "attack yon fellow, all of you, and let him meet death at my hands, for it is tabu for you that a youth should join in your game without ensuring his protection from you. Attack him all together, for we know that he is the son of an Ulster chieftain, and let them not make it a habit to join your games without putting themselves under your protection and safeguard."

Then they all attacked him together. They cast their thrice fifty camain at the boy's head. He lifted his single play-stick and warded off the thrice-fifty sticks. Then they cast the thrice fifty balls at the little boy. He raised his arms and his wrists and his palms and warded off the thrice fifty balls. They threw him the thrice fifty toy spears with sharpened butt. The boy lifted up his toy wooden shield and warded off the thrice fifty spears. Then he attacked them.

The king put on his light travelling garb and went to bid farewell to the youths. Conchubhar went to the playing field and saw something which astonished him: thrice fifty boys at one end of the field and a single boy at the other end, and the single boy winning victory from the thrice-fifty youths. When they played the hole-game (cluich-pholl) - a game which was played on the green of Eamhain - and when it was their turn to cast the ball and his to defend, he would catch the thrice fifty balls outside the hole and none would go past him into the hole. When it was their turn to keep goal and his to hurl, he would put the thrice fifty balls unerringly into the hole.

*[Extract from **An Leabhar Laighneach** - in translation]*

LIKE A MARCH WIND

Then the champion of the invaders threw off his battle-dress and put on a distinguishing decorated dress and he took a *camàn* and a *liathròid*. He struck the ball from the west of the strand to the east and he caught it in his right hand before it fell. He put the ball on his foot the second time and he went with a rush from the west of the strand to the east tossing the ball from one foot to the other without touching it with his hand and without its touching the ground. He put it on his knee the third time and he ran to the other end of the strand putting it from one knee to the other without its touching the ground. Then he tossed it on his shoulder and rushed like a March wind from one end of the strand to the other tossing the ball from shoulder to shoulder without touching it with his hand without its touching the ground. And he challenged all the Fianna to perform that feat.

[Cath Finntràgha, edited by Cecile O'Rahilly (1962), pages 17-18.]

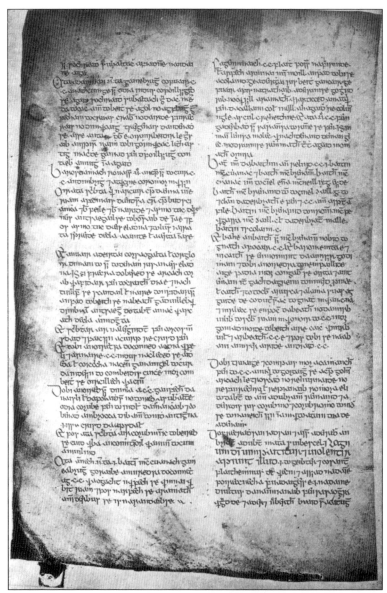

Facsimile of Rawlinson B. 514, Life of Columcille

MAR DH'FHÀG COLUM CILLE EIREANN: OF THE EXILE OF COLUMCILLE FROM EIRIN

167. Here beginneth the sending of Columcille to Alba and the causes of his exile to Alba, as his *Life* anon will show.

168. On a time Columcille went to stay with Finnen of Druim Finn, and he asked of him the loan of a book, and it was given him. After the hours and the mass, he was wont to tarry behind the others in the church, there transcribing the book, unknown to Finnen. And when evening came there would be candles for him the while he copied, to wit, the five fingers of his right hand blazing like five passing bright lights, so that they lit up and enlumined the whole temple. And on the last night that Columcille was copying the end of that book, Finnen sent one to ask it of him. And when that one had come to the door of the church where Columcille was, he marvelled at the greatness of the light he saw within. And passing great dread seized him, and he peered timorously through the hole in the leaf of the church door. And when he was aware of Columcille in the manner we have set forth, fear suffered him not to speak nor to require the book of him.

Howbeit it was revealed to Columcille that the youth was thus watching him, and he waxed passing wroth at this thing, and he spake to a pet crane he had there, and said: "Thou hast leave of me, if thou hast leave of God, to pluck out the eye of that youth that cometh to spy upon me without my knowledge."

Anon withal arose the crane at the words of Columcille, and he gave a peck with his beak through the hole of the door into the eye of the youth, so that he plucked out his eye from his head, and left it upon his cheek. Then went the youth to Finnen, and related to him how it had gone with him from beginning to end. Illpleasing to Finnen was this thing, and he blessed and sained the youth's eye and put it again in its place as it had been afore, without hurt or harm thereon. And when Finnen heard that his book had been copied without leave from him, he accused Columcille and said it was not lawful for him to copy his book without his leave.

"I shall require the judgment of the King of Erin between us," saith Columcille, "to wit, the judgment of Diarmaid, son of Cerball."

"I shall accept that," saith Finnen.

Anon withal they went together to Tara of the Kings, to Diarmaid son of Cerball. And Finnen first told the King his story, and he said:

"Columcille hath copied my book without my knowing," saith he, "and I contend that the son of my book is mine."

"I contend," saith Columcille, "that the book of Finnen is none the worse for my copying it, and it is not right that the divine words in that book should perish, or that I or any other should be hindered from writing them or reading them or spreading them among the tribes. And further I declare that it was right for me to copy it, seeing there was profit to me from doing in this wise, and seeing it was my desire to give the profit thereof to all peoples, with no harm therefrom to Finnen or his book."

Then it was that Diarmaid gave the famous judgment: "To every cow her young cow, that is, her calf, and to every book its transcript." "And therefore to Finnen belongeth the book thou hast written, O Columcille."

"It is an unjust judgment," saith Columcille, "and punishment shall fall on thee therefor."

At this time Curnan, son of Aed, son of Echaid of Tir in Charna, that is, the son of the King of Connacht, was with the King of Erin as hostage from his father. And there befell a quarrel between him and the son of the seneschal of Tara as they were playing, touching a hurling ball. And in the quarrel the boy struck the son of the seneschal upon the head with his playing-club. And he died straightway. And the son of the King of Connacht betook him to the safeguard of Columcille. And King Diarmaid bade him be dragged from the bosom of Columcille and put to death for the deed he had done.

169. And then Columcille said: "I will go to my kinsmen, the clan of Conall and of Eogan, and I will make war against thee to avenge the unjust judgment thou hast given against me touching the book, and to avenge the killing of the son of the King of Connacht that was under my safeguard, for it sufficeth me not that God take vengeance on thee hereafter, save myself take vengeance on thee in this world."

170. Then said King Diarmaid that none of the men of Erin should be suffered to accompany Columcille from that place, nor a man of them to go into battle with him against himself. Then Columcille went his way from the place without leave of the King of Erin. And the safeguard of God was upon him in such wise that he was invisible to all as he departed from their sight. And he went to Monasterboice that night. And all men warned him to be on his guard in Sliabh Breg on the morrow morn, for Diarmaid and his folk were in ambush for him on the way, lest he reach his kinsmen to set them against the King

171. And so on the morn Columcille rose early and set his following on one side of the mountain, whilst he took another way alone. And there he made the lay:

"Alone I am on the mountain O King of Suns,
may the way be smooth.
No more am I affrighted
Than if I were three score of hundreds."

And unknown to the King of Erin God bare Columcille and his folk through the midst of the mountain.

172. And then he came to the clans of Conall and of Eogan, and to them all he made complaint of the evil judgment that the King of Erin had pronounced upon him. And they upheld his cause, and went with him to give battle in the place that is now called Cuil Dremne in Connacht, between Sligo and Druim Cliab.

173. And these are the kings that were of the clan of Conall and Eogan in that time, to wit, Ainmire son of Sedna son of Fergus Cennfada son of Conall Gulban son of Niall of the Nine Hostages, King of the clan of Conall and Ferghus and Domnall, kings of the clan of Eogan, that is to say, the two sons of Muirchertach the son of Muiredach the son of Eogan son of Niall of the Nine Hostages. And to aid Columcille there came to that place moreover Aed son of Echaid of Tir in Charna, King of Connacht and of the Ui Maine of Connacht. Then did Columcille fast on God the night before the battle, to give him victory over the King of Erin, and to cause no hurt to his kinsmen or their host.

174. Then came to him Michael the Archangel, and told him that illpleasing to God was the boon he had asked of him. Natheless naught that he required could He refuse him. And therefore he should obtain it. But because he had asked so worldly a thing, God would not be reconciled with him until he should go into exile beyond the sea. And he should not come back to Erin again forever, nor partake of her food nor her drink save the time he was on the journey, nor should he look upon her men nor her women forever. And then the angel told him there should not fall of his folk there save one man. And the angel charged Columcille that no man of his following should cross the stream that was betwixt the two armies that were doing battle, and if one went he should be slain.

175. It was in this wise Columcille was: at the back of the host the while the battle lasted, in cross vigil praying to God. And the seat of Columcille is the name from that time to this of the place where he was in that hour. And Michael the Archangel was seen in the form of a passing great warrior, — on his shoulder a shield, and a naked sword in his hand, in the vanguard of the folk of Columcille, routing the King of Erin in the fray. Columcille besought God not to kill the King of Erin in the battle. And Garb son of Ronan of the clan of Conall Gulban would have slain him, had not Columcille prayed for his protection.

176. And Finnen was likewise in cross vigil in the rear of the King of Erin and his men. And Columcille sent his messengers to him to forbid him to pray thus. And the reason he gave was that the King would not yield the while the saint was thus in cross-vigil in his rear, so that all his folk would be stain save he leave his praying and his cross vigil to the end they should accept defeat and not wait to be slain. And Finnen knowing that this was true, and that Columcille had never spoken lie, and that God was right firmly in league with him, dropped his arms from his cross vigil, and left the place where he was. And in that battle of Cuil Dremne, the King of Erin was routed, and there were slain ten and a score hundred of his men. And of the folk of Columcille were none slain, save one man only that went across the stream betwixt the two hosts against the command of the angel and Columcille.

177. When the King of Erin had been routed in the battle of Cuil Dremne, Columcille made peace with him and gave back to him his kingdom, for he thought it enough to punish him for his unjust judgment.

And Columcille might have had the Kingdom of Erin for his own that time, had he not renounced it for God's sake; for him were liefer to have the greater kingdom, to wit, the Kingdom of the Realm of God.

178. The Cathach for a sooth is the name of that book by reason whereof the battle was fought. And it is covered with silver under gold. And to open it is not lawful. And if it is borne thrice sunwise round the host of the clan of Conall when they go into battle, they come back safe in triumph. And it is in the bosom of a cuccessor or a cleric that is so far as may be without mortal sin, that the Cathach should be borne around the host.

179. And Columcille said to his kinsmen and his people: "It behooveth me now to go on my pilgrimage and to leave Erin, and to return hither no more forever, as the angel told me, by reason of the numbers ye have slain for my sake in the battle of Cuil Dremne and in the battle of Cuil Fedha when ye overcame Colman Mor son of Diarmaid for vengeance because his son Cumaine son of Colman killed Baedan mac Nindedha, King of Erin, at Leim an Eich, in despite of my sureties, and in the battle of Coleraine where you routed the King of Ulster, to wit, Fiachna son of Baedan and Clan Rugraide, by reason of my contending for Ross Torothair, to wit, the land touching which there was a quarrel between me and Comgall. And to prove that his kinsmen fought these battles for his sake, the poet said, to wit Dallan Forgaill:

> *"The battle of Cuil Dremne of strife*
> *The men of Erin have heard thereof;*
> *The battle of Cuil Fedha, a good cause;*
> *And the battle of Cuil Rathain."*

180. And the saints of Erin fell to murmuring against Columcille, and they condemned him for all the folk that were slain in those battles of his making. And by the counsel of the saints of Erin, Columcille went then to Molaise of Devenish to accuse himself thereof. And this was the sentence Molaise laid upon him, even the sentence of the angel had lain on him afore, to wit, to leave Erin and to behold her no more, her food and her drink to eat not or to drink, nor to see her men nor her women, nor to tread on the soil of Erin forever.

181. And great sadness fell on Columcille therewith, and he said: "It shall be the worse for Erin to cast me out from her, and were I not cast out from her I would obtain from God that no sickness or distemper should be on the men of Erin forever, save the sickness of death." And he hath said it in this quatrain:

"Were it not for the words of Molaise,
At the cross above Ath Imlaise
I would not leave in my life-time
Distemper or sickness in Erin."

182. After the battle of Cuil Dremne, Columcille went on a journey to where there was a holy man called Cruimther Fraech. Twelve men were in his company and it chanced that he was one night at Cill Mudain. And there he gat a poor welcome from Mudan, to wit, a dirty wretched kiln was given him as a sleeping place and a hairy pig on a Friday as food for him, and therewith was sent a cracked cauldron, and some damp branch-wood of the alder-tree to make a fire thereunder.

"It was with no good will toward us that this was sent us, but let us boil the meat and eat thereof," saith Columcille, "and our God will account it to our honor in Mudan's despite."

When the water was put in the pot to boil the meat, the cracked pot (it was no wonder) let the water through.

"Let us put a wisp under the cauldron," saith Columcille, "in the name of the Lord and Cruimther Fraech. "It was done thus, and forthwith the wisp clung thereto, and it clingeth to every cauldron from that time till now. And it is not that Columcille was not able to calk the cauldron himself, but he rejoiced in exalting the name of Cruimther Fraech. And at the command of Columcille his followers ate some of that meat.

And this was the food of Mudan and his folk: bread and butter and fish. And one of the varlets of Mudan took the leavings of Columcille's followers with him to set them by in the house where Mudan was. And he set by the leavings of Mudan and his folk in like wise. And this is how he found on the morn the dishes wherein were the leavings of Columcille's followers: full of bread and fish. And the dishes wherein were the leavings of Mudan: full of gore and blood. Columcille cursed that place, and said it should be barren and desolate for all time and that its clerics and scholars should be wolves at nones each day forever.

Then departed Columcille from that place, and he forgat the book of the gospels in the place it had been the night before. And the kiln took fire of itself, so that it was wholly burned and might not be saved. And the book departed of itself to the height that was above the place called Escert na Trath, so that it was found by the cleric that Columcille sent to seek it. And God's name and Columcille's were magnified thereby.

Then went Columcille on his way walking, till the end of day was closing upon him, and he heard the sound of the vesper bell of the church where Cruimther Fraech was. And there he made a stay, and his tent was spread, for it was not his wont to be journeying between the vespers of Saturday and Monday morn.

Pen drawing of St.Colum Cille from Adamn'an's Vita. Stiftsbibliothek St Gallen, Codex 555, page 166.

It was revealed to Cruimtheir Fraech that Columcille was not far from him. He came forth to meet him and bade him welcome. And then Cruimtheir fell to rebuking him for the battle that had been fought because of him.

"It is not I that am to blame therefor," saith Columcille, "but the wrong judgment of Diarmaid son of Cerball against me."

" It were more easy for a cleric to submit to a wrong judgment than to set about defending himself," saith Cruimtheir Fraech.

"When a man's wrath is up and he is sore tried, he can not submit, " saith Columcille.

"It is right to stifle wrath," saith Cruimtheir Fraech, "lest it make matter for regret."

"Though a man do much ill through anger," saith Columcille, "yet will God pardon him therefor if he do penance."

"It were better to shun evil than to seek forgiveness therefor."

"Knowest thou not, O Cruimtheir Fraech," saith Columcille, "that God and the folk of Heaven have more joy for a sinner that returneth to them with repentance, than for one that doeth no sin and remaineth continually in a state of virtue! For it is the wont of us mortals to have more welcome for those that are dear to us and that have long been absent, than for those that are ever with us. And wit thou well," saith Columcille, "that in the world is none that shall sooner reach Heaven than the sinner that repenteth. And there hath never been nor ever will be done a worse deed than did Longinum, " saith he, "and it was forgiven him by reason of his repentance."

"If it be so," saith Cruimtheir, "may God make us good men both together. "

"Amen," saith Columcille.

So then they made together the poem that is called the *Colloquy of Columcille and Cruimtheir Fraech*: 'Welcome, O Colum of the Bells' *et reliqua*.

Anon they sealed friendship and fellowship, and each bade other farewell.

183. Then went Columcille to Derry. And the place was dear to him and he was loth to leave it. And right greatly did he praise it, as the quatrain saith:

"This is why I love Derry: For its level fields, for its brightness, For the hosts of its white angels, From one end to the other."

And he said that not more numerous were the leaves on the trees, or the grass on the meadows, than the angels that hovered over that place. So that he uttered this quatrain there:

> *"There is not a leaf on the ground,*
> *In Derry lovely and faultless,*
> *That hath not two virgin angels,*
> *Overthwart every leaf there."*

184. And he said that not only were they hovering over the land, but they reached for nine waves on the sea around it, and he spake his quatrain:

"They find no room on the land, For the number of good gentle angels, Nine waves distant therefrom, It is thus they reach out from Derry."

185. And in especial above in the yew tree in front of the Black Church, where Columcille and his saints were wont to chant the hours were there ten hundred angels keeping guard, as Columcille hath said in these quatrains:

> *"This is the Yew of the Saints*
> *Where they used to come with me together.*
> *Ten hundred angels were there,*
> *Above our heads, side close to side.*
>
> *Dear to me is that yew tree;*
> *Would that I were set in its place there!*
> *On my left it was pleasant adornment*
> *When I entered into the Black Church."*

186. And though dear to him was that place, yet he made him ready to leave it and to go into exile to Alba at the counsel of the angel and of the saints of Erin. And so great was his love for that place that he let send his ship to Loch Foyle to a stead that is called Glais an Indluidh today. And he went himself by land to meet it then, and he washed his hands in that stream. Wherefore is its name Glais an Indluidh to this day. And he blessed a stone fast there beside, and made a circuit around it sunwise, and from that stone it was he went into his boat. And he said that whoso should make a circuit around it from that time, going on a journey or a pilgrimage, it would be likely that he would come safe. And for this he let send the boat beyond that place in the loch, as we have said above: that he might the longer have sight of that stead on his way up beyond it, and coming down again by its side.

187. And when Columcille and his saints were entering into the boat, there was a certain man in the port with a forked club in his hand. And he set the club against the boat-to push it off from land.

When Columcille saw this he said: "I leave upon thee the gift of unwilling exile by reason of the help thou hast given me in leaving Erin for exile, and to those after thee that have a forked club I leave the same gift forever."

188. The ship departed then. And his kinsfolk, to wit, the Conalls and the Eogans and all that dwelt in that place were there on both sides of Loch Foyle. And when they saw that Columcille was in truth depart,ing from them, they gave one cry of sorrow and lamentation for him.

189. "Woe is me for the cries I hear," saith Columcille, "the cry of the clan of Conall and of Eogan, my own beloved kinsmen, sorrowing and mourning my departure. Sorely have they troubled my spirit. I cannot listen to them nor endure them."

Then did Columcille shed tears passing many, and he said that it was right for his kinsmen to make dole for him, and so sorely would he grieve for them that there would not be a day of his life without his shedding tears lamenting them. And so he made these quatrains:

> *"Sad to me the lamenting*
> *On this side and that of Loch Foyle;*
> *The cry of Conall and Eogan,*
> *In truth, bewailing my going.*
>
> *Since I am to leave mine own kinsmen,*
> *I shall give them to know of my secret:*
> *A night shall not pass, I conceal not,*
> *That tears shall not come to mine eye.*
>
> *Since my leaving the folk of the Gael,*
> *On whom I have set my affection,*
> *It is naught to me though but one night*
> *Were the length of my life days thereafter."*

190. Then said holy Odhran that was in the boat with Columcille, "Be silent, and heed them not, and set thy mind on Him for whose sake thou hast given them up, to wit, Almighty God.

"Thou hast well said, Odhran," saith Columcille, "Howbeit it is a parting of the body from the soul for a man to part from his kinsfolk, and his native land, and to go from them to distant foreign places in pilgrimage and lasting exile." And he spake this quatrain:

> *Though well it is that thou speakest,*
> *O Odhran, noble and spotless,*
> *Yet the parting of body from soul*
> *Is the parting to me from my kinsfolk."*

191. Then sailed they onward till they left Derry behind them. And Columcille heard a passing great lamentation of the Derry folk; and he said, "Though sad to me is every cry that I hear, yet sadder and heavier to me than any is this great weeping of the folk of Derry. And in my breast it hath made of my heart four fragments, and the sound will not go from my ears till death."

So it was then that he made these quatrains:

> *"Since I have heard this lamenting*
> *Why do I still live my life days!*
> *The loud wail of the people of Derry,*
> *It hath broken my heart in four fragments.*
>
> *Derry of Oaks, let us leave it*
> *With gloom and with tears, heavy hearted;*
> *Anguish of heart to depart thence,*
> *And to go away unto strangers.*
>
> *Forest beloved,*
> *Whence they have banished me guiltless!*
> *On the women of Niall's clan a blemish,*
> *And on each man of them, is my exile.*
>
> *Great is the speed of my coracle,*
> *And its stern turned upon Derry;*
> *Woe to me that I must on the main,*
> *On the path to beetling-browed Alba."*

192. Then steered they the boat through Loch Foyle to the place where the lake entereth into the great sea, that is called the Tonna Cenanna today. And it was not the folk only of his land that were heavy and sorrowful after Columcille, but the birds and the senseless creatures were sorrowful after him. And in token of this thing, the seagulls and the birds of Loch Foyle were pursuing on both sides of the boat, screaming and screeching for grief that Columcille was leaving Erin. And he understood that they were uttering speech of sorrow as he would understand it from human folk; and so great was his gentleness and his love for his land and the place of his birth that no greater was his sorrow in parting from her human folk than his sorrow in parting from the seagulls and the birds of Loch Foyle. So that he made this quatrain:

> *"The seagulls of Loch Foyle,*
> *They are before me and in my wake;*
> *In my coracle with me they come not;*
> *Alas, it is sad, our parting."*

And in witness of this story a crane went to seek Columcille from Erin to Iona in Alba, as Saint Adamnan maketh mention.

193. And then they saw a monstrous beast rising out of the sea; and not more vast to them seemed a mountain peak than seemed she; and she raised a storm and a great tempest on the sea round about them, so that the boat was in peril of sinking therefrom. And great fear fell on Columcille's folk, and they besought him to pray God for them to bring them out of the great danger they were in.

194. And anon Columcille said: "For the sake of all of you, it is needful that ye give one of your folk to propitiate that beast. And better were that, than for all of you to be in danger from her, and whose goeth unto her for the sake of all of us, to him will I give the Kingdom of God."

195. Then spake a lad of the household of Columcille, "I will go for your sakes into the jaws of that beast, and I shall be given the Kingdom of God in reward therefor."

And therewith he made a bound out of the vessel, and by hap he fell into the jaws of the beast. And the monster made off with him then over the sea. And they gat peace from the sea thereafter.

196. Anon said those of his household to Columcille: "It grieveth us for the death of the lad that was coming with us from his own land to distant foreign shores for love of us."

Then prayed Columcille to God in behalf of the youth and it was not long thereafter that they beheld the beast coming toward them, and she gave back the youth to Columcille entire. And no hurt had the beast done him nor any more did she do harm to the boat thereafter.

197. Anon went Columcille with his holy men from Loch Foyle beyond the Bann, and they halted not till they came to land in Dal Riada; and he went to the house of a certain man there, and Coisgellan was the name of the man of that house. And there was none in the house save three women and a little child with them. And the child came toward Columcille and kissed him. And Columcille took him to his bosom and gave him a kiss. It was then he made the famous quatrain:

"O conscience clear,
O soul unsullied,
Here is a kiss for thee;
Give a kiss to me."

And Columcille made a prophecy about him, and said he would be a wise and learned man and a faithful vassal to God, and he would be great in the knowledge of the Scriptures, and it would be he would give the illustrious judgment between the men of Erin and Alba touching Dal Riada at the Assembly of Druim Ceat. And it was Colman son of Comgellan. And every word that Columcille said was verified.

198. Then Columcille and his household departed from Erin, and this is the number they were: twenty bishops, two score priests, thirty deacons, and two score sons of learning that had not yet the rank of priest or deacon, as the poet, even Dallan Forgaill, hath said in this quatrain:

> *"Forty priests their number,*
> *Twenty bishops, lofty their virtue,*
> *For psalmody, without doubting,*
> *Thirty deacons, fifty boys."*

199. And these folk were full of wisdom and knowledge and the graces of the Holy Ghost. And the years of Columcille at that time were two and two score. And other fourteen and twenty years of his life he spent in Alba in pilgrimage and exile.

200. Then went Columcille and his household into their ship. And there he made his quatrain:

> *"My foot in my tuneful coracle;*
> *My sad heart tearful;*
> *A man without guidance is weak;*
> *Blind all those without knowledge."*

201. And he bade farewell to Erin then, and they put out into the ocean and the great deep. And Columcille kept gazing backward on Erin till the sea hid it from him. And heavy and sorrowful was he in that hour. And it was thus he made this quatrain below:

> *"I stretch my eye across the brine,*
> *From the firm oaken planks;*
> *Many the tears of my soft grey eye*
> *As I look back upon Erin.*

There is a grey eye
That will look back upon Erin;
Never again will it see
The men of Erin or women.

At dawn and eve I lament;
Alas for the journey I go!
This is my name - I tell a secret -
'Back to Erin'."

[Betha Colaim Chille, Life of Columcile, A. O'Kelleher and G. Schoepperle, 1918, pages 177-201.]

CÙ CHULAINN AGUS AN CAMAN

Part of the twelfth century version of the feats of Cù Chulainn with the word caman indicated. The reproduction here is from the transcript made by Seosamh o Longain from An Leabhar Laighneach and published in facsimile by the Royal Irish Academy, with introduction, etc. by Robert Atkinson, 1880, page 62.

A panel from the side of a silver and enamel cruet which was one of an alter-set made in Paris in 1333. The set may once have belonged to the monastery of Soro in Denmark which was dissolved in 1586.

(Reproduced by permission of the Director of the National Museum of Denmark.)

"Chaidh mi moch gu cùl na sràide,
Rug mi air ceann na caman is chuir mi bàir leis,
Rug mi rithisd air is chuir mi bàir leis."

"Early on I went to the back of the street,
I picked up the caman and scored a goal,
I caught it again and scored another."

[Traditional verse -16th century - quoted in Ninian MacDonald, Shinty, page 70.]

The fifteenth century grave-slab in the ruined church of Clonca in
Inishowen, County Donegal.
(Reproduced by permission of the Commissioners of Public Works.)

44

ONE COMMON ANCESTOR

Fifth century BC; found in Athens, 1922.

Another conclusion, which would seem to be legitimate, is that not only were all these games, which were played with "a clubbe or hurle batte" (to use the language of "Philogamus" in the 16th century) indigenous, but they all derive from one common ancestor, to wit from the game to which such frequent reference is made in Celtic story.

Thus hockey, golf, cricket, stool-ball, trap-ball, tip-cat: et hoc genus omne, no matter by what names they are now differentiated, no matter what modifications they may have suffered in the lapse of centuries, no matter what special rule of play may have crystallised around this or that individual variety and caused it eventually to stand out distinct from the others—all reveal an unmistakable community of origin.

True, we may not be able to point to the exact date at which any one emerged from the parent stem and acquired a distinct form and individual existence; like Topsy, many have "just growed," but they can one and all boast of a lengthy and honourable ancestry.

Of peculiar interest is the fact that new names have been given to many of these varieties simply by ringing the changes on the Caman, the club used in the original game. So in Hockey, Bandy, Golf, Camanachd, Cricket, La Crosse, etc. The Gaelic "caman" is merely the bent stick or club, hockey is the hooked stick, La Crosse is the crook, etc. Likewise, the most favoured derivation of cricket is from "crice" (Saxon cryce), an old English word for crook, and early illustrations of the game manifest the curved nature of the bat then employed.

TWO EARLY SPECIES.

The original game has thus become the prolific parent, of a numerous progeny - a striking proof of its inherent vitality. Even in the ancient Saga we read of an early offshoot from the main stem. A distinction is made between the "hole" game and the more common form, which one might term the "boundary" game. The latter was the game par excellence in which the team spirit predominated (it was called "ag iomain," the urging or driving), and in which the endeavour of one party was to drive the ball to a fixed bound or goal defended by the other.

In the former (called "cluich-dhesog," and now known universally as golf) the contest was less strenuous; it was a test of individual proficiency, in which two or more players engaged, the aim of each being to place the ball in a distant hole in the fewest number of strokes.

But all the above-mentioned sports have now their own individual histories; it is beside our present purpose to follow these ramifications in detail; and we shall confine our attention as far as possible to the story of Camanachd—the direct descendant of the ancient game.

ENGLISH EQUIVALENTS.

Its trail may be followed here, there, and everywhere, blazed across the story of social life in these islands for hundreds of years. Perhaps no stronger testimony to its onetime popularity could be adduced than is found in the variety of names by which it has been known in different districts.

From the root "cam" in Caman (the curve(l stick) arose the variants—Cammock, cammack, camac, camok, camoke, camake, camocke, camog, camag, camawg, cambock, cambok, cambuc, cambuck, etc.

From the "hooked" stick we have—Hockey, hockie, hawky, hawkey, etc.

Perhaps the earliest use of this variant is found in the Galway Statutes, 1527, where amongst prohibited games is included "the horlinge of the litill balle with hockie stickes or staves." (Hist. MSS., Com. 10th, Rep. app. V., 402).

Bandy (the bent stick) was also a term in common use, likewise "bandy-ball," and in Norfolk and Suffolk, "bandy hoshoe."

Hurling or hurley became the English equivalent used in Ireland (which must be carefully distinguished from Hurling as practised in Cornwall). In Cheshire we find "baddin," in Lincolnshire "crabsow," in Fifeshire "carrick," in Dorsetshire "scrush," and in Gloucestershire "not" (from the knotty piece of wood used as a ball). In other districts we find "chinnup, camp, crabsowl, clubby, humney, shinnup, shinney-law, shinney," etc.

*[**Shinty. A Short History. Father Ninian MacDonald, pages 53-56.**]*

TWO BOYS AT PLAY. (From a MS. Book of Prayers of 14th Century.)

DÀ MHAIDE DHÌREACH

Chuir Iain Moireasdan gille a Steòrnabhagh aon latha, a cheannach rudan a bha a dhìth air. Chuir e roimhe na bha e ag iarraidh leis an rann a leanas:

John Morrison once sent a servant-lad to Stornoway to make some purchases which he listed for him in verse:

> *Dà mhaide dhìreach gu caman,*
> *dà mhaide chama gu carn*
> *cliath, cas-dhìreach is bacan -*
> *cuimhnich, a mhacain, nach fhàg.*

> *Two straight sticks for shinty clubs,*
> *two bent sticks for a sledge,*
> *a harrow, a straight delving-spade and a tether-stake -*
> *take care, my boy, not to leave them behind.*

THEY ARE VERY NIMBLE AT IT

"They use for their diversions short clubs and balls of wood; the sand is a fair field for this sport and excercise in which they take great pleasure and are very nimble at it; they play for some eggs, fowls, hooks and tobacco; and so eager are they for victory that they strip themselves to their shirts to obtain it."

[Martin Martin, Description of the Western Isles, c. 1695, (1703).]

280 *A* DESCRIPTION *of the*　　　　*Weſtern Iſlands of* Scotland.　281

St. *KILDA*, or *HIRT*.

THE firſt of theſe Names is taken from one *Kilaer*, who lived here; and from him the large Well *Tonbir-Kilda* has alſo its Name. *Hirta* is taken from the *Iriſh Ier*, which in that Language ſignifies *Weſt*; this Iſle lies directly oppoſite to the Iſles of *North-Viſt, Harries*, &c. It is reckon'd 18 Leagues from the former, and 20 from *Harries*. This Iſle is by *Peter Goas*, in a Map he made of it at *Rotterdam*, call'd St. *Kilder*; it is the remoteſt of all the *Scots* North-Weſt Iſles: It is about two Miles in length, and one in breadth; it is faced all round with a ſteep Rock, except the Bay on the South-Eaſt, which is not a Harbour fit for any Veſſel, tho in the time of a Calm one may land upon the Rock, and get up into the Iſland with a little climbing. The Land riſes pretty high in the middle, and there is one Mountain higher than any other part of the Iſland. There are ſeveral Fountains of good Water on each ſide this Iſle. The Corn produc'd here is Oats and Barley, the latter is the largeſt in the Weſtern Iſles.

THE Horſes and Cows here are of a lower Size than in the adjacent Iſles, but the Sheep differ only in the Bigneſs of their Horns, which are very long.

THERE

THERE is an antient Fort on the South end of the Bay, call'd *Dun-fir-Volg*, i. e. the Fort of the *Volſcij*: This is the Senſe put upon the Word by the *Antiquaries* of the oppoſite Iſles of *Viſt*.

THE Iſle *Soa* is near half a Mile diſtant from the Weſt-ſide of St *Kilda*; it is a Mile in circumference, very high, and ſteep all round *Borera*, lies above two Leagues North of St. *Kilda*; it is near a Mile in circumference, the moſt of it ſurrounded with a high Rock. The largeſt and the two leſſer Iſles are good for Paſturage, and abound with a prodigious Number of Sea-fowl, from *March* till *September*; the *Solan* Geeſe are very numerous here, inſomuch that the Inhabitants commonly keep yearly above twenty thouſand young and old in their little ſtone Houſes, of which there are ſome hundreds for preſerving their Fowls, Eggs, &c. They uſe no Salt for preſerving their Fowl; the Eggs of the Sea Wild-fowl are preſerv'd ſome Months in the Aſhes of Peats, and are aſtringent to ſuch as be not accuſtom'd to eat them.

THE *Solan* Gooſe is in ſize ſomewhat leſs than a Land-Gooſe, and of a white Colour, except the tips of the Wings, which are black, and the top of their Head, which is yellow; their Bill is long, ſmall pointed, and very hard, and pierces an Inch deep into Wood, in their

Deſcent

A SENSE OF SIN

Reported some of the East and West Gate to have played schinnie on Sabbath last in the afternoon, to be at the Session the next day.

January 15, 1671

The Session being informed the Sabbath this day month bygone to have been broken by severals playing on the Sands in the afternoon, who being convened before them this day and the day poreceding, and brought to a sense of thir sins and acknowledgment therof before them, were willing to be enacted and by their opresent enact as follows: - That if ever they should be found guilty of the above particular... should pay four lib. and make public acknowldegment thereof before the congregation. And... the Session statutes and ordains that what other persons shall be found guilty of the like, or going in great numbers together on the sands on the Lord's Day in all time coming, every particular person shall be liable to the like pounishment and fine, which will be exacted of their parents and masters whom they serve.... and ordains public intimation to be made the next Lord's day, that none pretend ignorance thereof.

[North Berwick Kirk-Session Minutes anent playing 'Schinnie' on Sunday.]

NO RESENTMENT IS TO BE SHOWN

And now I think I may say something to you of the sports used among the Irish on their holidays. One exercise they use much is their hurling, which has something in it not unlike the game called Mall. When their cows are casting their hair, they pull it off their backs and with their hands work it into large balls which will grow very hard. This ball they use at the hurlings, which they strike with a stick called a comaan about three feet and a half long in the handle. At the lower end it is crooked and about three inches broad and on this broad part you may sometimes see one of the gamesters carrying the ball tossing it for 40 or 50 yards in spite of all the adverse players and when he is like to lose it, he generally gives it a great stroke to send it towards the goal. Sometimes if he miss his blow at the ball, he knocks one of the opposers down: at which no resentment is to be shown. They seldom come aff without broken heads or shins in which they glory very much. At this sport sometimes one parish or barony challenges another; they pick out ten, twelve or twenty players of a side and the prize is generally a barrel or two of ale, which is often brought into the field and drunk off by the victors on the spot, though the vanquished are not without a share of it too. This commonly is upon some very large plain, the barer of grass the better, and the goals are 200 or 300 yards one from the other; and whichever party drives the ball beyond the other's goal wins the day. The champions are of the younger and most active among them, and their kindred and mistresses are frequently spectators of their address. Two or three bag pipes attend the conquerors at the barrel's head, and then play them out of the field. At some of these meetings two thousand have been present together. They do not play often at football only in a small territory called Fingal near Dublin the people use it much, and trip, and shoulder very handsomely. These people are reckoned the best wrestlers of the Irish, though I think the best would come off but badly in Moorfields. They have a sort of jargon speech peculiar to themselves, and understand not one word of Irish, and are as little understood by the English.

[O Caithinia, Sceal na hIomana, pages 6-7.]

Sgàthach - Simon Fraser.

ANCIENT SPORTS

Soon after Culloden we find Pennant, in a "Tour in Scotland" (1769), recording that

"Of the ancient sports of the Highlands those retained are: throwing the stone of strength (clach neart), which occasions emulation who can throw it the furthest; the shinty, or the striking of a ball of wood or hair; this game is played between two parties furnished with clubs in a large plain; whichever side strikes it first to their own goal wins the match."

McIan's Highlanders at Home, 1848, page 204

THE DANGERS THAT THE SHINS RUN

James Boswell's "*Journal of a Tour to the Hebrides*" with Samuel Johnson in 1773 is quite rightly praised as one of the greatest travel books of all time. As Roger Hutchinson points out (*West Highland Free Press*, 10.12.94) Boswell missed very little in his travels, but in the previously published versions of the book, they appear to have missed shinty.

However, in his researches for his book on Boswell and Johnson, "*All the sweets of being*" (Edinburgh, 1995), Roger Hutchinson discovered a short description of shinty on Coll in the 1770s which had been edited out of the published version of the tour by the editor Edmond Malone.

"About ten days at Christmas time, the people in Coll make merry. All the men in the island are divided onto two parties. Each party is headed by a gentleman. the Laird perhaps heads one, and Captain Maclean another; or other two gentlemen of the family are leaders. There is a ball thrown down in the middle of a space above the house, or on a strand near it; and each party strives to beat it first to one end of the ground with clubs or crooked sticks. The club is called the "shinny". It is used in the low country of Scotland. The name is from the danger that the shins run. We corrupt it to "shinty". The leader of the party which prevails receives the bet which the opposite leader has lost to him, and gives it to the people to drink."

This description of shinty would appear to confirm a number of hitherto unconfirmed assumptions. As Hutchinson points out, there are not many first hand accounts of shinty surviving from the 18th century. The paragraph confirms the feudal format of the ceremonial games at the time; the fact that even Gaelic speakers such as Boswell's hosts in Coll accepted that "shinny" came from the shins, rather than from the Gaelic "*sinteag*" (leaping motion); the fact that the game was known in the Lowlands and that the term "shinty" had, in fact, become a commonly used corruption more than 200 years ago.

The sentences quoted were removed from the published version of Boswell's *Journal* along with one or two of his more vicious insults of the local lairds.

Edmond Malone wrote thus to Boswell: "The description of Coll you may remember I had some apprehension about, on account of the great number of small particulars."

A VERY ANCIENT CUSTOM

About 1776, Arthur Young describes for us a custom which then obtained in Ireland:—

"There is a very ancient custom here for a number of country gossips among the poor people to fix upon some young woman that ought as they think to be married. They also agree upon a young fellow as a proper husband for her. This determined, they send to the fair one's cabin to inform her that on the Sunday following she is to be horsed—that is, carried in triumph on men's backs. She must then provide whisky and cider for a treat, as all will pay her a visit after Mass for a hurling match.

"As soon as she is horsed, the hurling begins, in which a young fellow appointed for her husband has the eyes of all the company fixed on him; if he comes off conqueror he is certainly married to the girl; but if another is victor, he as certainly loses her, for she is the prize of the victor."

[Ninian MacDonald, Shinty, A Short History, 1932, page 66.]

THE BRIGADE'S HURLING MATCH

In the south's blooming valleys they sing and they play
By their vine-shaded cots at the close of the day:
But a game like our own the Italians never saw -
The wild sweeping hurlings of Erin gu bràth.

Our tents they were pitched upon Lombardy's plain;
Ten days nigh the foemen our army had lain;
But ne'er through their walls we made passage or flaw,
Till we showed them the game played in Erin gu bràth.

Our sabres were sharp and a forest was nigh;
There our hurleys we fashioned ere morning rose high;
With the goal ball young Mahon had brought from Dunlawe,
We showed the game played in Erin gu bràth.

Our captain stood out with the ball in his hand;
Our colonel he gave us the word of command;
Then we dashed it and chased it o'er eskir and scragh ,
While we showed the game played in Erin gu bràth.

The enemy stood on their walls high and strong,
While we raced it and chased it and dashed it along;
They opened their gates as we nearer did draw,
To see the wild game played in Erin gu bràth.

On a sudden we turned from the ball's swift career;
And rushed through the gate with a grand ringing cheer;
Ah, the ne'er through our bright strategem saw,
While we showed them the game played in Erin gu bràth.

Their swords clashed around us, their balls raked so sore,
But with hurleys we paid them in hard knocks galore;
For their bullets and sabres we cared not a straw,
While we showed them the game played in Erin gu bràth.

The fortess is taken! our wild shouts arise;
For our land and King Louis they swell to the skies,
Ah, he laughed as he told us a game he ne'er saw
Like the wild sweeping hurlings of Erin gu bràth!

(Robert Dwyer Joyce, M.D., c.1750.)

THE HURLING

Of all the sports that please the rural throng,
The goal first claims the effort of my song;
Where mimic war its evolutions shows,
To fly, to harass, to pursue and close.
By games like this imperial Rome began,
Where beardless childhood play'd the warlike man.

Some hoary sage, rever'd by all the train,
Who long had been the champion of the plain,
With placid smile, not with tyrannic sway,
Waves back the crowds, the willing crowds obey.
With knowing ken he marks the level ground,
And plants the willow at the well-known bound.
Reflection fans the half extinguish'd flame,
With fond remembrance of his former fame;

Where oft he Nisus-like skim'd o'er the plain,
Or stood the butt of ev'ry tilting swain;
When shouting maids extoll'd him with their cries,
The rolling orb dim fading in the skies;
Whilst wond'ring they the cloud-veil'd ball pursue,
And whisp'ring ask the place to which it flew:
Fain wou'd he join the youthful band once more,
His heart yet willing - but his strength is o'er.
Affection kindles in each swelling breast,
And all his fame unenvy'd is confess'd.
When thus the sage, of former prowess proud,
Becks the attention of the prattling crowd.

"Such were my pow'rs when once I here have stood,
Where strongly flow'd the current of my blood;
Ere envious age an hoary winter spread
O'er the thin'd honors of my silver head."

The lusty youths advance in equal rows;
Each parent's breast with blushing transport glows;
Silk kerchieves bind their close compacted hairs;
Each strong-nerv'd hand a polish'd hurly bears;
Contrasted wreaths their hardy breasts display,
To mark each partner thro' the mazy play;
With ribbon gay which her fair head array'd,
Or homely garter that herself hath made,
Which from her leg with native blush she stole,
Of her chaste love the great, tho' humble dole,
Each buxom lass her fav'rite lad intwines,
Each sturdy band in rustic splendour shines.

The signal made aloft is flung the ball,
All anxious watch impatient for its fall:
The steady back their bossy weapons rear,
And twirl them nimbly in th' intrenchant air;
Men above men in quick succession bound,
Hips justle hips, the clashing hurlies found;
Till one, essays, versed in the wiles of play,
And nimbly sends th'elastic ball away.
The cause remov'd here ends the contest too,
The active whips with hasty steps pursue;
Scud o'er the plain swift as the fleeting wind,
Or tilting leave the prostrate foe behind.
(Foe of the hour, hence harmony and peace,
And friendship clasps them in its close embrace.)

Back to the green the pliant orb they roll,
Each party pointing to the adverse goal;
Now high it flies, then skims the turf below,
As chance, or skill, directs the sounding blow;
'Till stop'd its course the flying wings essay,
Or sturdy force, or quick finesse of play.
Close as the phalanx fam'd in ancient song,
They crowding press the rolling ball along;
Now those succeed, now these reluctant yield,
As crested legions on th'embattl'd field,
O'er some fall'n hero wage the stubborn fray,
To bear triumphantly the spoils away.
True to his charge the goal-man calm surveys
The various efforts, and the winding maze,
Hopes, doubts, fears, alternativley arise,
As friends or foes possess the bounding prize,
To lend his aid, tho' eagerly inclin'd,
Still duty binds him to the post assign'd.
Enough the prowess of each swain display'd,
He bids them cease, who first the band array'd.

[Robert Devereux, 1779.]

THE CONVICT OF CLONMEL

How hard is my fortune,
And vain my re-pining!
The strong rope of fate,
For this young neck is twining,
My strength is departed,
My cheek sunk and sallow,
While I languish in chains,
In the gaol of Cluainmeala.

No boy in the village,
Was ever yet milder,
I'd play with a child,
And my sport would be wilder.
I'd dance without tiring,
From morning till even,
And the goal-ball I'd strike,
To the lightning of Heaven.

At my bed-foot decaying,
My hurlbat is lying,
Through the boys of the village
My goal-ball is flying;
My horse 'mong the neighbours
Neglected may fallow, -
While I pine in my chains
In the gaol of Cluainmeala.

Next Sunday the "pattern"
At home will be keeping,
And the young active hurlers
The field will be sweeping.
With the dance of fair maidens
The evening they'll hallow,
While this heart, once so gay,
Shall be cold in Cluainmeala.

(J. J. Callanan, d.1827)

BANDO

Bando is a Welsh game, never established on an organised basis, although popular throughout the country. Bando is probably borrowed from the English bandy, and the earliest example of the word in Welsh occurs in the great English-Welsh dictionary published by the Glamorgan lexicographer, John Walters, in 1770-1794.

Bando was common in the nineteenth century; John Elias, the famous Calvinistic Methodist preacher was a player, as was David Lloyd George in the parish of Llanystumdwy, Caerns. The "Margam Bando Boys" were immortalised in a ballad of that name. Rules were often agreed immediately before matches, which, in similar fashion to shinty, often took place between parishes, with teams of as many as 30 members each. Games were often played on sandy beaches; the aim was to send a small wooden ball between two posts at either end of the pitch which acted as goals. Teams often wore coloured ribbons to distinguish the sides. The players also took their bando seriously enough to practise by long-distance running before the game.

The club was known as the "bando". Two examples of a bando stick are preserved in the Welsh Folk Museum; both are approximately 2'3" long with a curved end of about 6". One stick is 1" thick and oval in section and also has a leather strap handle; the other is circular in section and has no handle.

It is quite obvious that bando was a popular game in Glamorgan throughout the eighteenth century, holding the place occupied by rugby football in the twentieth century.

The bards composed poems in praise of famous players - unfortunately none of these 'Pindaric' odes have survived. According to the Llangyfelach hand-bill of 1780, members of the winning bandy team had "a bottle of brandy each", while the footballers had to be content with "a bottle of gin each", a cheaper (and much less satisfactory, apparently!) commodity.

Iolo Morganwg has an interesting note on bandy in a review he wrote in 1796:

Bandy playing is a very popular diversion of young men that ought to be suppressed, and by severities if milder courses will not prevail. It is in some things similar to cricket but the bat is made of a young ash or elm sapling, having one end bent,....with this they strike the ball. When I was a boy from 8 to 12 or 14 years of age, I was esteemed dexterous at making these Bats or Bandys. I well supplied my pockets with money for every boyish purpose by making bandies for which I should have from 3d or 6d each. I have for this purpose destroyed from time to time some hundreds of fine elm and ash saplings that I found of spontaneous growth in the hedges."

[Based on Glamorgan Customs in the Eighteenth Century.]

LA GRIANACH SOILLEIR

Se fear de na cunntasan as mionadaiche agus as fheàrr de ghèam camanachd aig toiseach na naoidheamh linn deug, an cunntas a th'aig Tormod MacLeòid anns an Teachdaire Gàidhealach. An seo, tha e ag innse mar a bhathas ris a' chamanachd san sgìre aige fhèin.

One of the most realistic Gaelic sketches written by Dr Norman Macleod in his " Teachdaire Gáidhealach" is one on the game of shinty, as played about the year 1800 in his native parish:-

Thog an latha oirnn gu grianach soilleir, air na cnuic mu'n cuairt do'n Bhlár-ruith. Bha na mnathan agus na leanabain, maighdeannan na tìre, uasal agus ìosal, eadar dà chloich na Dùthcha, air teac a dh'amharc na camanachd. 'Nuair a thug mi fhèin sùil a nunn nam measg, cha'n fhaod mi ràdh, nach robh mi glè thoilichte gun d' thug mi bhoineid chonnlaich, agus an cleoca sgàrlaid dhachaidh, a bha air Mairi, is i thall 'nam broilleach. Chomharraicheadh a mach an tadhall, agus thòisich iad air na daoin' a tharruing.

" 'Buaileam ort, Alasdair', arsa Dòmhnull; "leigeam leat", ars' Alasdair. 'Is leamsa Dòmhnull Bàn chuil-fho-dair', an aon duine bu shine bh'air an fhaiche; thug Dòmhnull leum gu taobh, agus shaoileadh tu gu'n leumadh an dà shùil as le h-aighear. 'Nuair bha na daoin' air an roinn, dà fhichead air gach taobh, buideal aig gach ceann de'n tadhall, thilg Alasdair Ruadh an caman suas. "Cas no Bas, a Dhòmhnull nan Gleann. "Bas a Sheumas ri d'chas gu h-oidhche." 'Sann air Alasdair a thainig an ceud bhuille bhualadh, agus air dha am ball iomanach a shocrachadh, mar bha e togail a chamain, ghlaodh Domhnull òg: "Deis-dé, Alasdair, rinn sinn dearmatl air eleaehda an latha, ach math an t-àm fhad's a dh'fheudar a leasachadh. Thig air t'aghart Eoghainn Bhain, agus aithris riaghailtean na h-iomain.' Chruinnich gach aon mu thimchioll, agus thoir-misg Eoghann ann an ainm cinn-fheadhna na camanachd, agus a reir nos an sinnsearachd connsachadh no trod, focal àrd no mionnan, buille no dorn, caonnag no misg, agus bhrosnaich e iad gu farpais chàirdeil, co-strigh dhuineil, fhearail, gun bhaeag gun cheap—tuislidh.

"Bhuail Alasdair a' cheud bhuille agus thóisich a' chamanachd. Ach cha'n 'eil cainnt' agamsa gus na thachair a chur sios. Chaidh a' cheud tadhall le muinntir an leathair, ach ma chaidh cha deach an latha. Rùisg Dòmhnull òg is a chuid ghillean, agus shaoileadh tù gu'n robh Blár-na-Léine a ris ga chur.

"Bha'n cath leinne. Bhuaileadh a' bhuille-choilleig le Eoghann Bán Leathair, fìdeag choimheach a chuir a thadhall am ball.

"Thog sinn caithream na buaidh, ach cha robh ann ach grádh agus fiúghantas. Chruinnich sinn m'an bhuideal, agus cha robh dith no ganntar oirnn. Na déigh sin chaidh a' cheatharna a chaitheamh na cloiche neirt, agus an dé iomadh urchair thabhachdach choisinn Eoghann Bán urram an latha."

THE GRAMPIAN'S DESOLATE

Chaidh a bhàrdachd seo a sgrìobhadh aig deireadh na h-ochdamh linn deug. Tha i a' toirt dhuinn dealbh àraid air na h-atharraichean a bha a' tighinn gu ìre air a'Ghàidhealtachd, tro shùilean a'bhàird, Alasdair Caimbeul.

In this epic poem, writen mainly in 1799, the poet Alexander Campbell sets out his vision of the changes which were taking place in the Highlands. This is how he explained his reason for writing such a poem:

> "to call to the attention of the good men, wherever dispersed throughout our island, to the manifold and great evils arising from the introduction of that system which has within these last forty years spread amongst the Grampians and the Western Isles, and is the leading cause of the depopulation that threatens to extirpate the ancient race of inhabitants of those districts. The system alluded to is that of Sheep-stores, a species of monopoly beneficial to a few, but prejudiced to the state, in as much as it leads to Emigration, and consequently to a train of national calamaties, the bare idea of which awakens apprehension and danger."

Book Sixth

"A ludicrous sketch of a shinty-match, dinner, and dancing, illustrative of the sports, mode of living and pastimes of the inhabitants of the Western Isles."

> *Th' appointed day is come - th'eventful day,*
> *When on the snowy field in firm array,*
> *Glen meeting glen - (yet not with tempered blades,*
> *But sapling-oaks cut from the neighbouring glades,)*
> *Engage with ardour keen - in jovial guise -*
> *A cask of whisky strong, the victor's prize!*   (note)
> *'Tis noon - but half the narrow plain is bright,*
> *The sun just tips the southern hills with light;*
> *The mountains gleam that shade the vale below,*
> *Clear and reflective with incrusted snow.*
> *Now DERMID, dextrous in manly art,*
> *And DOUGLAS of the dale, with dauntless heart,*
> *Lead to the contest fierce their marshall'd ranks;*
> *To wield their weapons - namely, skinny-shanks. -*

And Dermid dignified in manhood's prime
Draws up his warriors - punctual to the time:
Lo, Douglas daring scowls with lofty brow,
(To gain the prize who form'd the secret vow)
As in full march he comes, and eyes askance
The adverse leader and his troops advance. -
Now front to front the armies are in array,
Await the signal to begin the fray;
Hark! - 'tis the signal - an ear-piercing smack,
Which bending echo peals as briskly back;
the well-struck ball whirls whizzing thro' the air,
While each keen combatant with with eager glare
Is on th'alert to hit it ere it fall,
And to the destin'd goal urge home the ball:
Sheer in the centre of the hostile train,
the orb now rolls along the glittering plain;
How brisk the onset! - fearless man meets man,
In kindling ire, of old as clan meet clan,
Aims at the globe, as swells the bickering din,
Yet hits it not - but hits his neighbour's shin!
Club rings on sapling oak, - or shin, or thigh,
As in the contest champions keenly vie,
Behold the ball hurled nearly to the goal, (original has "gaol")
But Dermid deftly strikes it with his pole,
When back it cleaves the gelid air again,
And laughs to scorn the contending efforts vain.
The doughty Dermid glorying in his might,
"Cheer up my lads! - the prize is ours ere night!"
Exulting cries, - his heroes - one and all,
Charge with redoubled vigour at his call.
As when in ire, contentious kites and crows,
High poised on wing, from chattering come to blows,

65

Sublime they mingling wheel from hill to hill,
And caw and scream, and whet the beak and bill -
'Tis horrid uproar all! - while crow meets kite,
Lo, how they tug and thwack, and peck and smite!
So fiercely in the fray our warriors bang,
While victory declares for neither gang;
And still they urge the dubious orb along,
Till Sol declines the Atlantic waves among;
When with a powerful arm and sapling-oak,
Lo, Douglas to the goal with giant stroke
Home sends the ball! - high peals the joyous "hail!"
While Dermid and his heroes gnaw the nail!
Thus ends the contest - but not so the play,
Our jovial frolicks close not with the day.
Behold the victor with joy-beaming eyes,
Triumphant marches with the well-won prize,
And in the hall aloft 'tis placed with care,
That all aloft may drink a liberal share"

[Alexander Campbell]

Ag ionndrain nam feara.

The hurler.

BLOOD RUNNING HOT

Tha beachd laidir ann gur ann bhon aon fhreumh a thanaig an dà gheam, golf agus camanachd. Chan eil iad idir air a bhith a' tighinn beò gu saorsnail le chèile tro eachdraidh ged tha, ged bhiodh an aithris fìor.

The games golf and shinty almost certainly spring from the same ancient sporting stock. But they have not always crowned their good with brotherhood.

According to the "Chronicle of the Royal Burgess Golfing Society of Edinburgh 1735-1935" by J Cameron Robbie, in 1816 blood was running hot between the golfers and the shinty players of the capital. So hot that the former reported the latter to the city magistrates.

In a memorial (or petition), dated 1816 the Burgess Golfing Society complained to the magistrates of Edinburgh "of the dangers and annoyance to the golfers through playing on the links of a game which resembles shinty—only it is more dangerous".

"From the numbers engaged in the game," carped the golfing fraternity, "the peculiar manner in which it is played, requiring the players to run with great violence and to station themselves over great portions of the ground, from the noise occasioned and the crowd of spectators attracted to witness it, the golfers find it impossible to continue the exercise of golf without great danger to those established on the links and claim the magistrates' protection."

It is not known whether the magistrates granted that protection. Perhaps the golfers were just jealous of that "crowd of spectators".

[J. Cameron Robbie, Chronicle of the Royal Burgess Golfing Society of Edinburgh 1735-1935, 1816.]

CALGARY SANDS: A STIRRING CONTEST

Two further paragraphs in the *Edinburgh Evening Courant* (Jan. 22nd, 1821) are worth recording:—

"On Tuesday last, one of the most spirited camack matches witnessed for many years in this country (Badenoch), where that manly sport of our forefathers has been regularly kept up during the Christmas festivities, took place in the extensive meadows below the inn of Pitmain."

"On Christmas and New-Year's Day matches were played in the policy before the house of Drakies, near Inverness, at the camack and football, which were contested with great spirit."

About the same date took place a stirring contest between the Campbells and Macleans of Mull, details of which have been preserved in the *Highland Home Journal*. During the troubled times of the Hanoverian rebellions these clans had entered the field under opposing banners, and the memories of those days had not been effaced. The Campbells challenged the Macleans to a trial of strength in Camanachd upon Calgary Sands.

"Everything was done on both sides to set their men to turn out on the day appointed, and so great was the feeling and excitement that Colonel Campbell of Knock, whose farm was nearly twenty miles from the Calgary Sands, ordered all his men to appear at Calgary and take part in the contest for honours. Mrs Clephane of Torloisk sent word round to all her tenants and crofters to be sure and attend the match to assist her cousin (Hector Maclean). The day was all that could be desired, and the number that turned out was much beyond the expectations of either party. At the appointed time the Shinty was tossed for sides. Then the wooden ball, as was then customary, was deposited in a hole in the sand, when a struggle took place to unearth it. Whoever was fortunate enough to get it out made off at full speed towards the goal, driving it before him, this being considered the feat of the day if well done. The playing was furious and determined. The Torloisk estate players placed their best men in reserve; they lay hid in the brushwood to the west of the Sands, whence they watched the play. From time to time a fresh man would dash out upon the Sands and enter into the fray. Ultimately they were one and all upon the the field. The contest grew hot and furious. Hail after hail was scored by the Macleans, until the Campbells were compelled to give in and leave the field, vanquished and crestfallen."

[Ninian MacDonald, Shinty, pages 79-80.]

THE CAMACK AND FOOTBALL

In recent years the term "Shinty" has come into general use amongst English speakers; whereas in the last generation it was more usual to speak of "camack." Thus in the Edinburgh *Evening Courant*, January 22nd, 1821—

"On Christmas and New-Year's Day matches were played at the camack and football." Gaelic speakers continue to use the term "camanachd," which has been applied to the pastime from time immemorial; although, as has been observed, in the oldest writings, "ag iomain" (the driving or urging) is of most frequent occurrence.

Regarding the origin of the word "Shinty" a term which has been applied indifferently to the club, the ball and the game—various suggestions have been put forward. The Standard Dictionary derives it from sinteag, a bound or spring; Jamieson suggests shon, a club; while the Oxford Dictionary refers to the cry used in the game, viz., "Shin ye, shin your side," and compares it to "Hummie" and its cry, "Hun you, shin you." These cries apparently were admonitions addressed to a player who attempted to approach on the wrong side.

The present writer thinks that the word "Shinty" may be derived from an old Celtic word meaning "to play," and used much as "ag iomain" was used among Gaelic speakers. Evidence for this is found in an Irish manuscript of the sixteenth century, where, amongst the marginal "probations pennae," may be read the following line:— "Sinnter linn do locht an fhoghluim," which means "we play, or let us play, for the pupils."

[Ninian MacDonald, Shinty. A Short History, 1932, pages 56-57.]

BLACK ISLE WITCHES

Tha aithrisean a 'nochdadh ann an *Courier Inbhir Nis* ann an 1827 mu thachartasan àraid anns an Eilean Dubh. Bha seo an luib grunn gheamanan a chaidh a chur air dòigh eadar muinntir Ghlinn Urchadain, agus sgioba bhon Eilean Dubh fhèin.

It is reported in the *Inverness Courier* in 1827 that extraordinary events were witnessed at a shinty match at Redcastle on the Black Isle. At the time, several matches were organised by Patrick Grant of Redcastle (near the author's home in North Kessock) and his friend Grant of Lochletter between Redcastle and Glenurquhart.

The first game was at Redcastle and, on approaching the field, the players found the gate intercepted by one of the Black Isle Witches who was knitting with a ball of thread thrown across to the other side. The Glen captain, Donald Maclean, cut the thread, made the sign of the cross on the witch's forehead and, calling out to his team to follow him, leapt over the fence. The Glen won and in a return at Lochletter, they won again.

At Redcastle, the ball was of hair and worsted, but at Lochletter, by request of the Redcastle men, it was of wood (cnag). At that time, a player catching the ball in the air was allowed to throw it, or even run with it, even through the goals. On one occasion, Donald Maclean, captain of the Glen team, did this and made for goal. He was tackled and caught by one of the Redcastle men, but, being big and strong, he lifted his opponent and ran with him between the posts. There were obviously no rules then, local custom being the unwritten law. This same incident between the Redcastle and Glenurquhart men was recorded in a letter published in the *Inverness Courier*, December 5, 1887, which states that these matches took place some sixty years previously (that is, around 1827).

[Peter English, Glenurquhart, page 18.]

AN SAGART

A boy posted on guard lest priest should catch the hurlers. This illustration accompanies the description of such an incident in Legends and Lakes of Killarney , Crofton Croker (1829), vol. 11, p. 63. Is there some attachment to the bas of two of the sticks, the one in the foreground and the higher of the two in the background? If there is, it is on different sides of the bas. Note the right hand under with both of the players.

(Is cosuil gur raibh cosg ag na sagairt air an iomanaiocht ar an Dòmhnach - it appears that priests had banned the playing of hurling on Sundays)

Scarcely had we reached the double row of lime trees on the Flesk Road, when we perceived a number of shock-headed youths enjoying a game of goal (the cricket of Ireland) in an adjoining field. Their amusement however was soon interrupted by the appearance of Father Fitzmaurice, which was immediately perceived by a tall boy, with a hurley in his hand, who had evidently been posted as a watch upon the movements of his reverance....... and in an instant they all scampered off before the priest could arrive at the field of action and recognise the transgressors.

[Crofton Croker, Legends and Lakes of Killarney, II, (1829), page 63.]

MYSTERIOUS PEOPLE FROM WESTERN SEAS

Among the Antrim hills men speak the very broadest of broad Scotch. On the way to Red Bay I managed to find out some old people who still speak Gaelic. Jeany McCallum, one of these, spoke the Argyllshire dialect withe certain forms which occur in old ballads, and with a new kind of brogue. When these old people, who have never been out of their native glens, spoke English, their accent was that Highland twang familiar to my ear from childhood. These know something about "Urageul" and some heroic names, but I got little out of them. The strange thing about these Saxon Antrim people is that they have forgotten the plantation of Ulster, without learning the traditions of Ireland, while they do remember some old British folk lore. I tried every name I knew with one man, and got no rise until I named King Arthur and Robin Hood. He knew about them. "Do you speak Irish?" I said to a polite farmer. "Old man," said this Irishman, "gin a body was to speak Irish till huz, we wad jeest lach at him Folks come here askin me whaur Sir Patrick herded the swine. I jeest tell them I dinna ken". "You must be a Scotchman," I said. "Na," said he, "I am an Irishman, and my fethers and my forebears dwalt here. What may your name be?" he asked. "Weel bruik your name," he said, when he heard it. At Coshendal, on Red Bay, I went to an old dame who keeps a whisky shop, and listened to her and her customers, and understood them. A man named Macdonald told me that his ancestors and most of the people about came from Scotland with Colla-Ciotach, and that many of them are left-handed still. Coll was hanged by order of the Marquis of Argyll, who was indicted for the deed, amongst others, and was beheaded 1660. Farther west, opposite to Ceantire, I conversed with men by the wayside in Gaelic as freely as I conversed in English with those Irishmen who spoke Lowland Scotch. In Rathlin they speak Argyllshire Gaelic with its accent, but use some different forms. On the other side of Ulster, at Ballyshannon, I got people to tell me stories about Diarmid and Graidhne. On the south of Donegal Bay runs a ranged of scarped hills, and high up in the face of a cliff is a cave which is called "leaba Dhiarmaid," or, in English, "Darby's den". This romance is very widely known as tradition all over Gaelic countries. It is very old, and somewhat like the story of Lancelot and Arthur's Queen. Beinn Boolbin, a peak 2000 feet high, is said to be Beinn Gulbin of the ballad. The topography of the head of Donegal Bay fits ballad topography better than any place I know. The great salmon fall at Ballyshannon is the place so often mentioned in ballads. The iron horse has taken the road which Caoilte and Fiona took when they chased the Old Norse witch who stole the cup and leaped the river at Bas Ruagh; and that same track must have been followed by marauding bands in real wars of old. The small harbour has the bearings given in ballads which describe the arrival of mysterious people from the western seas at Eas Ruagh of the sheltered streams.

[From "A Turn Through Gaelic Ireland in 1872," in Frazer's Magazine; in
The Oban Times, July 26, 1873.]

IN DEFIANCE OF THE EXCISE MAN

Parish of Layd

There are several caves along the coast of this parish. The most extensive is that in Sleans townland near the village of Cushendun and opposite the site of Port Crommelin harbour. It enters the rock very near the high water mark, and passes through it, extending about 80 feet in length, 16 in width and from 6 to 18 feet high. In it are fitted up by Mr Crommelin (whose property it is) a powder magazine, smith's forge, 2 store rooms and a cow house. The rock is conglomerate.

Near to Red Bay and on the roadside is Nanny's Cave, which has been inhabited by an old woman, who in defiance of the excise man has sold illicit whiskey. The cave is about 12 feet high and 15 wide at the entrance, extending about 40 feet inwards and gradually diminishing in size.

Close to Nanny's Cave are 3 others of a similar size; one is fitted up as a store for fishing nets etc. and the other as a smith's forge.

Under Red Bay Castle, in the conglomerate rock, is a cave about 20 feet above the level of the sea and 10 feet above the road. There are 2 entrances to it, each on a level with the floor. It is of an irregular form, rather small and 6 feet high. It does not seem to be connected to the castle.

Parish of Lochguile

Amusements

Their principal amusements are dancing, cards and cock-fighting. The latter are on the decline. A sort of hurling or "cammon playing", as it is called in the north, is still kept up here, chiefly among the Catholics. Going to fairs is also an amusement they are fond of.

[Ordnance Survey Memoirs of Ireland: Glens of Antrim, Volume 13, 1992, Institute of Irish Studies, Queen's University, Belfast, pages 45, 65.]

THE MARGAM BANDO BOYS

Due praises I'll bestow,
And all the world shall know,
That Margam valour will keep its colour
While Kenffig's waters flow.

Our master straight and tall,
Is foremost with the ball,
He is, we know it and must allow it
the fastest man of all.

Let cricket players blame,
And seek to blight our fame;
Their bat and wicket can never lick it,
This ancient and manly game.

Our fame shall always stand,
Throughout Brittania's land;
What men can beat us, who dare to meet us,
Upon old Kenffig sands.

Should Frenchmen raise a noise,
To crush our peaceful joys,
They'll get by storming, a precious warning,
From Margam Bando Boys.

Like lions we'll advance,
To charge the sons of France,
The Straits of Dover, we'll ferry over,
And make the traitors dance.

Napoleon shall repent,
If war is his repent,
He'll sadly rue it, if he'll pursue it,
Proud Paris will lament.

Brave Britons rule the main,
And many a hill and plain,
With every nation throughout creation,
Our rights we will maintain.

[Thomas Bredyn Jones, 1859.]

GUTH O MHACTALLA

Cha 'n ni 'nollaig ùr
A tha aca 'measg nan dù-ghall,
A leanas sine, ach dùchas
No dùthch' as an d' fhalbh sinn."

Lath-nollaig so chaidh, anns an t-seann chùnntas, chruinnich mòran de Ghaidheil Ghlaschu air machair mhòr an Rìgh, a h-uile fear sa chaman air chùl dùirn, agus ged thuit an oidhch' orra cha deach an là air taobh seach taobh. Chuir iad rompa gun coinnicheadh iad a rìs air Diluain an t-sainnseil; agus b'ann mar sin a thachair: ma mheadhan là chunnacas a' tighinn còrr is mìle Gàidheal le Pìobaire air an ceann agus fear a' giùlain buideil de Mhac-an-Tòisich. Bu bhòidheach da-rìreabh leam fèin an sealladh. Am fear air nach robh boineid bha osain bhreac' air, agus am fear air nach robh osain bhreac bha ite an fhìrean na aid.

Chaidh an comunn a roinn - thòisich an ùpraid, agus gu dearbh nuair ghabh na gillean teas cha bu near-achd fear briogais a bhiodh an rathad! Bha cho math is trì mìle Gall ag amharc air a chluiche, agus mòran de Ghàidheil cho measail's tha'n Glaschu, a dh'fhàs aon chuid ro reamhar no ro mhòrchuiseach airson ruith. Fhuair mi fèin caman o fhear de na ceann-stuic, agus mar tug mi teas don bhall-iomain thug esan teas dhòmhsa. Gach uair a rachadh am ball a thadhall, ghabhta sgailc de Mhac-an-Tòisich, agus dh'èrigheadh a'phìob sith rè tamuill.

Mu thuiteam na h-oidhche thàinig sinn dhachaidh trom, sgìth 's am pìobaire a' cluiche *"Soraidh o slàn do ghillean an fhèillidh."* -

Chuir mi seo thugaibh a Theachdaire, a leigeadh fhaicinn d'ar càirdeabh ann an tìr nam beann nach do dhì-chuimhnich sinn gu h-uile iad fhathast. Tha cuid de mhinistirean tha mi a' tuigsinn a' searmonachadh an aghaidh camanachd; theagamh gur ann dhiu so sibhse. Chan eil fhios agam fèin; ach se mo bheachd mar eil agaibh dad as miosa na iomain ri searmonachadh na aghaidh gu bheil 'ur sgìreachd ann an deagh staid da-rìreadh. Air mo shon fhèin bheir e maithachadh air mo chridhe, cuiridh e tiomachd aoigheil air m'anam, agus lasaidh e gràdh 'nam inntinn do'm uile cho-chreutairean nuair chluinneas mi ann an tìr chèin nuall na pìoba, òran maith Gaìdhlig, eadhon nuair a bheachd smaoinicheas mi air.

[MacTalla, Glaschu, 1830.]

DEIL TAK' THE GLASS

"Deil tak' the glass! Gie me a capp,
That I may drink a heart drap
In health to ilka honest chap
Wha loses that game of shintie.

[Leabhar Comunn nam Fìor Ghael, (The Book of the
Club of True Highlanders), Book of Sports, Chapter V, Orain na Camanachd, 1881.]

THE SHINNIE MUSTER ROLL

Air - "Bridge of Perth"

'Twas on June, the twenty second,
Eighteen hundred, thirty six,
That the Gael met at Shinnie,
On Blackheath their joints to rax.
Bagpipes raving, tartans waving,
Philibegs 'boon naked knees;
Banners flying, clouds converging,
Souls of heroes on the breeze.
Hearts inspiring, bosoms firing;
With the deeds of other days,
Flinging, dancing, bounding, prancing,
As the muse who sings their praise.

Our chief, Logan, rais'd the slogan,
Tait and Sievewright sung encore;
Brave Macewen and Macian,
Quickly joined the gallant corps.
Warrens, Martin and Macpherson,
Last of whom, a bard of note;
With Macdonalds, and good Reynolds,
Rush'd to keep their vigour hot.

Scott, Mackay and Macdonald,
Better pipers could not be;
Blew so loud that Scottish sailors,
Heard it on the German sea.

Menzies, Lossie and Macian,
Whitear, Grant and Rouvery;
Watsons bold and bright Glendinning,
Nicol, Gifford and Macphee;

Dauntless Siccar, bold Earwacker,
Forbes, Watts, and Dykes and Bell;
Robertson and Murchison,
And Mackintosh, all mountain Gael.
Henchman Gallie, our brave Gillie
Brandish'd his Lochaber axe,
As if to stretch on earth the wretch
Who would our wives and sweethearts vex.

Off they cast their plaids and bonnets,
Jackets, sporans, dirks, and belts;
For the signal wait the Celts.
Sides being chosen in the fashion
Of the hardy mountaineer;
And as the ball flew, on they follow'd,
Bounding with the speed of deer;
Straining, striving, all contriving,
Each his neighbour to excel;
Running, racing, rolling, chasing,
Eagerly to join the hale.

Oh! were Fingal, son of Cumal,
Present at the sport that day;
With his son, th'immortal Ossian,
Such were worthy of his lay.
Done no sooner, than for dinner,
Beef and haggis, mutton, veal,
Tatties, cheese and kail, and pease,
With streams of whisky, lochs of ale.
Then on the heath, till out of breath,
They danc'd their native Highland fling;
Now 'tis ended, thus commended,
As an honest bard can sing.

[David MacDonald, The Mountain Heath, London, 1938, pages 160-162.]

A UNIVERSAL AND FAVOURITE GAME

Football, curling, and golf, are too well known to need description; and we must content ourselves with a notice of the Camanachd, as not only being a favourite sport of the Club of True Highlanders, but as being undoubtedly the oldest known Keltic sport or pastime. The game is also called Cluich bhall, shinnie, shinty, bandy, hurling, hockey, and at one time was a universal and favourite game of the whole of Keltland.

We have already mentioned that it formed an important part of Keltic military education. Repeated reference is made to this game in the ancient laws. The enrichment of the camacs with different metals is mentioned, and "no one was to be fined for hurling on the green, because every green was free." The game must always be classed as the most valuable means for promoting agility, speed, presence of mind, endurance, truth of eye, and sureness of foot; no game is better calculated to bring into play all the muscles of the body and faculties of the mind, without over-straining; and we must trust that the day is not far distant when the youth of Great Britain will as keenly contest the hale as their fathers did. The origin of this game is lost in the mist of ages; MacPherson says:- "In Ireland it has been always the national game - indeed, it is said, and, no doubt, with great truth, that the game of *Camanachd*, or *club playing*, was introduced into the Green Isle by the immediate descendants of Noah. On such authority we may rationally conclude that it was played by Noah himself; and if by Noah, in all probability by Adam and his sons." As we have, however, no contemporary account of the game at that period we must be content with later records.

Many authorities have endeavoured to prove that the game was an importation of the Romans, but Menzies effectively demolishes the flimsy fabric.

All ball playing was suppressed by Edward 111, by a public edict, the ostensible reason for suppressing these sports being that they impeded the progress of archery.

"The game is played in its utmost perfection in the districts of Strathdearn, Strathnairn, Strathspey, Braidalbane, Rannoch, Lochaber, in many parts of the West Highlands; but particularly so in *Baideanach*, where the late Colonel Duncan Macpherson, the father of the present chief, greatly patronised it."

"The number - one each side - on the Prad of Cluny was never above ten, and the distance of the hales from each other was always about half a mile. This is, however, not practicable in all situations. The width of each goal was about seven feet." This game has always been a great favourite with the members of the Club, and the "mire chath" of the combatants in the mimic fray has again and again aroused the enthusiasm of the bards of the Club. The first recorded game shows that the members in order to enjoy the sport had to start at ten o'clock in the morning per coach from the British Coffee House. The game was held at Blackheath, and the day's amusement was finished with the dance, the song, and the shell. Blackheath for many years was the favourite spot, but increasing railway facilities having made it the resort of a crowd of pleasure-seekers, Wimbledon Common, the racecourse of the Alexandra Palace, &c., have of late years been selected for the annual gatherings.

Críoch.

Leabhar Comunn nam Fíor Ghael.
(Book of the Club of True Highlanders)

The members of the Club in formal setting

The game as played by the Club of True Highlanders has always been opened with a certain amount of ceremonial, the due order of which is as follows:-

First: The players march from the place of rendezvous two by two, club over shoulders, to the field, preceded by the warder and piper.

Second: When arrived in from the marquee, the members lay aside those parts of the dress which would become cumbersome and prevent activity in the game.

The arrangements of the field are under the direction of the chief, and the teams are under the direction of the two chieftains or captains who stake out the ground. The distance that the hales are placed apart varies with the extend of the ground and the number of players; each hale being formed of two flags placed ten feet apart, the mid-hale, or place from which the game is started, is also marked.

Third: The chieftains then select by lot, as customary, their respective parties. The usual manner is for one of the chieftains to toss the caman towards the other, who catching it with one hand, a grip is taken hand over hand until the end is reached, and the man who can take the last grip has the first choice.

The players are drawn up in two lines, as they are to be opposed to each other in order of play; the chief and chieftains will then pass between the men, and the chief will read out the following rules :-

Rules and regulations of the game (as generally observed throughout Scotland).

1. The club or caman to be used for no other purpose than that of propelling the ball; neither to trip the foot of an opponent not in any way to molest him, except to turn away his club that you may gain the ball.

2. No player on any account must push the player he is in pursuit of, for that is attended with great danger; it being evident that an extra force applied to a person at full speed may easily throw him on his head. No player must voluntarily shoulder his opponent; the *fair game* being to get before him and take the ball from him, *not by force , but by dexterity*.

3. Each player must play on his own side, that is, right-handed, and no-one shall be deemed accountable for any accident that may happen to a left-handed player.

4. The ball must be driven in between the two sides of the goal (Eader dha bhith an taoghail), either on the ground so as not to touch either side; or if it hails by a raised blow, the course of the ball must be fairly over the space between the sides of the goal.

5. If any dispute arise it must be left to the chief, whose decision shall be final.

6. The side that hails plays the next game in the opposite direction, and must be allowed to drive the ball *from the goal* into the middle space as far as he can in one blow, and he who hails has the right to give the first blow to the ball in the next game, or he can transfer his privilege to any one of his own side.

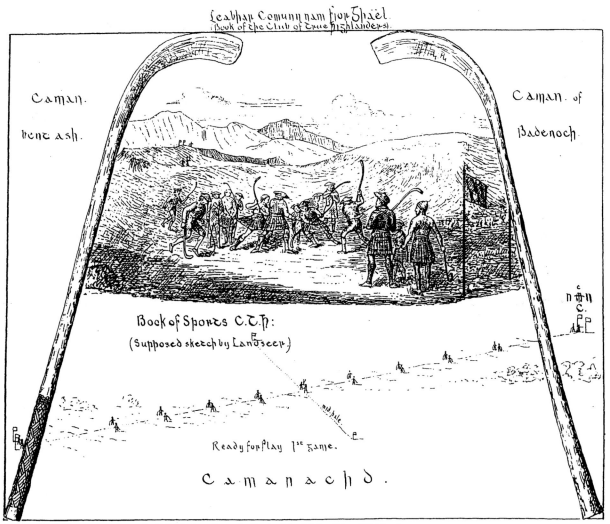

Leabhar Comunn nam fior Ghael.
(Book of the Club of True Highlanders)

Caman.

bent ash.

Caman. of

Badenoch.

Book of Sports C.T.H:

(Supposed sketch by Landseer.)

mid hole

Ready for play 1st game.

Camanachd.

The method of setting teams on the field of play: from the Book of the Club of True Highlanders.

The rules proclaimed, the next duty of the chieftains is to decide in which direction each side is to play the first game; one sends a caman spinning in the air, crying, "Bas na cas"; the other chieftain cries to one or the other, and his side plays to the hale to which the selected end points; they then see that their men are placed in the best position. At this stage of the proceedings great care should be exercised as to the manner in which the men are placed; one or two steady, cool hands should be placed to guard the hale, and the younger and more active members should be placed towards mid-hale, or forward towards the opponents' hale. The men should be cautioned to play into each other's hands, as many a good game has been lost by an over-eager player driving the ball anywhere, regardless of consequence, so long as he could get a good lick at it. Each player should also be careful to play the ball so that it can be taken up by his comrades, and not by his opponents.

When the chieftains reach the mid-hale and are face to face, the warning given by one chieftain, *"Buail'm ort"* (I'll strike), is answered by "Leagadh me leat" (I'll allow you), the chief then exclaims, "Suas e," throws up the ball, and the game commences. The hush of expectancy gives place to the excitement and animation of the camanachd; the ball is driven hither and thither, from caman to caman; sometimes a smart blow sends it flying in the air, at others it is kept bounding along by the skilful play of a fleet runner, and it is bandied about with varying fortune until it comes dangerously near one of the hales; the hale-keepers and the rear backs are anxiously on the alert; the players draw together, darting backwards and forwards like a swarm of midges, until a well directed blow either sends the ball flying between (or over) the hale-posts or towards the centre of the field; and so the struggle is kept up until the buail-choilleag (or stroke that gains the hale) has been given. The next game is then *started from the hale which has just been gained* by one of the winning sides driving the ball from the centre of the hale towards the middle of the field.

If the progress of the game of the ball should be driven past the hales, the party defending the same has the right to one hit to drive the ball as far towards the middle as he can. [or in the most suitable direction].

This manner of playing the game has been carefully handed down in the records of the Club of True Highlanders, and, we think, is the best mode of play; but it is played in a slightly different manner by other societies. The Highland Camanachd Club has a boundary line of flags, and when the ball passes that line it is dead, and is brought in six paces, and thrown up again. This system has its advantages and its disadvantages. On the other hand, a great deal of time is wasted in stepping the distance and throwing up the ball, and there is a great temptation for a player, when he is hard pushed, to strike it out of bounds, and then get breathing time. This is especially noticeable on the hale boundaries: a player, no matter how unskilful, can by a power blow drive the ball past (no matter how wide of) the hale; the six paces are stepped, the players have time to draw near, and the ball is started within six paces of the hale, and this dangerous advantage is gained either by bad play or an exhibition of mere animal force. Another point of difference is that at the commencement of each game the ball is thrown up by one of the captains at *mid-hale*. The illustrations of the game (copied from a sketch woodcut in the possession of the Club, which is supposed to have been from the pencil of Landseer) give a very good idea of the game. The caman on the left hand was made by ourselves of bent ash.

The old Badenoch caman was about four and a half inches long in the bas or flat, and was about two inches thick at the back or keel, but not above one-half inch thick at the top, thus admirably contrived for raising the ball, and sending it to the greatest distance at one blow; it was always made of birch.

The ball was generally a small cricket ball, covered with stout twine, but is not so reliable as the old-fashioned one.

The game when played on ice is one of the most exciting it is possible to conceive; the ball, however, is replaced by a lump of cork, or bung, and the players wear skates.

We may add that the season for the game generally extends from two months before to two months after New Year's time. The annual Cruinneachadh Camanachd of the Club of True Highlanders, however, is generally held about Belteine, or even later, in order that the ladies may participate with comfort and pleasure in the outing. Play is generally kept up for two or three hours, and, after a dance or two to John McKenzie's piping, the zest with which the "beef and greens" are attacked may be (as the newspaper reporter would say) more easily imagined than described.

[MacIntyre-North, Leabhar Comunn nam Fior Ghael (Book of True Highlanders), 1871.
See also Hutchinson, Camanachd!, page 73 and thereafter for references.]

"O MUSTER MY LADS FOR THE SHINNIE"

The Thistle Club Shinnie Medal

O! muster, my lads, for the shinnie,
Come, rush like waves of the sea;
Come, sweep as the winds from the heavens,
Nor these than the Gael more free.

Let national fervour inspire you,
As bounding you march to the heath;
O! think of your anscestors' glory,
Who smiled at the triumph of death.
O! muster, my lads....

The heather blooms sweet on the mountain,
The thistle waves proud in the vale,
Where hover the ghosts of your fathers -
The brave Caledonian Gael.
O! muster, my lads.......

To witness their progeny summon'd,
And joyously view their combine;
With camacks to play at the shinnie,
The pastime and sport of Langsyne.
O! muster, my lads.....

How fine is the muscular action -
So highly conducive to health -
O! Hygeia's glances are sweeter
than all the caresses of wealth.
O! muster, my lads...

'Tis worthy the soul of true heroes
In exercise such to contend;
Promoting their wealth and their vigour,
Their sacred rights to defend.
O! muster, my lads....

Then cast off your plaids, lads, and to it,
And when you've gained three times the 'hail',
March straight to the barn or the bothy,
Your sweethearts and wives to regail..
O! muster, my lads.....

For Logan has tapp'd you Scots whisky,
And Lossie broached you good ale,
And Currie has made a Scots' haggis,
And Menzies prime savoury kale.
O! muster, my lads.....

I've purchased some cheese in Glen Muidart,
Which Gallie has fetch'd in a sack;
Though great and astounding the distance,
He carried it all on his back.
O! muster, my lads........

On, that ye may feast at the shinnie,
And thank the Great Giver with awe;
And ere ye arise from the table,
Let harmony animate all.
O! muster, my lads....

Then dance to the tune of the bagpipes,
Quick reading till panting for breath;
And may you all meet the next season,
As happy again at Blackheath.
O! muster my lads....

[1836]

Hurling in summer. This pen and ink drawing of a hurling match is signed MacKenzies Delin, 1805. The artist was possibly Charles MacKenzie, a landscape painter in Dublin at the beginning of the nineteenth century. This and a companion sketch of a football scene apparently by the same artist are preserved in the National Library of Ireland.

(Reproduced with thanks to the Trustees of the Library)

THE PENNY MAGAZINE

OF THE

Society for the Diffusion of Useful Knowledge.

181.] PUBLISHED EVERY SATURDAY. [JANUARY 31, 1835.

THE GAME OF SHINTY.

[Game of Shinty.]

THE DIFFUSION OF USEFUL KNOWLEDGE

In the Highlands of Scotland it is customary for persons to amuse themselves, in the winter season, with a game which is called "shinty". This sport has a considerable resemblance to that which is denominated "hurling" in England, and which Strutt describes under that name. The shinty is played with a small hard ball, which is generally made of wood, and each player is furnished with a curved stick somewhat resembling that which is used by golf players. The object of each party of players is to send the ball beyond the boundary on either side; and the skill of the game consists in striking the ball the greatest distance towards the adversaries' boundary, or in manoeuvring to keep it in advance of the opposing side. Large parties assemble during Christmas holidays, one parish sometimes making a match against another. In the struggles between the contending players many hard blows are given, and more frequently a shin is broken, or by rarer chance some more serious accident may occur. The writer witnessed a match, in which one of the players, having gained possession of the ball, contrived to run a mile with it in his hand, pursued by both his own and the adverse party until he reached the appointed limit, when his victory was admitted. Many of the Highland farmers join in with eagerness in the sport, and the laird frequently encourages by his presence this amusement of his labourers and tenants.

A Highland Landscape with a game of shinty. c1840, attributed to D. Cuncliffe.

"A gentleman announces that he is to give a shinty play on a certain day in a certain place. The meaning of the announcement is that a certain quantity of whisky is to be distributed at the place to the players and the spectators. The quantity of whisky provided varies according to the wealth, the liberality and the vanity of the donors, from ten to fourteen imperial gallons."

(The Rev Donald Cameron, describing one aspect of the preliminaries to a shinty match in Laggan in 1841)

JOYOUS OCCASIONS AT DORNOCH

Sgrìobh an t-Urramach Dòmhnall Sage Memorabilia Domestica faisg air ceud gu leth bliadhna air ais. Se seo tè de na cunntasan as fheàrr a th'againn air dòigh-beatha nan Gàidheal aig an àm - mar a bha iad a'tighinn beò agus mar a bha iad a'fulang aig làmh nan uachdaran.

A-measg gach nì eile air am bheil e a'toirt luaidh, tha an aithris bheag seo air mar a thachair aig gèam camanachd.

One of the most interesting and evocative accounts of life in the Highlands 150 years ago is Reverend Donald Sage's Memorabilia Domestica, or parish Life in the North of Scotland. Written originally by Donald Sage, minister of Resolis, the description of life in the north was edited by his son and published under the title Memorabilia Domestica . Reverend Sage died in 1869. His diary accounts were largely written in 1840 and published fifty years later.

The intriguing account of life 150 years ago includes, on page 118, reminiscences of his school-boy days at Dornoch, one of the very few accounts which have been discovered of an apparent death on the shinty field.

When at school at Dornoch we had our holiday games. Of these, the first was "club and shinty" (cluich' air phloc). The method we observed was this - two points were marked out, the one the starting-point, and the other the goal, or "haile". Then two leaders were chosen by a sort of ballot, which consisted in casting a club up into the air, between the two ranks into which the players were divided. The leaders thus chosen stood out from the rest, and, from the number present, alternately called a boy to his standard. The shinty or shinny, a ball of wood, was then inserted into the ground, and the leaders with their clubs struck at it until they got it out again. The heat of the game, or battle as I might call it, then began. The one party laboured hard and most keenly, to drive the ball to the opposite point or "haile;" the other to drive it across the boundary to the starting point; and which party soever did either, carried the day. In my years the game was universal in the north. Men of all ages among the working classes joined in it, especially on old New Year's day. I distinctly recollect of seeing, on such joyous occasions at Dornoch, the whole male population, from the grey-headed grandfather to the lightest heeled stripling, turn out to the links, each with his club; and, from 11 o'clock in the forenoon till it became dark, they would keep at it, with all the keenness, accompanied by shouts, with which their forefathers had wielded the claymore. It was withal a most dangerous game to young and old. When the two parties met midway between the two points, with their blood up, their tempers heated, and clubs in their hands, the game then assumed all the features of a personal quarrel; and wounds were inflicted, either with the club or the ball, which, in not a few instances, actually proved fatal. The grave of a man, Andrew Colin, father of one of my school-mates, was pointed out to me, as that of one who was mortally wounded at a club and shinty game. The ball struck him on the head, causing concussion of the brain, of which he died.

THE GAME OF THE PEASANTRY

"But the great game in Kerry, and indeed throughout the South, is that of 'Hurley'—a game rather rare, though not unknown in England. It is a fine, manly exerise, with sufficient danger to produce excitement; and it is for excellence the game of the peasantry of Ireland. To be an expert hurler a man must possess athletic powers of no ordinary character . . . . The forms of the game are these:—The players, sometimes to the number of fifty or sixty, being chosen per each side, they are arranged (usually bare-footed) in two opposing ranks with their hurleys crossed to await the tossing up of the ball, the goals being previously fixed at the extremities of the hurling-green, which from the nature of the play is required to be a level, extensive plain. Then, there are two picked men chosen to keep the goal on each side, over whom the opposing party places equally tried men as a counterpoise, the duty of these goalkeepers being to arrest the ball in case of its near approach to that station and return it back towards that of the opposing party, while those placed over them exert all their energies to drive it through the goal. "All preliminaries being adjusted, the leaders take their places in the centre. A person is chosen to throw up the ball, which is done as straight as possible, when the whole party, withdrawing their hurleys, stand with them elevated to receive and strike it in its descent. Now comes the crash of mimic war; hurleys rattle against hurleys; the ball is struck and restruck, often for several minutes, without advancing much nearer to either goal. When, however, someone is lucky enough to get a clear "puck" at it, it is sent flying over the field, and it is followed by the entire party at their utmost speed; the men grapple, wrestle and toss each other with amazing agility, neither victor nor vanquished waiting to take breath, but following the course of the rolling and flying prize. The best runners watch each other, and keep shoulder to shoulder throughout the play, and the best wrestlers keep as close on them as possible to arrest or impede their progress. The ball must not be taken from the ground by the hand, and the tact and skill shown in taking it on the point of the hurley and running with it half the length of the field, when too closely pressed striking it towards the goal, is a matter of astonishment to those who are but slightly acquainted with the play. At the goal is the chief brunt of the battle. The goalkeepers receive the prize and are opposed by those set over them; the struggle is tremendous: every power of strength and skill is exerted; while the parties from opposite sides of the field run at full speed to support their men engaged in the conflict; then the tossing and straining is at its height, the men often lying in dozens side by side on the field, while the ball is returned by some strong arm again, flying over their heads, towards the other goal. Thus for hours has the contention been carried on, and frequently the darkness of night arrests the game without victory on either side. It is often attended with dangerous, and sometimes fatal results.

[Hall, Ireland, its scenery, character etc, c.1840.]

The game of the peasantry

THE HIGHLANDERS IN LONDON - CHRISTMAS DAY

The 25 December being a general holiday in London, the sons of the *Gael* resident in the metropolis, to the tune of several *scores*, assembled as usual on the splendid and spacious grassy plain called *Black heath*, behind Greenwich Park, to have a bout at the good old national game of "*shinny*," where the *cammock* chest of the "Society of True Highlanders," in the charge of a trusty Macleod, awaited their arrival, and contained some of the finest specimens, in British oak, of the *club* or *cammock*, we ever saw, each branded with the initials of the Society, and bound above the bass with a knot of green or red ribbon, to distinguish the sides of the respective players. About 11 o'clock A.M., Messrs Gollan (of Gollanfield) and Mackenzie, were chosen *head-stocks*, and while the operation of calling sides was going forward we were wafted in imagination to the land of the "mountain and flood," as the clannish names of Mackintosh, Macleod, Maclean, Maclennan, Mackenzie, Chisholm, Cameron, &c., flanked by -

"na Frisealaich 's na Grantaich"

Sounded in our ears. The Highlanders then laid aside their belted plaids, stripped to their shirts, and commenced the game in right good earnest, to the no small amusement of the wondering Cocknies present, who evidently regarded every blow struck, and crash of the *cammocks*, as they met in the manly strife, with the most intense interest, and the ladies were apparently only deterred from taking part in the sport, by the unfortunate recollection of their petticoats! After the first four games had been played, during which the most admirable tact and activity was displayed on both sides, (the last one having lasted two hours), the Highlanders repaired to the "Princess of Wales," adjoining the heath, where they had refreshments in the shape of the true blue and "Reid & Co's entire," after which they again sought the heath, and renewed the contest until Phoebus had hid his head in the Eastern horizon and warned the Gael that the strife must cease. The unaccountable absence of the bagpipes on the occasion was much felt and regretted.

On returning to London by way of the Greenwich railway, the Highlanders crowded together in the train, as it sped along, a reel (as best they could) was got up, to the Gaelic airs of a Chisholm of Strathglass, which, had it been persisted in, would have endangered the bottom of the carriage, and probably have brought their feet in contact with the rails! As it was, however, they arrived in safety, much pleased with the manner in which the day had been spent. *Correspondent.*

[Inverness Courier, January 3, 1844.]

THE SONS OF THE MOUNTAINS

The fourth of April being a holiday, the sons of the mountains, resident in this province, had determined to try a game of shinty for auld lang syne. Though the weather was very threatening in the morning, the players were not to be daunted, but crossed the Bay in boats, and marched to the ground (a plain at the foot of the mount, from which Montivideo derives its name), under the inspiring strains of the bagpipes, to the tune of "The Campbells are Coming," where they were greeted by a large concourse of people, assembled to witness the game.

After sides were called, and a few other preliminaries arranged, playing commenced, and was carried on with great spirit till four P.M., when the players sat down on the grass and partook of an asado de carvo con cuero (beef roasted with the hide on,) and plenty of Ferintosh (Aldourie and Brackla being scarce.) Dancing then commenced, and the Highland Fling danced by Messrs Maclennan and Macrae; Gille Callum, by Captain MacLellan; Sean Truise, by Mr MacDougall; and several other Scotch reels were greatly admired.

At half-past seven o'clock, the bagpipes struck up the "Gathering" and the whole, forming two deep, marched from the field to the place of embarkation, to the tune of "Gillean na Feileadh," amidst loud cheering, and still louder vivas from the natives.

At nine o'clock, the players sat down to a comfortable supper at the Steamboat Hotel; and, after the cloth was removed, and bumpers quaffed for the Royal family, and the President of the Republic, Don Frutuoso Rivera, the Chairman called for a special glass for the toast of the evening and, in a neat and appropriate speech, interspersed with Gaelic, proposed, "Tir nam bean, 's nan gleann, 's na gaisgich," which was drunk with great enthusiasm amidst deafening cheering.

Several Gaelic and other songs were sung during the evening, and the health of our chairman, Captain Maclellan, of the ship Orpheus, being proposed, and the thanks of the company returned him, for the spirited manner in which he conducted the proceedings of the day, the whole separated at two in the morning, after drinking "Deoch an dorus," highly delighted wit the day's amusement.

[Inverness Courier, July 13, 1842.]

[Duke of Argyll, Scotland as it was and as it is , Volume II; Appendix II, pp328-329.]

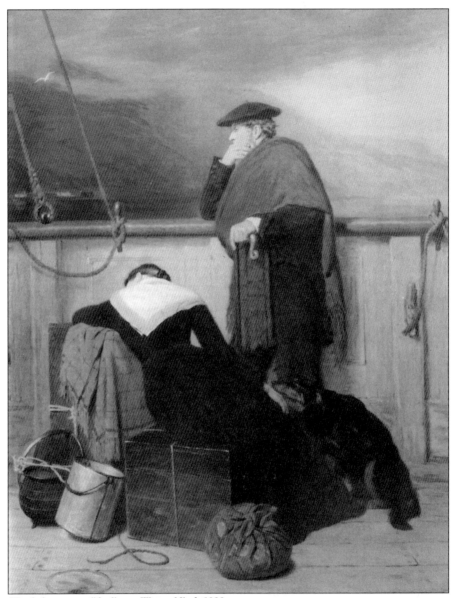

"Lochaber no more" by James Watson Nicol, 1883

SHEAS MI CAR TAMUILL

Sheas mi car tamuill
Le ioghnadh gun smalan,
a'coimhead nam fearaibh
Le'n camain chruaidh ùr;
Gaoth tuath is clach-mheallain
'Gam bualadh 's 'gan dalladh;
Bha 'chuideachd cho dannair
'S nach aithnicht' orr mùth'.

Laoich chalma le 'n camain
'Gan dearbhadh 's gach bealach,
Laoich eutrom 's na caraibh
Mar cheathach nan stòc;
Cur ball anns an athair
Le luathas na dealain,
'Nuair gheibh i ri spealladh
Ri talamh 'toirt cùil.

Gur bòidheach an treud iad
Air faiche le chèile,
'S iad ruith mar na fèidh
Air slèibh nam beann àrd;
A rèir cumha an fhèidhe
Bha mactalla ag èigheach;
Sud 'nis, òlaich threubhach,
Nach gèilleadh gu bràth.

O'n dualas a lean ribh
O ghuaillibh 'ur seanair,
Bhiodh cruadalachd daingeann
Nis leanachd ri 'n àl;
Ard-inntinneach fearail,
Foinnidh, fuasgailte, fallainn;
Bhiodh suathadh de 'n fhallus
Mu'n mhal' air an tràigh.

A sketch of Geeelong, Victoria, soon after the arrival of the infamous "Georgiana", with the immigramts from the Isle of Skye in 1852. From "Voyage & mutiny of the 'Georgiana'", by Lorraine MacKenzie, Geelong, 1994.

GUMA SLAN DO NA FEARAIBH

In the year 1838, a large number of people emigrated to Australia from the neighbourhood of Kingussie. The St George, by which they had taken passage to Sydney, lay at Oban, so it was necessary for them to make the long journey to Fort William in carts, and thence to the place of embarkation by steamboat. Their departure from Kingussie took place at mid-summer, and on the day of St Columba's Fair - Latha Feill Chaluim Chille. This fair was the occasion of a general gathering of the inhabitants of Badenoch; and to it many resorted from distance for purposes of trade or mere amusement. Several near relatives of the writer, who were among those present on the memorable day referred to, used to describe with deep emotion the scenes of heart-rending grief which they witnessed.

A band of strolling musicians in connection with some entertainment, readily entered into the situation and temper of their assembled patrons at the fair. Playing airs suited to the occasion, and followed by crowds of people, they made their way to the top of the Little Rock, which commands a view of the whole of Badenoch downwards from Glen Truim. From that height, where a few years before, "the young men of Kingussie" had erected a cairn in memory of Duke Alexander, many eyes were turned wistfully to take a last farewell of much-loved haunts and homes. One strain of song touched every heart, and snatches of it were ever associated with recollections of the affecting events of the day:

> Let Fortune use me as it may,
> I will think on Scotland far away.

After descending from the Creag Bheag, the emigrants set out on their westward journey, accompanied as far as the old stage-house of Pitmain by relatives and friends. Here, those who were departing for the New World and those who were remaining behind took leave of each other as persons who would never meet again on this side of the grave.

Among those who then bade farewell for ever to the banks of the Spey, there was one of whom I should like to make passing notice. This was a young man named John Eason. His parents were natives of Morayshire, and had come to reside in Kingussie, no doubt in consequence of some employment on the Gordon Estates. A stone-mason to trade, he found time to devote to reading and the cultivation of the muses. Being possessed of much public spirit, he was the recognised leader of the forward youths of the village, and a universal favourite throughout the country. Half a century after he had gone, those of his companions who still survived, liked to speak of him often. I understand that he died not long after his settlement in the New World.

The bard, Dòmh'll Phàil, was another resident in the neighbourhood of Kingussie, who had resolved to seek his fortunes beyond the seas. Circumstances, however, prevented him from carrying out his intention. It was when in prospect of leaving his native land, and when the advantages of emigration were constantly under discussion, that he composed this song, which makes bantering allusion to the various inducements that might be supposed to suggest themselves to his mind.

It may be remarked that the good ship, St George, took no less than five months to make the voyage to Sydney, which must have been a tiresome one indeed for the unfortunate passengers.

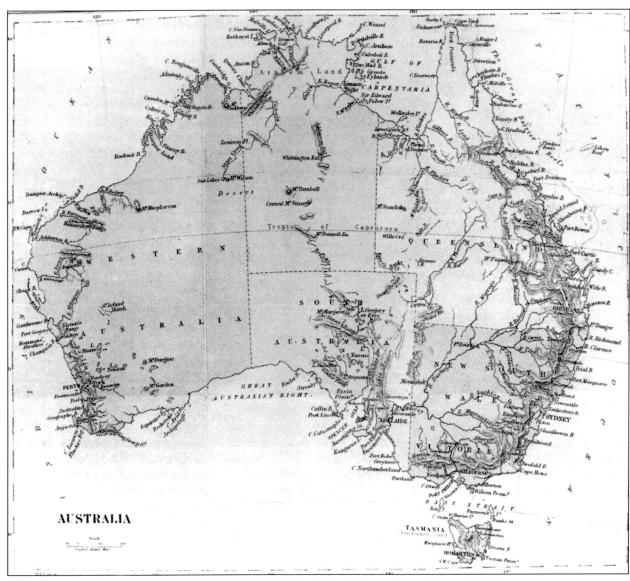

Guma slan do na fearaibh, Australia, 1865.

Gu 'm a slàn do na fearaibh
Thèid thairis a' chuan
Gu talamh a' gheallaidh,
Far nach fairich iad fuachd.
Gu 'm a slàn etc.

Gu 'm a slàn do na mnàthan
Nach cluinnear an gearan,
'S ann thèid iad gu smearail,
'G ar leantuinn thar 'chuan;
Gu 'm a slàn etc.

'Us na nìghneagan bòidheach,
A dh'fhalbhas leinn còmhladh,
Gheibh daoine ri'm pòsadh,
A chuireas òr 'nan dà chluais.
Gu 'm a slàn etc.

Cha bi iad 'g ar dùsgadh,
Le clag Chinne-Ghiubhsaich;
Cha bhi e gu diùbhras,
Ged nach dùisg sinn cho luath.
Gu 'm a slàn etc.

**[Sinton, Poetry of Badenoch
pages 34-38.]**

105

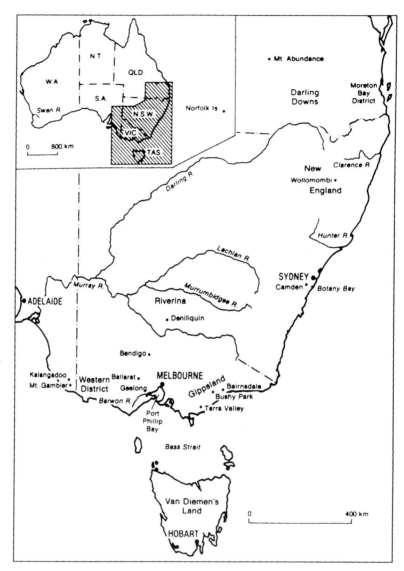

Centres of Scottish settlement in Australia, from The Scots Abroad: Labour, Capital, Enterprise, 1750-1914, ed. by R.A. Cage. London, 1985. By permission of Croom Helm Ltd, Publishers.

AG IONNDRAIN NAM FEARA

"Ag ionndrainn nam feara, a' cheathairne chòir
A bheireadh dhomh cuireadh le furan gun ghó;
Cha chluinn mi's cha'n fhaic mi na fleasgaichean òg
'Dol cruinn air an achadh le'n camain 'nan dòrn."

[Dr Maclachlan, Rahoy, Transactions of the Gaelic Society of Inverness, XXX, page 35.]

A' feitheamh son a'bhàta.

Between decks on an emigrant ship. Illustrated London News, 17 August 1850.

THERE WAS NO ALTERNATIVE

The Highland and Island Clearances, and potato famine, brought much devastation and heartache to many families on Skye. There was no alternative, they were forced to emigrate or starve. How difficult it must have been for the many families leaving behind loved ones, to sail with young children, to a strange land far away over the seas. They had no idea how long the voyage would take or even if they would survive the journey.

The Scottish Immigrants from the Isle of Skye sailed from Greenock, Glasgow, for Australia on the Barque "Georgiana" on July 13, 1852, and berthed at Point Henry, Geelong, on 16th October 1852. A mutiny, on arrival, by some of the crew, who wanted to desert the ship for the gold diggings, was a terrifying experience for the Scots.

One hundred and forty two years later descendants of the Scottish Immigrants from the Isle of Skye, who arrived on the "Georgiana" gathered in Geelong to celebrate the lives of their brave Scottish ancestors, who were Australian Pioneers. The reunion on 15 October 1994, was attended by 300 people from all over Australia.

Visitors could have been forgiven for thinking they were in Scotland, as the different clans arrived in their Kilts, to the skirl of the Bagpipes. The day began with a short Thanksgiving Service, with the singing of the 23rd Psalm, which the Immigrants had sung as they sailed down the Clyde in 1852. There was hardly a dry eye in the hall.

A Roll Call, by the Town Crier of the 372 original Passenger's names, united many families. Family histories, photos and treasured possessions were displayed. A clock, brought to Australia, by Angus and Mary McKenzie (Nee MacKinnon) and a shawl woven by Mary McKenzie, on Skye, also a Gaelic Bible which was presented to Martin Robertson on the "Georgiana," were displayed. A map of Skye showed where the families emigrated from.

Guest Speaker Roderick Balfour, from Inverness, Scotland, an expert on the Highland and Island Immigration Scheme, shared his wonderful knowledge with all, and his contribution was a highlight.

Scottish Country Dancers, Highland Dancers and Singers, who sang the old Scottish songs stirred the crowd of Australians whose roots are still deep in Scotland. No one can ever take that away. Many families found long lost relatives, or different branches of their families who were previously unknown.

A book was produced on " The Voyage and Mutiny of the Georgiana." Names of all the original Immigrants and families are now on a Computer Database, with the names and addresses of known descendants in Australia.

The missing links left behind in Scotland, we wonder what became of them.

A return pilgrimage to the Isle of Skye is being planned for July and August 1996, by some of the descendants of the Scottish Immigrants.

[Lorraine Mackenzie, Geelong, Victoria, Oban Times, 1994.]

LET'S PLAY THE GAME

LINES SUGGESTED BY HEARING OF THE ESTABLISHING OF A HURLING CLUB IN GEELONG

All hail! thou ancient game, all hail!
Come, welcome, join my friends,
And patronise such sport with zeal,
And party strife thus end;
Let's play the game with energy-
Compete - yea,"man to man,"
With lithesome limbs, in rivalry,
And win, let he who can.

Come let us join, both one and all -
No matter creed or clime,
Instead of legs, let's strike the ball,
In sportiveness - not crime -
And thus in union shall we meet
Henceforth, and crush all spleen,
And brotherly each other greet
Upon the "Hurling Green."

The anniversary of the birth
Of our good gracious Queen,
Is wisely chosen for the mirth
Of the "Hurlers on the Green,"
Let the Shamrock, Rose, and Thistle
Unite upon that day;
And, without a ruffled bristle,
"Goal," on the 24th of May.

[The Geelong Chronicle, May 5, 1863.]

[Port Philip Herald, July 16, 1844.]

110

GOAL KEEPER

AN OPEN 'PUCK'

'RISING'

A FLY CATCH.

JOHN SWAIN ENG

ORMOND HURLING CLUB

The annual meeting of the Ormond Hurling Club was held at Ryan's Ormond hotel on last Thursday evening; Mr. P. Cusack (the president) in the chair. There were about fifty persons present, the utmost enthusiasm prevailed, and it was confidently asserted that the club must have a very prosperous season. It was decided that the colours of the club be green and white. On the motion of Mr. J. Linehan, seconded by Mr. J. Gilbert, it was decided to change the name of the club to Bungaree Hurling Club. The election of officers for the ensuing season resulted as follows :- Patrons - Messers E. Murphy, M. L. A., J. J. Fitzgerald, J. P, P. J. Slattery, P. Bourke, J. Coghlan, T. Maher, A. Lee, M. Newton, W. J. Coghlan, R. S. Foley, M. Cremin, J. Noonan, J. Lynch, and R. Trebilcock; president, Mr. P. Cusack (re-elected); vice-president Mr. D. Clohesy. There were two nominations received for the captainship. Vice-captain, Mr. C. Lee; secretary Mr. M. Reidy; treasurer, Mr. T. Ryan (re-elected); committee- Messers J. Gilbert, M. Hogan, Michael Reidy, M. Cunningham, W. Doolan, and J. Curtain. A letter was received from the secretary of Bendigo and Sandhurst United Hurling Club, inviting this club to take part in a hurling contest to take place on the Bark Creek cricket ground on the 21st of August for a valuable trophy, and also a silver hurley. It was unanimously decided to send a team to compete for the above mentioned trophy. After a deal of routine business had been transacted the meeting closed with a vote of thanks to the chair. The members of the club are particulary requested to attend practice regularly.

[Ballarat Courier, July 23, 1889.]

TO THE ANNOYANCE OF PASSENGERS

And be it Enacted, That every person shall be liable to a penalty of not more than forty shillings who on any road, bridge, or quay within the limits of this Act shall commit any of the following offences (that is to say,)

Every person who shall slaughter or dress any beast, swine, calf, lamb, or other cattle, except in the case of any over-driven cattle, or which may have met with any accident, and which it may be impossible to get to any slaughter-house, and which the public safety and other purposes may require to be killed on the spot;

Every person who shall suffer any sow or pig to be at large so as to root up or damage any road, or the fences or ditches, or the sides thereof;

Every person who shall suffer to be at large any troublesome work, and having a door, window, or aperture fronting, or opening into or towards any thoroughfare within the limits of the Act, and who shall not close such door, or fasten the shutters or other fastenings of such windows, or close such aperture every evening within one half hour after sunset, so as effectually to prevent the light from shining through the doorway, window, or aperture, upon the thoroughfare;

Every person who shall fly any kite, or play at shinty, foot-ball, or other game, to the annoyance of passengers;

Every person who shall place any line, cord, or pole, or hang or place any clothes, linen, or other such article thereon, or on the hedges and fences of the thoroughfare, to the danger or obstruction of any person;

Every person who shall suffer any water, filth, dirt, or other offensive matter or thing to run or flow into or upon the thoroughfare;

Every person who shall throw or put any ballast, earth, dust, ashes , stones, or other thing into the sea within three hundred yards of the extremities of any of the quays within the districts respectively:

Every person who shall assault, interrupt, or hinder any collector, surveyor or other employed in the execution of this Act;

Every gipsy, hawker, higgler, or other person who shall pitch any tent or encamp upon by the side of any thoroughfare; etc...

[Argyllshire Roads Act, 1843.]

Facies Cinitatis ABERDONIÆ Veteris. The Prospect of Old ABERDIEN.

THE HEALTH OF THE SONS OF THE NORTH

NORTH OF SPEY SHINTY CLUB, ABERDEEN. - The members of this club met on Monday, the 1st January, for the purpose of contesting the long-established Celtic game. The club met on the Links, when they were divided into two sides, the halekeepers appointed, coats were cast, the ball thrown, and off they went in right good earnest, shinties flying in all directions, and the ball winding its way to its destination. Keenly, indeed, was the game contested, and it occupied nearly two hours before either of the sides could be declared the victor. However, those wearing the red signals were declared the winners. The after part of the day becoming somewhat rainy, the piper of the club sounded his pibroch, and, in an instant, all were around him, and in an orderly manner they proceeded to the North of Scotland Hotel, where an elegant repast was in readiness. When assembled, Mr Sutherland was called to the chair, and in a neat speech complimented the club upon the orderly manner in which they had conducted themselves during the former part of the day. The croupiers were Messrs Craigan and Low. The cloth having been removed, the Chairman then proposed "The health of the Sons of the North", which was acknowledged by Mr Mitchell. - During the interval, Mr MacBean entertained the company with a song. - Mr Low then proposed "Success to the Culloden monument, coupled with the health of Mr Forbes, the present proprietor;" Mr Low having made a pithy and well-directed appeal to their feelings on behalf of the Culloden Monument Fund; and, at the same time, showing the liberality of the Forbes family. He considered it was the duty of the club, as Highlandmen, to contribute their mite to commemorate the heroes who fell on that fatal field. Mr Macbean, the only party present thoroughly acquainted with the biography of the Forbes family, returned thanks for the manner in which the toast was received. - Mr Gow next entertained the company with a song appropriate to the occasion. The bagpipes played; and a number of other songs and recitations kept up the harmony of the evening until an early hour. It is almost superfluous to state that the supper was served up with Mr Carnegie's usual good taste. A vote of thanks was then passed to the Chairman, and the meeting separated. - Correspondent.

[Inverness Courier, January 11, 1849.]

HOT AND FURIOUS

I was once at a hurling match in Ireland. The game was played on ice on a lake, and after some hours the owner of the lake sent down a Scotch butler with bread an cheese for the players. They gathered about the cart in perfect good humour, when suddenly, without cause, and excited banker's clerk shouted, "Hurroo for —" (the nearest post town), and performed a kind of war dance on the outside edge of his skates, flourishing a stick wildly, and chanting his war song, "I'll bet ere a man in England, Ireland, Scotland." A knobby stick rose up in the crowd, and the Scotch butler was down; but an Irish boy who had not opened his mouth was the next. He went head-foremost into a willow bush amongst the snow, and three men in frieze greatcoats kicked him with nailed shoes. In ten minutes the storm was over, the butler was up in his cart dispensing the refreshments, the man in the bush was consoling himself with a dram, and all was peace. But that night the country party took a position behind a stone wall, and when the others came, they sallied forth, and there was a battle-royal.

So I have seen a parish shinny match in the Highland become so hot and furious, that the leaders were forced to get two pipers and march their troops out of the field in opposite directions, to prevent a civil war of parishes.

And so, as part of her majesty's guards having gone out to exercise at Clewer, and being stationed as "the enemy" at some point, obstinately refused to "retreat in disorder;" but stood their ground with such determination, that the officers had to sound the retreat on both sides to prevent a serious battle.

So at Eton, shins were broken in my tutor's football match against my dame's; and boys injured themselves in rowing frantically for the honour of upper or lower sixes.

Two twins, who were so like, that one used to skip round a pillar and answer to his brother's name, and who probably would have died for each other, still fought in private so earnestly, that one carried the mark of a shovel on his forehead for many a long day; and so boys fight, and men fight, individually and collectively, as parties, races, and nations, all over Europe, if not all over the world.

[J. F. Campbell, Popular Tales of the West Highlands, Vol 1, pages cxxix -cxxx]

COMMITMENT,
SKILL AND ENDURANCE.
QUALITIES
WE APPRECIATE.

SHINTY, THE SPORT of the Gaels, embodies the very spirit of Scotland. In Glenmorangie's 150th year, our Sixteen Men are proud to support the brave teams of twelve in their centenary year.

GLENMORANGIE
SINGLE HIGHLAND MALT SCOTCH WHISKY.

A VERY DETERMINED AIR

INVERARAY

Grand shinty match at Inveraray

The great annual challenge match between the opposite sides of Upper Lochfyne was played at Inveraray on Friday, the 3rd instant. The much-talked-of meeting took place on the Castle lawn, which affords excellent and ample scope for the purpose, and where from time immemorial each Yule-tide has seen its well-fought battle in the favourite pastime of the district.

The Ardkinglas men, under command of their young laird, arrived per steamer 'Fairy' shortly after 11 A.M., and headed by their piper immediately marched with a very determined air on to the field of battle. Here the Inveraray forces were being rapidly marshalled by the Lords Archibald and Walter Campbell, assisted by their trusty general William Mackenzie. All was soon ready, - the rival sides distinguished by a badge worn round the left arm: Inveraray, orange; Ardkinglas, pink. The number was restricted to 40 on either side - the course about 500 yards long; and the goals marked by a couple of flags at each end, twelve yards apart. J. Campbell, Esq., Islay, acted as judge of the game.

Exactly at noon it began; the Ardkinglas side getting choice of direction, and of course choosing to play with their backs to the sun. Starting from the central point the battle at first rather inclined to the Ardkinglas goal, and after a little took a decided turn in that direction. During this round the pinks showed some powerful play; but, by and by, the Inveraray "boys" managed, by coolness and pluck to stem the adverse tide. Forced steadily back to the centre of the field, the contest raged there keenly and long. As it surged heavily from wing to wing, for a considerable time one could scarcely note any decided advance on either side. And so the tug of war went on. It was an exciting sight for the spectators that had come from far and near, and now occupied the grassy slopes overlooking the field. At last, seemingly by a supreme effort, the ball got away a little from the ruck, inclining ever so slightly towards the Inveraray goal; and now those of the orange, putting forth all their energies, and bringing into requisition some of their best strategy, began gradually to gather momentum. Then swiftly and surely they urge their way onwards, close up to the very "hail". Yet even now there are not wanting on the part of their opponents two or three gallant but desperate attempts to recover their lost ground. Thrice the young laird of Ardkinglas succeeds in turning the battle wave at the very last push. But still ominously and persistently it surges up against the flag-posts. At length, by a quiet stroke judiciously planted, the ball is shot through between them. Up go the Inveraray caps, and cheer on cheer follows all around. Tough work it has been, as witness the panting foemen while they gather round. And thus within and hour ended the first round in favour of Inveraray.

Presently, almost without a moment's breathing space, they are at it again, this time starting from the winning post. Up and down, across and across, sometimes far, at others near, the struggle goes on. Both parties seem to ply with a vehemence ever increasing. Hard knocks are given and received; but all is taken in good part. Now and again in the shock of battle one after another bites the sod, but only to rise again and plunge more keenly than ever into the fray. Suddenly there is a halt and a gathering round at one particular spot, as if something unusual has occurred. The pause, however, is only for an instant; on they move, now one way, now another. But what kilted warrior is that, with one or two attendants, moves quietly off the field? It is one of the chiefs o' Inveraray; it is Lord Walter Campbell, who in the thick of the fray has been hit by that hardwood ball right in the middle of the upper lip, with such force as to cut it clean open half its length. The doctor, summoned from a distant part of the field, follows with all speed. And so the wound is dressed - simple suture - the young hero wincing not the while. Meantime the battle has gone on, gradually recovering back to the starting post; Ardkinglas side, urged on by the shouts of their veteran general, Brodie, and cheered by the approving voice of their commander-in-chief, plays with the utmost determination and force - a force, indeed, which in one or two instances degenerated into coarseness. Getting, at last, within easy range of the goal, one of them caught the ball as it bounded off the ground, and instantly threw it out, thus claiming the game and raising the shout of victory. Immediately, however, the other side objected that it was not allowable to throw the ball except when caught before touching the ground. But the umpire, on being appealed to, decided that according to the written regulations, it was quite sufficient if the ball was caught in the air, no matter whether it had previously touched the ground or not. And so, by this ruling, the second game went to Ardkinglas.

After a short delay in settling the disputed point, another start was made by the last winners from the same goal under very favourable circumstances; but somehow or other the Inveraray "boys" brought it back with a run, and in less than five minutes popped through and won, thereby carrying off two out of the three.

Thus ended this well-contested match. The playing on both sides, and especially on the Ardkinglas side showed a decided improvement since last year. One thing, however, have rise to a good deal of remark, namely, how very few of the Ardkinglas party were in any way injured, whereas in the case of their opponents cuts and bruises seemed to be the order of the day. Having resumed their warm attire the combatants were then marched off the field to the Argyll Arms Hotel, when a comfortable lunch was in readiness. A number of patriotic and complimentary toasts having been enthusiastically pledged, and a friendly challenge renewed for next year, the company adjourned to the open air in front of the Hotel, and there danced several reels with great spirit. Shortly before 4 p.m. the Ardkinglas party marched on board and left amid loud and general cheering.

COMPLIMENTARY BALL TO THE SHINTY PLAYERS. - On Monday evening a ball was given to the shinty players upon the Inveraray estate in celebration of the victory they had won. There was an excellent attendance. Dancing commenced in the Burgh Parochial Schoolrooms at 9 p.m., and was continued with increasing spirit till an early hour. Tea and other refreshments were liberally provided during the evening.

[Oban Times, January 11, 1868.]

GRANT of GLENMORISTON

McIan's Grant of Glenmoriston, in the attitude of throwing the ball........

ENDURING CONTRIBUTIONS

Santee Dakota Indian ball-play on the ice, Minnesota from Schoolcraft.

The Earl of Selkirk had promised his Kildonan emigrants that they would be provided by him with a Gaelic-speaking - and Presbyterian minister. Indeed Donald Sage, a son of the Kildonan manse and after wards a well-known Highland clergyman in his own right, had been engaged for just this task. But Sage, who made no mention of the affair in his extensive memoirs, seems to have reneged on the deal, leaving Red River to make do with one John West, appointed the community's chaplain by the

Hudson's Bay Company. West, however, ministered in accordance with Church of England rites. 'And the Scotch,' as one of Red River's first historians remarked, 'could see no spirituality in such forms; besides which, the English language was to them a foreign tongue and they longed to hear their native Gaelic.' So it came about that, rather than rely on alien rituals, Red River's Highland settlers made one of their own number, James Sutherland, responsible for baptisms, marriages and other matters of that kind.

These same Highlanders imported more than Scotland's predominant religion. Their agricultural techniques began as variants of those to which they had been accustomed in Sutherland - with the first Red River farms being laid out in much the same way as those which their occupants had previously worked in the Strath of Kildonan. Fields were small initially. Sheep and cattle were pastured on what amounted to a common grazing of the Highland type. There was, after all, no alter native pattern on which the Red River settlers might draw. But new circumstances clearly called for new methods. Adaption and innovation of a sort which the men responsible for the Sutherland evictions were inclined to think Highlanders incapable - were consequently quick in coming. Soon pumpkins and melons were being grown in addition to barley, oats and potatoes. Soon wheat, which this part of North America would eventually produce in enormous quantities, began to be cultivated successfully - one visitor who reached Red River just before sunset on a cloudless day in early fall remarking on how each high stack of wheat sheaves sent 'its long eastward shadow over the closely shaven plain'.

Red River wheat was harvested with the help of sickles brought from Scotland. Whether or not some Red River Highlander's baggage also included the hooked stick or caman used by players of the ancient Highland game of shinty is unclear. What is certain is that shinty or 'shinny', as it was commonly called in North America, was being played at Red River from the moment of the Kildonan people's arrival - just as it was played by other Highlanders in Glengarry County and the American South. What is equally evident is that shinny, in Red River as in Glengarry, rapidly made the transition from snowy fields to the much smoother, faster surface provided by frozen lakes and rivers. Not the least of the many still enduring contributions made by Scottish Highlanders to North American life, it thus seems likely, is the modern sport of ice hockey.

[James Hunter, A Dance Called America, pages 203-204.]

UNIVERSAL AMONG THE TRIBES

Santee Dakota Indian ball-play on the prairie, Minnesota from Schoolcraft.

Shinny is especially a woman's game, but it is also played by men alone (Assiniboin, Yankton, Mohave, Walapai), by men and women alone (Sauk and Foxes, Tewa, Tigua), by men and women together (Sauk and Foxes, Assiniboin), by men against women (Crows). It may be regarded as practically universal among the tribes throughout the United States. As in racket, the ball may not be touched with the hand, but is both batted and kicked with the foot. A single bat is ordinarily used, but the Makah have two, one for striking and the other for carrying the ball. The rackets are invariably curved, and usually expanded at the striking end. In some instances they are painted or carved.

The ball is either of wood commonly a knot, or of buckskin. The wooden ball occurs chiefly on the Pacific coast and in the Southwest. The buckskin ball is generally used by the Eastern and Plains tribes, and is commonly flattened, with a median seam. the opposite sides being painted sometimes with different colors. The Navaho use a bag-shaped ball. The goals consist of two posts or stakes at the ends of the field, or two blankets spread side by side on the ground (Crows); again a single post is used (Menominee, Shuswap, Omaha) or lines drawn at the ends of the field over which the ball must be forced (Navaho, Eskimo, Omaha, Makah). The distance of the goals is not recorded, except among the Miwok (200 yards), the Omaha (300 yards), Mono (1,400 yards and return), and the Mnkah (200 yards).

In a California form of the game the players were lined up along the course and struck their ball along the line, the game corresponding with one in which the ball was kicked, struck or tossed, played by the same tribe.

The game of shinny is frequently referred to in the myths. It was commonly played without any particular ceremony. Among the Makah it was played at the time of the capture of a whale, the ball being made from a soft bone of that animal. The shinny stick may be regarded as analogous to the club of the War Gods.

In his Wichita Tales a Dr George A. Dorsey relates how the first man, Darkness, who began to get power to foretell things after the creation of people, told the woman Watsikatsia, made after his image, that when he was as about to go to a certain being, Man-Never-Known-on-Earth he reached down at his left side with his right hand and brought up a; ball. Then he reached flown with his left hand at his right side and brought up a belt. Then he reached down in front, touched the ball to the belt, and brought up a shinny stick. He took the ball, tossed it up, and struck it with the stick. As the ball flew, he went with it. Thus guided, he went to the place where he expected to find Man-Never-Known-on-Earth. The object of his visit was that power be given him so that there should be light on the face of the earth. He tossed and struck the ball again, but not arriving at the place, he knew he could not depend upon the ball, and so took his bow and arrow and shot an arrow and flew with it. This he did a second, third, and fourth time, but without avail. Then he remembered he could run. He made one long run and stopped to rest. Then he ran again and a third and fourth time. He had made twelve trials and knew he was near the place of his journey.

Later, in the same narrative, it is related how Darkness, arriving at a certain village, instituted the game of shinny:

The crowd came, and he told them they were to have such a game as shinny ball. He reached down with his right hand on his left side and produced a ball, and then ranched down on his right side with his left hand brought up a shinny stick. These he showed the people and told them they were for their use. Then he commanded the people together just outside the village at about evening time, and then he set the time for play. They went as he told them. When they were all there he tossed the ball toward the north and travelled with it. It went a long ways. When it lit, he picked it up and struck it with the stick and drove the ball back south, then said that the point where he stood when he struck the ball would be called "flowing water" (the goal). Then he took the balkl, tossed it, went with it, and again struck it southward. Where it hit

was the second "flowing water", or goal. Between these two goals or bases was level ground, and in both directions as far as you could see. The he divided the men into two parties, and placed one at each goal. Between these two parties and in the centre of the field he placed two men, one from each of the two parties. He gave one man the ball and told him to toss it up. As the ball was tossed he told the other man to strike it towards the south. He did so and drove the ball towards his opponents to the south. Now they played, and the north side drove the ball to the south and won. Then they changed goals, and the other side won. Then Darkness said they had played enough.

Dr George A. Dorsey also relates that in the Wichita creation legend the first man, Having-Power-to-carry-Light, gave the men a ball smaller than the shinny ball.

He told them this ball was to be used to amuse themselves with; that the men were to play together and the boys were to play together. Whenever a child was born, if it was a boy this kind of ball was to be given to it, that he might observe it and learn how to move around. The ball had a string to it. The farther the ball rolled - that is, the older the child should get - the faster it would move around. He went on and taught the men how to play the game, for the people were ignorant and did not know what the things were for. Finally, the men were shown how the ball should be used. He showed them the clubs for the shinny game. He told them they should be divided equally in the game, one party on one side and the other party on the other side. Many were interested, for the game was new to them. Many of the men were fast on their feet. The game was to be won by the side that should get the ball to the goal first. Having-Powerto-carry-Light also told them how to travel with the arrows and ball. This marks the time when they learned to travel fast from one place to another. The men went out hunting animals after they had been taught that animals existed for their use, and they travelled with their arrows and ball. They would shoot an arrow in the direction they wanted to go; then they would go with the arrow as it went up. This is the way they travelled. They would hit the ball, and as it flew the person would be on the ball. When the ball hit the ground they would hit it again, and so they would go from place to place.

[S. Culin, Games of the North American Indians, Volume 2, pages 616-7, 626-7.]

Rann Colain

Thanaig mise nochd air Chalain,
Mar a chanas iad san tìr seo;
Gus a ruige tigh bhràthar mathar,
Smòr mo bheachd nach h-eil e spiochdach.
Tha e shiol nan daoine coire,
Clann Dòmhnuil dan deòin nach striochdadh;
'S aig an tric an d'fhuaras biatachd,
Do na ciadan sgial tha fior e
Ciod e'n stadh dhomh bhi gad mholadh,
'S nach h-eil dhut san rioghd so;
Leis an sin cha chluinn thu 'n còr dheth,
Gus an deun thu 'n stop a lionadh.
Chuala mi gun d'fhuair thu buideal.
Sgun robh glugan ann don Ileach;
'S co dhiubh bhann mòran na beaghan,
Gun robh eleven O.P air.
Chan eil fhios agam man sgial sin.
Dhiubh si bhriag a thann nan fhìrinn;
Ach ma fhuair na bi ga àicheadh,
Fiach a nusa dhuin làn 'na fideig.
Sion a h-aon dhiubh lion a dha dhiubh;
Sùgh fallainn fìorghlan an eòrna.
Cha'n fhaigh mi mo leòr dheth gu siorraidh,
Se fhèin a thigeadh ri mo shluigein,
Scha be spùd dubh* a thaig Irig;   *(*Spud dubh - porter)*
Ged dhòlain dheth làn na Cuinneig,
Cha traigheadh e uile m'iotadh.
Eirich thusa a nis a Sheònaid,
Fosgail an seòmar ud shuas dhuinn;
Sma tha diar idir sa phige.
Lion an t-shlige sna bi spiochdach.

ALPHA
(Iona, 12th Dec., 1871)

[Oban Times, January 20,1872.]

A'CHALUINN - NEW YEAR IN THE HIGHLANDS

An old Highlander recalls the customs of his youth:-

"My father was piper to Glendessarie, as was his father before him, and every son of mine, as soon as weaned, has taken to the pipe-chanter just as naturally as the young kid takes to scrambling up the rocks. It was the habit of this family to gather for Calluinn Night (New Year's Eve) all the tenantry on their lands, young and old... and according to wont, Evan Ban Maor (fair-haired Evan, the ground officer) went round amongst them a few days before the time.

"It is the wish of the family,' says he, 'that we should observe the Calluinn as of old; and see, my lads, that you have your *camain* (shinties or clubs) right and ready for New Year's Day.'

"The piper set off in his full Highland garb about the height of the evening. We reached the great house. The young ladies of the family met us with bows of ribbon for the chanter of the pipe. The piper played a round on the green before the door, as the men gathered.

"The time of *Calluinn* came.

"'Who will carry the hide this year?' says Evan Bàn.

"'Who but Para Mòr?' says one.

"'Who but Broad John?' says another.

"'Out with the hide, Pàra Mòr !' says Evan Bàn; 'and you, Broad John, stand by his shoulder in case he may stumble.'

"Pàra Mòr drew the hide about his head, taking a twist of the tail firmly about his fist.

"*Cothrom na Feinne!*" (fair play as among Fingalians, or Fingalian justice) he exclaimed, as he drew near the place where the Laird was standing with his caman in his hand.

"*Calluinn* here !', says he, giving the first rattle to the hide.

"Pàra Mòr set off, but, swift of foot as he was, the men of the glen kept at his heel, and you would think that every flail in the country was at work in the one threshing-floor as every mother's som of them struck and rattled at him, shouting, 'A *Calluinn* here! The Calluinn of the yellow sack of hide! Strike ye the skin! A *Calluinn* here!'

’S tu a bhuaileadh le d’ chaman,
’S a leanadh i teann
Cho luath ri boc-earba,
An garbhlach nam beann.

"Three times they went *deas-iul* round the house.

"Blow up, piper!' says Evan Bàn, 'and when the company are in order let them assemble in the rent-room.'

"My father played *Fàilt' a' Phrionnsa* (The Prince's Welcome). Often have I seen him, shedding tears on hearing that thrilling music which had stirred his forefathers to deeds of manliness on the field of battle.

"We went into the chamber where the family and the neighbouring gentry were assembled. He, himself, the graceful president of the feast, stood in the midst, and his winsome lady by his side. The lovely young branches of the family were around them. The Laird of Corrie was standing at the door to guard against anyone slipping in without saying his *Calluinn* rhyme, and John Bàn of the Casks (the butler) beside him with a bottle in his hand. John Bàn dealt round the drink, and the bread and cheese, piled up plenteously, were distributed freely.

The songs began. He himself (the Laird) gave us an iorram (boat song), and well he could do it. The fox-hunter gave us Duan a' Choin Ghlais (the Song of the Grey Dog), and Angus of the Satires repeated a tale of the Fingalians.

"After the songs and dancing began, very different from the slow, soft, silken steps of the present day. First came in a smart dame, dressed like a housekeeper, with a bunch of keys jingling by her side. The woman sang *port a' beul* (a tune from the mouth), selecting *Cailleach an Dùdain* (the Old Wife of the Mill-Dust), and it was she who capered and turned and sprang nimbly. After this they danced the *Dubh-Luidneach* (the Black Sluggard). But the best fun was when the Goat Dance (*Dannsa nam Bòcan*) , Weave-the Gown (*Figh an Gùn*) and the Thorny Croft (*Croit an Droighin*) were danced.

"The time of our parting came. The gentry gave us the welcome of the New Year with cordiality and kindliness, and we set off to our homes.

"'My lads,' says he himself, ' be valiant on the field tomorrow. The seaboard men boast that they are to meet us Glen-men at the shinty-match this year.'

"On New Year's morn, the sun was late of showing his countenance, and after he came in sight his counteneace was pale and drowsy. The mist was resting lazily on the hill-side; the crane was rising slowly from the meadow; the belling stag was heard on the mountain; the black-cock was in the birch-wood, dressing his feathers, while his sonsie mate, the grey-hen, was slowly walking before him.

"After I had saluted my family and implored the blessing of the Highest on their heads, I prepared the Christmas sheep (*caora Nollaig*), gave a sheaf of corn to the cattle, as was customary, and was getting myself in order when in walked Pàra Mòr and my gossip, Angus Og (young Angus). They gave me the welcome of the New Year. I returned it with equal heartiness. Then Pàra Mòr produced a bottle from his pocket.

"'A black-cock,' says he, 'whose gurgling voice (crowing) is more musical than any ràn that ever came out of any chanter of thy pipe.'

"We toasted to one another, and then Mary, my wife, set before us a small drop of the genuine Ferintosh, which she had stored up long ago in the big chest for grand occasions.

"It was my duty to gather the people together this morning with the sound of the pipe. So we set off, going from farm to farm up the Glen, making the son of the cave rock (the echo) answer to my music. I played *A Mhnàthan a 'Ghlinne S*o (The Women of the Glen), and if the pipe had been dry that day it had ample means of quenching its thirst! The company continually increased in numbers until we came down by the other side of the Glen to the ground-officer's house, where it was appointed for us to get our morning meal. The lady had sent a three-year-old wedder to his house. We had a roe-buck from the corrie of yew-trees; fish from the pool of whitings; and such qualtities of cheese, butter and solid oatcake, sent by the neighbours round and about, as would suffice for as many more - though we were fifty men in number, besides women and children. Grace was said by Lachlan of the Questions (*Lachlan ceistear*), the Bible-reader. We had an ample and cheerful breakfast.

"Breakfast over, I set off and played the tune of the *Glasmheur* while Red Ewen, the old soldier, was mar-shalling the men. We reached *Guala-nan-Càrn* (the shoulder of the cairns) where the gentry were to meet us; and before we knew where we were, who placed himself at our head but our own young Donald, the heir of the family! Dear heart, he was the graceful sapling! The people of the seaboard then came in view, Alistair Roy of the Bay at their head. When the two companies observed each other, they raised a loud of mutual rejoicing. We reached the field, and many were the salutations between friends and acquaintances exchanged there.

"The sun at length shone out brightly. On the eminences around the field were the matrons, the maidens and the children of the district, high and low, all assembled to witness the *Camanachd* (shinty match). The goal at each end of the large field was pointed out, and the two leaders began to divide and choose each his men.

"*Buailidh mi ort*," (literally, I will strike on thee), says young Donald.

"*Leigidh me leat*" (I permit you), says Alistair Roy of the Bay.

"If so," says young Donald, 'then Donald Bàn of Culloden is mine.'

"This was by far the oldest man present, and you would think his two eyes would start from his head with delight as he stepped proudly forth, at being the first chosen.

"When the men were divided into two companies - forty on each side - Alistair Roy flung his shinty-stick high in the air.

"*Bas no Cas*" (head or handle), Donald of the Glen?' said he.

"Handle, which will defy your handling until nightfall!" replies Donald.

"Alistair gained the throw, and was about to strike the ball immediately when the other exclaimed, 'A truce! Let the rules of the game be first proclaimed, so that there may be fairness, good fellowship and friendship observed among us, as was wont among our forefathers.'

"On this, Evan Bàn stepped forth and proclaimed the laws, which forbade all quarrelling, swearing, drunkenness and coarseness; all striking, tripping or unfairness of any kind; and charged them to contend in a manful but friendly spirit, without malice or grudge, as those from whom they were descended were wont to do.

"Alistair Roy gave the first stroke to the ball, and the contest began in earnest; but I have no language to describe it. The seaboard men gained the first game. But it was their only game. Young Donald and his men stripped to their work, and you would think the day of *Blàr na Lèine* (Battle of the Shirt) had come again. Broad John gave a tremendous blow, which sent the ball far beyond the goal. We thus gained the day, and we raised the shout of victory; but all was kindliness and good feeling among us.

"In the midst of our congratulations, Pàra Mòr shouted out, 'Shame on ye, young men! Don't you see those nice girls shivering with cold? Where are the dancers? Play up the reel of Tullochgorum, Finlay!'

"The dancing began, and the sun was bending low towards the western ocean before we parted. We returned to the house of nobleness, as on the preceeding evening. Many a torch was beaming brightly in the hall of hospitality. We passed the night amid music and enjoyment, and parted not until the breaking of the dawn guided us to our homes.

"Many good results followed from this friendly mingling of gentles and commons. Our superiors were at that time acquainted with our language and our ways. There were kindness, friendship, and fosterage between us, and whilst they were apples on the topmost bough, we were all fruit of the same tree.

.....(Now) our superiors dwell not among us; they know not our language, and cannot conserve with us .... All this has passed as a dream."

[F. Marian MacNeill, The Silver Bough, Volume 3, Chapter XI, pp 117-121]

HIGH EXCITEMENT, HALF UNDERSTOOD

Shinty at Kilberry, Old New Year's Day

The custom of playing Shinty on Old New-Year's Day, January 12, began at an unknown date and continued until January 1938; that year the then owner of Kilberry estate, Miss R. M. I. F. Arbuthnot, died shortly before Christmas, and as a mark of respect it was generally decided not to hold the match, and the subsequent Ball in the Home Farm Barn in January, 1939. After 1945 the mood was against trying to revive either Match or Ball, rationing was in force; we were all trying to pick up the pieces of our lives, and the district was beginning to depopulate. But there are still some of us who can remember the former ways.

My first memories of 'The Twelfth' are of high excitement half-understood, and a great many large people towering over me. (I was born in late 1919, so I suppose the first pictures come from 1921 or '22). My Father died in 1928 and from 1929-1931, we were away from home, returning when Father's cousin Miss Arbuthnot came to live here. Our absence had not interrupted the match sequence - it cannot be said to be something dreamed up by "them in the big house". There was, however, a sort of ritual about the whole proceedings, partly developed in the 19th century, but pre-existing in some respects.

This is how I remember it:-

The day was 12 January or the nearest convenient day, usually 11th, if the 12th itself fell on a Sunday. People assembled at the Home Farm after dinner, about 1.00pm, and 'marched' (more or less) to the field, behind one or more Pipers if any were on hand. If you wanted to play, you came with a caman on your shoulder; (these were selected from the woods during the spring and summer when parties were working at getting stack-poles or pea-stakes, and there was a lot of interest in a good stick and how it was being made into a caman). The field of play was one to be ploughed shortly; it was not going to be much good for anything else in fact, but there might have been an element of ritual - (anointing the good earth with blood?) - as well.

Arrived at the field, two sides were picked - by my Father or uncle versus a Farm Manager or another Heid Man. Everyone with a caman was chosen eventually, anything up to 30 or so a side. There was also some kind of Referee, though who I can't think - or possibly the team captains broke up the more difficult situation themselves. It was a busy scene, and again a little older ritual may have edged in, as scores could be settled in the general ruck. It was not unknown for people to jump on other people's backs, and one dear friend of mine reported later that he had 'gone ofer and ofer like a wee barrel' (not so wee).

I'm not sure how long they played each way (45 minutes I think, but there was another, though less important, game to get in to the short hours of daylight). Eventually they came to a halt; my Mother had brought up two large two-handled laundrybaskets with the help of other women - one basket with First

Aid dressings and the other with thick biscuits ('Captain's Biscuits', also called 'Funeral Biscuits' on other occasions) which had a raised rim and were about the size and texture of the lid of a Scots Pie. The rim held a large slab of yellow cheese in place. There may have been kettles of tea - I don't remember - and there was a bottle or so, strictly to revive elderly spectators and controlled by some specially respectable bystander. The players, unless in need of First Aid, had no access to this comfort. Instead, after a biscuit or so, they returned to the field and played Football for half an hour each way or until the light failed - with the same sides or the survivors. The ball was round, the rules were beyond me, and I considered the whole thing a come-down after the Shinty.

We were not done as yet, by any means. We returned to the Castle, from whichever field we had been ritually furrowing, and there the Piper(s) took station on the front steps and the company danced Eightsome Reels, one or more, on the gravel. The gravel-sweep was not level at the best of times, and the gardener(s) had devoted some days to raking it clear of leaves and getting it 'nice and deep'. Luckily were all in boots or brogues; even so, ankles were turned only too easily. Then the company dispersed to lick its wounds.

During the match itself, there were sometimes efforts to get either a Junior or a Women's game going - mostly we wanted to watch the main game, but sometimes it was so bitterly cold that we had to do something to keep our hands and feet alive; but we seldom had camans, and grown-ups were not willing to part with their walking sticks.

If the 12th fell on a weekday (not Saturday) the Match was followed by a Ball in the Barn the same night, usually lasting until it was time to get home for the milking next morning. The Barn had been built with a dancing floor (1883) in which a 'spring' built up, so that small girls not allowed to go could lie in bed and hear the whump of the beams as well as the hoochs of the dancers. If the 12th was a Saturday, of course the Ball had to be held either on the Friday (bad play next day) or next week.

People walked out from Tarbert, 16 miles, to attend either or both the events, and women sent their dance-dresses on ahead to friends' houses where they would change.

There were some modifications to the Ball arrangements by the time I was going to it - a Band as well as Piper; and not the lavish 'refreshments' of the old Press reports. There was a supper-room of sorts in my Father's time, with I think sandwiches and mainly soft drinks (and probably beer, which was never held to be DRINK). I don't think this was revived in the 1930s.

What I think emerges from family diary entries, and from the strength of the tradition which survived here, is that the Shinty must have been in full swing before my Grandfather began to record it. Kilberry estate had an absentee landlord of sorts from 1788 to 1839, in which time it was owned by an man whose home was an Minard, Loch Fyne, and who came here only for shootings and rent-days. His son, my great-grandfather, rebuilt the old castle (damaged by accidental fire in 1773) and brought his family to live here, including his eldest son. He died in 1861 and his son went to join the 93rd Highlanders in India in 1863, coming back with them in 1870. In 1871 he was away from home, getting married and honey-mooning in Italy, and 1872 is the first reference to the Old New Year at home. It is noticeable that he and his two brothers all played enthusiastically, and had presumably learned the game in childhood. All in all, it looks to me as if they were joining in, and carrying on, a long-established tradition.

[Miss Marion Campbell of Kilberry, October 1, 1992.]

BALL GHLINNTRUIM

The distinctive person of Donald Campbell, honorary captain of Kingussie Camanachd at the time of the club's Highland versus Lowlands clash with Glasgow Cowal in the 1880's.

to the tune of "The Laird of Cockpen"

Chorus:
Ho ro, cha bhi mi nad chaoidh na's mòth'
Ma thrèig thu mi, regrettidh mi thu
Ma thilleas thu fhathast, 's tu m'aighear 's mo rùn
Perhaps I will marry you, 's t-earrach co-dhiubh.

Yesterday evening, 'sann feasgair an raoir,
We marched away to ball Ghlinntruim ,
We couldn't get lasses, cha rachadh iad leinn,
and going without them, bu mhuladach sinn.

When we arrived, gum sinn ho-rè!
They all enquired "nach tug thu leat tè?"
We're better without them, gun fhreagair mi fhèin,
But never let on nach fhaighinn a h-aon.

And when we entered, an rùm san robh 'n danns',
The lasses were dressed anns na fasanan Galld',   *(original unclear)*
With muslin white frocks and crotaibh nan ceann,
They would cheer up your heart, ged a bhiodh tu fann.

With gum flowers and ribbons, gur iad a bha breagh,
All trimed in the fashion, nach fhaca mi riamh,
With hoops in their skirts, sann annta bha'n liad,   *(leud?)*
They thought nach robh'm leithid, rim faighinn mas fhìor.

When the dancing commenced, cha robh iad cho gann,
And you would get plenty, a reidheadh leat a dhanns'
The house was so crowded, bha an t-ùrlar cho trang,
You never saw leithid de rabble 'sa bh'ann.

The butter then went, leis an toddy mun cuairt,
When they got the whisky, sann aca bha'm fuaim,
The lads were with lasses ri barganan cruaidh,
And I went to listen an taice ri'n cluais.

The wind was hard-blowing in sabhal Ghlinntruim,
The candles were dripping a mhàin air an druim,
They painted our coats gun fhaireachdainn dhuinn,
If we stayed at home cha d ' dh 'èirich sinn dhuinn.

It was four o'clock sa mhadainn a bh 'ann
We started for home, anns a ' choach aig a'Ghall,
When we reached Ceann a 'Ghiuthsaich gun deach mi na Ghleann,
Regretting the loss bhith gun chadal san àm.

(c1870)

138

Kingussie - 1896 First winners of the Camanachd Association Challenge Trophy
(back row): John Campbell, A. MacPherson, John Campbell, A. MacPherson
(middle row): Col-Sergt. MacDonald, J. D. Pullar, James Grant, James Smith, Alex Cumming, John Campbell
(front row): Alex Gibson, John Dallas, Provost MacPherson, D. Campbell, Wm. Ross, Alex Campbell.

LAG NAN CRUACHAN

Ma thèid thu Lag-nan-cruachan,
Dean innseadh dhaibh, mur cual iad e,
Gur ann air moch Di-luain
Le gaoth-tuath a rinn sinn seòladh.

Nuair dhfhàg sinn a mach a Grianaig,
Bha ceò is fiath nan ian againn;
'S ged chuir sinn a h-uile stiall oirre,
Cha deanadh iad dhuinn crònan.

'N sin fhuair sinn mar a b'àill leinn i,
Is chroch sin na siùil àrda rith';
Nuair chuimhnich mi mo mhàthair
Bha ga fàgail, bha mi brònach.

'Dol seachad air Creag Ealasaid,
Bha 'ghaoth a'tighinn o'n ear oirnn;
Bha i ga ghearradh geal againn,
'Se oirre h-uile stròic dheth.

Dir-daoin bha latha èibhinn ann,
Ri taobh an fhearainn Eireannaich.
'S i againn mar a dh'fheumamaid
tigh'nn as ar deigh le sòlas.

Di-haoine thàinig gruaim oirre,
Is thòisich i ri tuairnealaich;
Gu'n ghabh sinn air a'ghualainn i,
An iar 's a tuath air Toraidh.

Di-Sathuirn gu'n do bhreeze i oirnn
Is dhèirich muir na sioban oirnn;
Cha d'fhuair sinn fois no diobradh
Bho riof-irinn fad Dhi-Dòmhnaich.

Am maireach bidh Bliadhn' Ur againn,
'S a righ! gur beag mo shùnndsa rith';
Mi ceangailte aig an stiùir aice,
'S na siùil a falbh na stròicean.

'S gur iomadh fear is aithne dhomh
'S a chaman ùr fo achlais
'Dol dh'ionnsuidh na Cloich Ghlaise,
Ged tha mise tarruing ròpa.

An àite dùil bhi fortanach,
'Sann thàinig oirnn a bhochdainne;
Bha cruadal agus gort againn
A'nochdadh ri Cape Horn.

Cha robh ach briosgaid chruaidh againn;
An fheòil chan èireadh buaidh oirre;
'S chan fhaighinn-sa uaireannan
De'n fhuar-uisge na dh'òlainn.

Gu'n dh'fhalbh an rail o'n bhial againn,
'S an ceabain chaidh na stiallan oirnn;
'S gu'n robh sinn anns an t-siorruidheachd
Mur b'iarrunn bha 's a'chòrr dhith.

[Rev. Hector Cameron, Na Bàird Thirisdeach, pages 222-224.]

MOLADH A'BHÀIRD

Moladh a'bhàird air a thìr fhèin air dha a bhith air farsan ann an tir choigrich.

Tha bard's praise for his own land, he being abroad in a strange land.

Uilleam Ros, Gairloch bard.

Tìr àn aigh, tìr nan armunn,
Tìr nan sàr-fhear gleusda,
Tìr an t-suairceis, tìr gun ghruaimean,
Tìr as uaisle fèile;
An tìr bhòrcach, nam frìth ro-mhòr,
Tìr gun leòn, gun gheibhinn;
An tìr bhraonach, mhachrach, raonach,
Mhartach, laoghach, fheurach.

Nuair thig Nollaig mhòr le sonas
Gu comunn gun phràbar,
Gur lìonar gaisgeach le sàr acfhuinn
Tighinn gu feachd na tràghad,
Mar shluaigh Mhic Chumhail le cruaidh fhiùbhaidh
Ruaig gun chùn air stràcan
Bidh Muireardach maide fo bhinn chabar
'Gu stad i anns a'Bhraighe.

Ged a tha mi siubhal Galldachd,
Chan ann tha mo mhi-chuis;
ged tha mi 'n taobh-s', 'sann tha mo rùin
Don chomunn chiùin nach priobal,
'N àm teirce don là thig sibh o'n tràigh,
Gu seòmar bàn nam pìsean;
Bidh ceòl nam feadan 's Eòin da spreigeadh
Gu beagadh 'ur mìghean.

A land of good, of hardihood,

A land of shrewd nobility,
Land of the gay withn courtesy,
And noblest trait, gentility;
The bursting land of forests grand,
The wholesome land, no fash therein,
The land of rain, of field and plain,
Calves and kine and grass therin.
Come Christmas with happiness,
To the meeting place with no splore;
The heroes will with no mean skill
Play shinty on the low shore.
Like host of Feen with weapons keen,
The rout spares none in affrays,
The champion ball's in the club's control
Till it cease to roll in the Braes.

Though here I tread the Lowlands braid,
Unstaid my avocations;
Tho' I'm in this part, still loves my heart
The resort without privations;
When day is o'er ye leave the shore
For the silver-trophied chamber,
The chanter's spring, John's fingering,
For lessening your cumber.

[G. Calder (ed.), Songs of William Ross in Gaelic and English, 1937, Extract, pages 68-71, 182.]

CAMANACHD GHLASCHU

le Mairi Nic a'Phearsain (Mairi Mhòr nan Oran)

Air Là na Bliadhn Uire, 1876, choinnich Gàidheil Ghlaschu is Ghrianaig son gèam camanachd. An ath bhliadhn a rithist bha gèam eile ann, le sgiobaidhean de thrì fichead air gach taobh. Bha Màiri Mhòr nan Oran a-measg an luchd-amharc.

On Old New Year's Day, 1876, the Gaels of Greenock challenged their compatriots of Glasgow to a shinty match, which was repeated the following year, at sixty-a-side.

> *Chan fhacas a riamh,*
> *A leithid de thriall,*
> *Air sràidean Ghrianaig cò-lamh ann.*
>
> *(There never was seen,*
> *such a procession,*
> *on the streets of Greenock, at one time.)*

A LETTER AND SONG BY MARY MACPHERSON, THE SKYE POET, IN 1876

(A Letter to John MacLean, Bernisdale)

Dear John,

I write this letter to let you know I am well, and hoping that you are not ill. Were I as wealthy as I am poor I would give a pound sterling to have you where I am tonight, in the Highlander's Great Hall in Glasgow; my sleeves rolled up to my shoulders, blinded with perspiration as I prepare and bake bannocks for the Hogmany lads; the President of the place is seated surrounded by three score shinty sticks, getting them ready for tomorrow. I'll tell you about the shinty when it's over. It will remind you of the days of our youth, when the people of Sgeabost and Carbost used to be on the great green by the stream, with a bottle at each end of the field, with plenty bannocks and cheese. We go tomorrow to Queen's Park - three score strong Highland lads; thirty in the kilt, and thirty in knickerbockers, with their sticks on their shoulders, pipers before and after them. and I with a horse and cart full of creels of bannocks, kebbocks of cheese as big as the moon, and a drop of Ferintosh to put spirit in the lads. Good-bye just now.

Your faithful friend,

Màiri Nighean Iain Bhàin.

[See Dàin agus Ghàidhlig le Màiri Nic-a-phearsain (Inverness 1891), pages 183 and following.]

Luinneag:

'S i seo a' Bhliadhn' ur thug sòlas duinn;
Siad gillean mo rùin
a'Bhliadhn' Ur thug sòlas dhuinn,
a thogadh mo shùnnd.
'S i seo a'Bhliadhn' ùr thug sòlas duinn.

'S iad gillean mo ghràidh,
Tha 'n Glaschu nan sràid,
Is fhada bho àit' an eòlais iad.

'S ann goirid roimh'n Challainn
A chruinnich an comunn,
'S a chuireadh an iomain an òrdugh leo.

Nuair thainig an t-àm,
Gun chruinnich na suinn,
'S bha caman an làimh gach òigeir dhiubh.

Aig aon uair deug
A rinn iad an triall,
Le pìob 's bu bhriagh' an còmhlan iad.

Nuair rainig na sàir
Gu ionad a'bhlàir,
Gun chuireadh gun dàil an òrdugh iad.

Bha glaineachan làn
Dhe'n Tòis'eachd a b' fhearr,
Is aran is càise còmhla ris.

Bha bonnaich gun taing
Is pailteas dhiubh ann,
'S clann-nighean nan gleann 'gan còcaireachd.

Nuair roinneadh na laoich
'S a ghabh iad an taoibh,
Bha mis' air an raon toirt cò-dhail dhaibh.

'S e 'n sealladh as breagh'
A chunnaic mi riamh,
Gach òigear gun ghiamh 's a chòta dheth.

Gach fleasgach gun mheang,
'S a chaman 'na làimh,
'S a' chnapag le srann 'ga fògar leò.

Bha cuid dhiubh cho luath
Ri fèidh air an ruaig,
'S cha chluinnt' ach "A suas i, Dhòmhnaill", leò.

'S ann ann a bha'n eadhlain
Le glagadaich chaman,
'S gach curaidh cur fallais is ceòthain deth.

Bha duine gun chearb,
Le siosa-còt dearg,
'S cha bhiodh am boc-earba còmhla ris.

Fear eile gun ghiamh
'S a chiabhagan liath
Chuir 'tigh' i bhàrr fiacail mòran diubh.

'S e duine gun tùr
Nach fhaiceadh le shùil,
Gu robh iad bho thùs an òige ris.

Nuair chuireadh am blàr,
Gun choisich na sàir
Le pìob gu Sràid an Dòchais leò.

Suidhibh, a chlann,
Is gabhaidh sinn rann,
Gu'n cuirear an dram an òrdugh dhuibh.

Gun dhealaich na suinn,
Mar thàinig iad cruinn,
Le'n cridheachan coibhneil, 's b'òrdail iad.

'S iad gillean mo rùin
A thogadh mo shunnd
'S i so a'Bhliadhn' ùr thug sòlas duinn.

Translation (part)

Chorus:

The lads that I love
would waken my joy;
it is this New Year that has gladdened us.

The lads I love dear
are in Glasgow here,
far from the land that reared them.

Just before Hogmany
they gathered together,
and plans were made for the shinty then.

When the heroes came
to the field of the game,
without delay they were lined up then.

There were glasses flush
with the best Ferintosh,
there was bread and cheese along with it.

And bannocks too,
more than would do,
that the girls from the glens had baked for them.

There was skill in plenty
and sticks at their denting,
perspiration and sweat were pouring there.

One player had
a waistcoat of red,
the roebuck could not keep pace with him.

Another that day,
though his sideburns were grey,
scored a goal in the teeth of defenders there.

Only one without sense
couldn't see at a glance
they had known the game since their cradle days.

When the battle was fought
the heroes trod
to the sound of the pipes to Hope Street.

CAMANACHD GHRIANAIG

Air Là na Bliadhn' Uire, choinnich Gàidheil Ghlaschu is Ghrianaig son an darna gèam. Agus bha Mairi Mhòr sa chuideachd a rithist.

This match took place at the New Year, 1877, between the Gaels of Glasgow and Greenock, sixty-a-side.

Luinneag: *'Si an t-Seann Bhliadhn' ùr thug solas duinn;*
Siad gillean mo rùin
A thogadh oirnn sunnd,
'S i an t-Seann Bhliadhn ur thug sòlas duinn.

' S i na dh'fhuiling mi phian
Le Sasunnaich chrion
Chuir gun cluinneadh sibh riamh ri òran mi.

Chaidh m'intinn a shnìomh
Le Bàillidh gun chiall,
Ach phàigheadh le riadh a'chòmhstri dha.

Mu'n taca seo a'n uiridh,
Gun rinn mi dhuibh iorram,
'S gum feuch mi ti tuilleadh chur còmhla ris.

Chan fhaca iad riamh,
A leithid a thriall,
Air sràidean Ghrianaig còmhla ribh.

Bha h-uile fear riamh
'S a chaman ri chliabh,
'S gum b'eireachdail fiamh nan òganach.

Bha 'm Pìobaire Bàn
Air thoiseach air càch,
'S Mac-Ranaild 's MacPhàrlain, 's b'òrdail iad.

'S iad baigearan crion'
Nach fhaca da riamh,
Nach cuireadh an iomhaigh sòlas orr'.

Bha mòran a chàch,
A choinnich ri 'n sàil,
'S a ràinig a'phàirce còmhla ruinn.

Bu toigh leam na seòid,
A leanadh nan tòir -
A Eilean a'Cheò bha mòran dhiubh.

Gur toigh leam na suinn,
A bhuinnig an geall,
Bha deagh Mhac-Cuinn agus Bogle ann.

Tha moran de sheòid
An Grianaig nan seòl,
A Eilean-a-Cheò na'n d'thainig iad.

'S am beagan a bh' ann,
Mar lean iad am ball,
'S mar shìn iad an eang bha pròis orn.

'S iad Clann-Asguil bhith gann,
Nach do bhuinnig sibh 'n geall,
Ach nochd na bha ann diubh mòralachd.

Bha fleagsgach gun chearb,
Le stocainean dearg',
'S bu luaithe na earb air mòintich e.

Cha tèid mi g'ur roinn -
'S sibh uile mo chlann -
'S ged tha mi ri ràin tha bròn orm.

Bho'n chaill sinn am fearann,
Gun chaill sinn an iomain,
'S cha mhòr gu bheil duin' ann tha eòlach oirr'.

Chail sinn a'Challainn,
Is chaill sinn a'chaithream,
Is chaill sinn na bannagan còmhla ris.

Chan fhaca sinn riamh,
Ach pailteas dhe'n bhiadh,
'S an drama ga riadhladh còmhla ris.

Na bannagan - Callainn,
A gheobhadh na gillean,
Bhiodh leith-pheice mhine is còrr annta.

Ged bha iad an uiridh,
Glè thiugh air am fuineadh,
Bha 'm bliadhna tuilleadh is òirleach annt'.

Bha cuid diubh car cruaidh,
Le teothad a'ghuail,
Ach am bliadhna fhuair sinn mòine dhaibh.

Gun soirbhich gu bràth,
Le buidheann mo ghràidh,
'S gum faigh sibh ur n-àit le chòraichean.

'S iad gillean mo rùin
A thogadh oirnn sunnd,
'S i an t-Seann Bhliadhn' ur thug sòlas duinn.

[Mairi Mhòr nan Oran, Dàin agus Orain, pages 187 - 190.]

NEW YEAR'S DAY SHINTY MATCH.
A TIME-HONOURED CUSTOM.

THERE is no event of greater importance in connection with the celebration of the advent of the New Year in the Highlands than the New Year's Day Shinty Match. It is a very ancient custom, and one which we hope will never lack observance. The game usually takes place on an extensive stretch of sand at the sea shore, where that is available, or in inland places on the largest field procurable, and to it flock young and old from the adjoining parishes. Usually there is no limit to the number of contestants, and the young men enter into the fray with a dash and energy that threaten danger to head and limb. Many romantic stories are associated with the observance of the time honoured shinty match on New Year's Day in the north.

In the south, Highlanders keep up the custom, and in Glasgow, Edinburgh, and London, the local shinty clubs never fail to engage in a game of *caman*, followed perhaps by a dance on the green, to celebrate the birth of another year. Those who care to visit Moray Park, Glasgow, on the forenoon of the 1st

GLASGOW COWAL *versus* EDINBURGH SUTHERLAND.

— The throw up. 2.—Scrimmage round goal. 3.—A disputed goal

January, will see how the members of the famous Cowal Shinty Club wield the *caman*. The views which we give represent incidents in a recent match between the Glasgow Cowal reserve team, which has so far an unbroken record of victories, and the Edinburgh Sutherland Club. The pictures speak for themselves, but only those who have actually played the game have any real idea of the excitement which a stiffly contested match creates. The ball is small in size, and it requires keen sight and an accurate stroke to hit it when travelling fast on the ground, or in the air. The New Year's Day match played by the members of the Camanachd Club in Edinburgh is always a picturesque and exciting game, as it is made a strict rule that every player must wear the Highland dress on the occasion. We hope that, with the extraordinary revival of shinty that has taken place of late, the time-honoured New Year's Day match will be duly observed by the Gaelic race, whether it be in the "land of brown heath and shaggy wood," the southern cities, or in distant lands across the sea.

AN EARLY TRIAL OF CONCLUSIONS

CHALLENGE TO THE SHINTY PLAYERS OF SCOTLAND.

The shinty players of the Vale of Leven, Dumbartonshire, would be very glad to have a shinty match with the Inveraray men, or any other society in Scotland, for £50 or a £100 each side; twenty players to play on each side; and we agree to take £10 and go to Inveraray, or give the Inveraray men £10 to come to Leven;. Communications addressed to John Sinclair, Seaforth House, Bridge of Allan, will be attended to.

[The Oban Times, November 26, 1870.]

Followed a week later by:

INVERARAY

SHINTY CHALLENGE

Considerable amusement was caused this week among the Inveraray boys of the terms of the challenge in name of the Vale of Leven which appeared in the columns of the *Oban Times* Saturday last. We understand that, while declining to play for money, the Inveraray boys have taken means for ascertaining the rules of the game as played in the Vale, with a view to an early trial of conclusions.

[December 3, 1870.]

AN T-SEANN SGOIL

Am meangan nach snìomh thu,
Cha spìon thu 'n chraobh e;
mar shìneas e gheugan
Bidh a fhreumhan a sgaoileadh.

Sgrlobhadh an earrann a leanas le Domhnall Fhionghuin Ard Ollamh na Gàidhlig an Oilthigh Dhùn-éideann. Chaidh a chur a mach an toiseach anns a' Ghàidheal, anns a' bhliadhna 1874. Tha e an so a' dèanamh iomraidh thaitnich air an sgoil anns an d' fhuair e fhéin a cheud ionnsachadh, ann an eilean Cholbhasa.

Chaidh Cathair na Gàidhlig a chur air bonn an Oilthigh Dhùn-éideann le saothair John Stuart Blackie, agus b'e Domhnall MacFhionghuin an ceud Ard-ollamh chaidh a shuidheachadh innte, anns a' bhliadhna 1882, àite a lion e le mòr urram gu mios meadhonach an t-samhraidh, 1914. Chaochail e air latha Nollaig anns a' bhliadhna cheudna an eilean Cholbhasa, far an do rugadh agus far an do thogadh e. Bha an t-Ard-ollamh tri fichead bliadhna agus coig deug a dheug an uair a chaochail e.

BHO linn an Ath-leasachaidh b' e, gun teagamh, lagh na rioghachd gum biodh Sgoil is Eaglais anns gach Sgireachd; ach bha Sgireachdan na Gàidhealtachd farsuing, agus cha robh Sgoilean ach tearc. Chomhdaich dorchadas taobh an Iar na Gàidhealtachd. Is ann a chum an dorchadas so fhuadach a chuireadh air bhonn, ochd fichead bliadhna roimh so, "a' Chuidheachd Urramach atà chum Eòlas Criosdaidh a sgaoileadh air feadh Gàidhealtachd is Eileana na h-Alba" — Cuideachd a bhreac an taobh an Iar le tighean-sgoil, is a chuir Gàidhealtachd na h-Alba fo chomain nach faodar innseadh. A réir riaghailtean na Cuideachd bha e mar fhiachaibh air Uachdarain an fhearainn tighean freagarrach a thogail, agus croiteag fhearainn a chur air leth do'n Mhaighistir-sgoil. B' ann leis a' Chuideachd so a bha an t-Seann Sgoil air a cumail suas.

Chan fhaicear, taing do 'n Fhreasdal, ach annamh a nis coimeas do 'n fhàrdaich ris an abairte an Tigh-sgoil. Tigh fada, farsuing, dorcha, le ballachan ìosal de chloich ghlais nach do ghearain air buillean an ùird, air an salachadh air an taobh muigh le crè, air an taobh stigh air an dubhadh le toit. Dorus air gach taobh de 'n tigh, ach gun chòmhla mar bu trice ri aon diùbh. Chìte anns a' gheamhradh sgathach fhraoich ri taobh an fhuaraidh de dhorus an t-soirbheis air a cumail 'n a seasamh le cas camain. Rachadh an sgathach a chaitheamh a lìon beagan is beagan a' lasadh na teine; agus bhiodh an sin boitein connlaich ag gleidheadh fasgaidh gus an tigeadh mart no each mìomhail an rathad a dh' itheadh e. Anns an t-samhradh bha an tigh fosgailte gu farsuing, fialaidh, do sgoilearan de gach seòrsa. Urlar de thalamh fuar, fliuch, ach làrach na teine a mhàin. Uinneagan leth-lìonte le pluic, 's an còrr còmhdaichte le lic is clach r' a cùl. Dà tholl air druim an tighe a leigeil a mach na toite nach iarradh a rathad

A' dol do'n sgoil

troimh dhorus no uinneig. Dà theine air an urlar dlùth air meadhon an tighe, agus clach eatorra. B' i a' chlach so "Stòl (no furm) an aithreachais." Is tric a rinn mi cron latha fuar geamhraidh a dh' aon ghnothuch air son faotainn air an stòl. Bha déileachan a gheibhte air a' chladach sìnte air clachan a' dèanamh àitean-suidhe; agus bha dà sheann bhord le casan briste air an urlar aig am faighte sgrìobhadh le beagan cunnairt. Agus ma bha àirneis an tighe-sgoil gann; cha robh àsuig an sgoileir duilich a ghiùlan. Leac-sglèat ghlas le ruith oibreachaidh oirre, paipeir-sgrìobhaidh cho saor 's a gheibheadh cailleach nan uibhean an Grianaig, dubh de shùghadh an daraich, peann de ite an t-sùlanaich, Gray, Leabhar Aithghearr nan Ceist, Biobull Gàidhlig air a chòmhdach le craiceann caorach, agus deagh chaman.

156

Bhiodh e eu-comasach do 'n fhear-theagaisg a bu chomasaiche sgoilearan maith a dhèanamh air a leithid so de chothrom; ach tha mi creidsinn ged bhiodh gach tigh is gach goireas a b' fhearr aig mo sheana mhaighistir (chan ann r' a chur 'na dhéidh e), nach faigheadh an sgoil an cliù a b' àirde o fhir-cheasnachaidh ar latha-ne. Cha robh eòlas a' mhaighistir ro fharsuing; agus cha d' fhuair e cothrom air na dòighean a b' fhearr air sgoil a riaghladh, no air a eòlas féin a theagasg d' a sgoilearan, fhaicinn no ionnsachadh. Bha e, gun teagamh, an Glaschu 'g a cheasnachadh, agus dh' innis an Dr. MacLeòid dha nach b' urrainn dàsan leasan Gàidhlig a thoirt da. Air dìomhaireachd an lagha "Leathan ri leathan, is caol ri caol," bha e mion-eòlach; ach nam biodh an sgoil air a pàigheadh a réir mar a fhreagradh na sgoilearan na ceistean a chuirear air cloinn an diugh, is mór m' eagal nach biodh tuarasdal a' mhaighistir a bheag na b' àirde na bha e......Duine breac-liath, mu dheich is tri fichead; deas na phearsa; aghaidh thuigseach; cridhe blàth; nàdur ath-ghoirid; a cheum air tromachadh is uilt air teannachadh; ach a spiorad gun taiseachadh - a mhisneach cho àrd is aignidhean cho togarrach ri aois ochd bliadhna deug. Cha robh balach anns an sgoil a bu deise breith air caman, na bu dèine a chur gu tadhal.

Saoilidh mi gu faic mi an seann duine sunndach a' tighinn am fradharc air maduinn reòta gheamhraidh, le a aid ghibich a bha uair-eigin dubh, le chòta clò, is le bhata glas-daraich 'n a làimh. Chi e a mhac féin a' leigeil seachad na cnaige. "A thuaisd, a thràill, a sgagaire bhochd!" their an t-athair, is a nuas leis a' chòta mhór. As déidh na cnaige gu lùthmhor bheir e, ag greimeachadh ceann caol a' bhata; agus an tiota tha i aig an tadhal as faide air falbh. Théid ar gairm a steach, is thèid na camain fo'n bhòrd. Tòisichear air obair an latha le ùrnuigh dhùrachdaich an Gàidhlig; thèid earrann de 'n Bhiobull a leughadh, is na Ceistean a chur. Tha an sin sgriobhadh is cunntas, cunntas is sgriobhadh, gu feasgar. Leughar am Biobull. Co-dhùnar le ùrnuigh. Bheirear na camain am follais, is bithear ag iomain gus an toir an oidhche as ar sùilean e.

[William J. Watson, Rosg Gàidhlig, Inverness, 1915, pages 3, 4, 5, 7.]

GLENDESSERAY

While the modern game of shinty may now be a stirring contest of one hour and a half, played between two teams of twelve players on a regulation surface, it was not always thus. In bygone days there was no limit to the duration of the period of playing, a stretch of four to five hours being common, or until dusk terminated the contest. This poem by Principal Shairp, in description of a game, has so many interesting observations on the mode of playing which then held, that one is tempted to quote fairly freely from the ballad:

> The mountains piled benorth Lochiel.
> Glen-Mallie and Glen-Camgarie
> Resounded to the joyful cry,
> Westward with the sunset fleeing,
> It roused the homes of green Glenpean;
> Glen Kinzie tossed it on—unbarred
> It swept o'er rugged Màm-Clach-Ard,
> Start at these sounds the rugged bounds
> Of Arisaig, Moidart, Morar, and Knoydart,
> Down to the ocean's misty bourn
> By dark Loch Nevish and Lochourn.

> VI

> Many a heart that news made glad,
> Hearts that for years scant gladness had,
> But him it gladdened more than all,
> The Patriarch of Glen Desseray,
> Dwelling where sunny Sheneval
> From the green braeside fronts noon-day,
> My grandsire, Ewen Cameron, then
> Numbering three score years and ten.
> Of all our clansmen still alive,
> None in the gallant Forty-five
> Had borne a larger, nobler part,
> Had seen or suffered more;

Thence forward on no living heart
Was graven richer store
Of mournful memories and sublime,
Gleaned from that wild adventurous time.

VII

For when the Prince's summons called,
Answered to that brave appeal
No nobler heart than Archibald,
Brother worthy of Lochiel.
Him following fain, my grandsire flew
To the gathering by Loch Shiel,
Thence a foster-brother true
Followed him through woe and weal.
Nothing could these two divide,
Marching forward side by side,
Two friends, each of the other sure,—
Through Prestonpans and Falkirk Muir.
But when on dark Culloden day
A wounded man Gillespie lay,
My grandsire bore him to the shore
And helped him over seas away.
Seven years went by; less fiercely burned
The conqueror's vengeance 'gainst the Gael—-
Gillespie Cameron fain returned
To see his native vale.
Waylaid and captured on his road
By the basest souls alive,
His blood upon the scaffold flowed,
Last victim of the Forty-five.
Thenceforth wrapt in speechless gloom
Ewen mourned that lovely head;
His heart become a living tomb

Haunted by memory of the dead.
Never more from his lips fell
Name of him he loved so well,
But the less he spake, the more his heart
'Mid these sad memories dwelt apart.

VIII

But when on lone Glen Desseray broke
The first flash of that joyous cry,
From his long dream old Ewen woke—
I wot his heart leapt high.
No news like that had fallen on him,
Within his cabin smoky dim
For forty summers long and more,
Straightway beyond his cottage door
He sprang and gazed, the white hair o'er
His shoulders streaming, and the last
Wild sunset gleam on his worn cheek cast:
He looked and saw his Marion turn
Home from the well beside the burn,
And cried, "Good tidings I Thou and I
Will see our Chief before we die."
That night they talked, how many a year
Had gone, since the last Lochiel was here,
How gentle hearts and brave had been
The old Locheils their youth had seen;
Aye as they spake, more hotly burned
The fire within them—back returned
Old days seemed ready to revive
That perished in the Forty-five.
That night ere Ewen laid his head
On pillow, to his wife he said:
"Yule-time is near, for many a year
Mirth-making through the glens hath ceased,

160

But the clan once more, as in days of yore,
Shall hold this Yule with game and feast."

IX

Next morning, long ere screech o' day,
Old Ewen roused hath ta'en the brae
With gun on shoulder, and the boy,
Companion of his toils and joy,
The dark-haired Angus by his side—
O'er the black braes o' Glen Kinzie, on
Among the mists with slinging stride
They fare, nor stayed till they had won
Corrie-na-Gaul, the cauldron deep
Which the Lochiels were used to keep
A sanctuary where the deer might hide,
And undisturbed all year abide.
Not a cranny, rock, or stone
In that corrie but was known
To my grandsire's weird grey eye;
All the lairs where large stags lie
Well he knew, but passed them by,
For stags were lean ere yule-time grown.
Crawling on, he saw appear
O'er withered fern one twinkling ear—
His gun is up—the crags resound—
Startled, a hundred antlers bound
Up the passes fast away;
Lifeless stretched along the ground,
Large and sleek, one old hind lay.
Straight they laid her on their backs,
And o'er the hills between them bore,
Up and down by rugged tracks,
Sore-wearied, ere beside their door
They laid her down—"A bonny beast
To crown our coming yule-time feast"—

As night came down on scour and glen,
From rough Scour-hoshi-brachcalen.

X

That night they slept the slumber sound
That waits on labour long and sore;
Next day he sent the message round
The glen from door to door,
On to the neighbouring glens - Glenpean
The summons hears and all that be in
Glen Kinzie's bounds ———Loch Arkaig, stirred,
From shore to shore the call was heard;
To Clunes it passed, from toun to toun,
That all the people make them boun,
Against the coming New Year's Day,
To gather for a shinty-fray
Within the long Glen Desseray,
And meet at night around Ewen's board,
In honour of Lochiel restored.

XI

Blue, frosty, bright the morning rose
That New Year's Day above the snows,
Veiling the range of Scour and ben,
That either side wall in the glen.
But down on the Strath the night frost keen
Had only crisped the long grass green,
When the men of Loch Arkaig, boat and oar
At Kinloch leaving, sprang to shore.
Crisp was the sward beneath their tread
As they westward marched, and at their head
The piper of Achnacarry blew
The thrilling pibroch of Donald Dhu.
That challenge the Piper of the Glen
As proudly sounded back again,

162

From his biggest pipe, till far-off rang
The tingling crags to the wild war-clang
Of the pibroch that loud to battle blown
The Cameron clan had for ages known.
To-day, as other, yet the same,
It summons to the peaceful game;
From the braeside homes, down trooping come
The champions of Glen Desseray, some
In tartan philabegs arrayed————
The garb which tyrant laws forbade,
But still they clung to, unafraid;
Some in home-woven tartan trews,
Rough spun, and dyed with various hues,
By mother's hands or maiden's wrought:
In hues by native fancy taught;
But all with hazel camags slung
Their shoulders o'er, men old and young,
With mountaineer's long, slinging pace,
Move cheerily down to the trysting place.

XII

Yonder a level space of ground ————
Two miles and more from west to east,
Where from rough Màm-Clach-Ard released
In loop on loop the river wound,
Through many a slow and lazy round,
Ere plunging downward to the lake.
On that long flat of green they take
Their stations: on the west the men
Of Dessreray, Kinzie, Pean Glen,
Ranged 'gainst the stalwart lads who bide
Down long Loch Arkaig, either side.
The ground was ta'en, the clock struck ten,
As Ewen, patriarch of the glen,

Struck off, and sent the foremost ball
Down the strath flying, with a cry;
"Fye, lads, set on," and one and all
To work they fell right heartily.

XIII

Now fast and furious, on they drive,———-
Here youngsters scud with feet of wind,
There, in a melee, dunch and strive;
The veterans outlook keep behind.
Now up, now down, the ball they toss;
Now this, now that side of the Strath;
And many a leaper, brave to cross
The river, finds a chilling bath;
And many a fearless driver bold,
To win renown, was sudden rolled
headlong in hid quagmire;
And many a stroke of stinging pain
In the close press was given and ta'en
Without or guile or ire.
So all the day the clansmen played,
And to and fro their tulzie swayed, (scuffle)
Untired, along the hollow vale,
And neither side could win the hail; ...
But high the clamour, upward flung,
Along the precipices rung,
And smote the snowy peaks, and went
Far up the azure firmament.
All day, too, watching from the knowes,
Stood maidens fair, with snooded brows,
And bonnie blithe wee bairns;
Those watching whom I need na say,
Those eyeing now their daddies play,
Now jinking round the cairns.

XIV

The loud game fell with sunset still,
And echo died on strath and hill;
As gloamin' deepened, each side the glen,
High above the homes of men,
Blinks of kindling fires were seen,
Such as shine out upon Halloween;
Single fires on rocky shelf
Each several farm-house for itself
Has lighted—there in wavering line
Either side the vale they shine
From dusk to dawn, to blaze and burn
In welcome of their Chief's return.
But broader, brighter than the rest,
Down beside Loch-Arkaig-head,
From a knoll's commanding crest
One great beacon flaring red,
As with a wedge of splendour clove
The blackness of the vault above.
And far down the quivering waters flung
Forward its steady pillar of light,
To tell, more clear than trumpet tongue,
Glen Desseray hails her Chief to-night.

XV

The while the bonfires blazed without,
With logs and peats by keen hands fed
Children and men—a merry rout;
In every home the board was spread.
On ev'ry hearth the fires burned clear,
And round and round abundant cheer....

[Glendessary and Other Poems - J. C. Shairp, London, 1888, pages 8-17.]

THE GREATEST SHINTY MATCH OF ALL TIME

The Glen Urquhart team of 1887 just prior to their epic encounter with Strathglass at the Bught Park, Inverness.

Back Row: (left to right) Angus MacDonald, Lewiston (No. 14), Peter John MacDonald, Balbeg (No. 8), Donald MacLean, Bearnock (9), Finlay MacLean, Upperton, (11), Donald MacPhee, Milton (15), Alexander Cumming, Drumnadrochit (17), Alex Fraser, Achmonie (19), Ewan MacDonald, Upper Lenie (21), John Campbell, Achtuie (23), John MacMillian, Balnaglaic (24).

Second Row: John MacDonald, Lewiston (13), Hugh MacKenzie, Achtemarack (6), Finlay Fanning, Lochletter (7), John MacDonald Jun., Balbeg (12), John Ross, Lewiston (18), John MacDonald Sen., Balbeg (22), Goalkeeper - unknown.

Kneeling: Ian MacDonald, Balbeg (10), Charles MacDonell, Kilmartin House (16), Alexander MacDonald, Bearnock (20).
Front: James MacDonald, Lewiston (5), Peter MacDonald, Balbeg (4), Donald MacDonald Jun., Balbeg (3), Donald MacDonald Sen., Balbeg (2), Andrew MacDonald, Balbeg (1).

Glenurquhart v Strathglass

The game was played at the Bught Park, Inverness on February 13, 1887. The venue was the field that today stands between the Glenurquhart road and the Ice Rink and it measured 300 yards by 200 yards.

The match was attended by a crowd of approximately 3,000 and soldiers and Inverness "bobbies" did duty on the line. There were 22 players on each side.

The Strathglass and Glenurquhart Shinty Clubs

Great Match at Inverness

On Saturday Inverness was the scene of a great shinty match between teams representing the Strathglass and Glen Urquhart Clubs—two of the champion clubs in the North. The game of shinty has long been a popular one in the Highlands; but owing to various causes, few matches of importance have taken place for many years. Recently, however, interest in the game has been revived, and keen and exciting contests have taken place between the Glen Urquhart and Glenmoriston clubs, and between the Strathglass and Lochcarron clubs.

The match was announced to begin at 12 o'clock, and shortly before this hour the Glen Urquhart men, under the command of their Chief, Mr Alistair Campbell of Kilmartin, marched into the field, to the music of the pipes. Dressed in blue jerseys, with white duck knickerbockers and blue socks, the men presented a very smart appearance. Shortly thereafter, the Strathglass men, headed by their players, and carrying several flags, arrived on the scene. They were under the command of Captain Chisholm of Glassburn, the Chief of the Club, and being generally taller and older men, they looked a more formidable body than their opponents. They were dressed in white shirts and 42nd tartan knickerbockers and hose, and wore Prince Charlie Glengarry bonnets, with rosettes, having the Chisholm crest and badge. The preliminary arrangements were soon made. Mr Gillespie of Tulloch acted as referee, Mr MacGregor, of the Hotel, Invermoriston, discharged the duties of umpire for the Glen Urquhart team, while Mr Charles Macdonald, Knocknagael, performed a similar service for the Strathglass men. At 12.15 p.m. the teams formed up in mid field.

The captains of both teams having intimated that they were ready for the fray, the referee threw up the ball and the game began in earnest. The Strathglass men had undertaken to defend the western goal, and it soon became evident that they would have to devote themselves seriously to the task. Getting on the ball, the Glen Urquhart team speedily carried it westwards, until it got into dangerous proximity to the defenders' goal posts. Just at the critical moment a member of the Strathglass Club got on the ball, and by fine play sent it well down the field. For a few minutes an exciting contest took place in mid-field, several members of the Glen Urquhart Club carrying the ball from right to left, where it was caught up and sent back by the opposing team. Again and again the ball was carried in this way across the field, the Glen Urquhart men on several occasions bringing it dangerously near their opponents' hail posts. The play was getting fast and exciting when, by a splendid run, Thomas Macgillivray, a member of the Strathglass team, carried the ball well down field. This success, however, was not followed up, and almost immediately the ball was brought back to the Strathglass hail posts. A keen struggle ensued, and in the excitement, a member of the Strathglass team unwittingly sent the ball through the posts, thus registering the first hail for the Glen Urquhart team, Rule 27 being to the effect that "when the ball is sent from the 'field of play' through the goal poles, and under the cross bar or tape connecting them, the game is won, even should an opponent, through mistake, send the ball through."

Sides were then reversed, the Glen Urquhart men now undertaking to defend the western goal. The ball was again thrown up, and elated by their success - after only a quarter-of-an-hour's play - the Glen Urquhart men set vigorously to work, and again carried the ball well into the Strathglass territory. The defenders, however, played a careful game, again and again driving back their opponents, thus enabling their flank men to get on the ball. This they did on several occasions with considerable success, but their efforts were quickly interrupted by their opponents, who played a fine, combined game. For fully half-an-hour the ball was kept moving about in Strathglass territory, the goalkeepers having again and again to defend their position with the greatest possible vigour. At length, by a well-directed shot, the ball was sent over the posts, and being thrown back by one of the crowd, it passed through the posts and a goal claimed. The matter was referred to the referee, who disallowed the goal claimed, and the ball was thrown out 15 yards from the posts. Almost immediately after, the ball was again shot over, and had again to be thrown up. An exciting struggle followed at the goal mouth; and just at the last half-hour of play was entered upon, a second goal was registered for the Glen Urquhart club.

Sides were again reversed, and the most exciting part of the game commenced. The Strathglass men played with great determination, and, for the first time during the game, carried the ball well into their opponents' ground. Again and again, however, the ball was driven back amid a scene of great excitement. At length, a member of the Strathglass club got on the ball in mid-field, and the line being clear, he had a good chance of distinguishing himself. Unfortunately, however, he missed his aim; and John Ross, Lewiston, getting the ball, carried it close to the enemy's goal posts. This was decidedly the finest run of the day, and Ross was rewarded with loud cheers. For a time, the ball was kept moving to and fro pretty near the Strathglass posts; but at a critical moment it was caught by Ronald Mackinnon and carried out of danger, where it remained when time was called.

The match thus ended in a victory for the Glen Urquhart team by two goals to nothing. The play throughout was fast and exciting; and the large crowd showed their appreciation of the game by repeated cheers.

The Strathglass Shinty Club of 1887.

Back: (left to right) Thomas MacGillivray, Cosac; Donald Cameron, Struy; James Fraser, Knocknashalauaig; Sandy Bain, Glen Affaric; Alexander Forbes, Leanassie; Donald Chisholm, Imir; Kenneth Chisholm, Carnich; James MacDonald, Tomich; Wallach MacDonald, Tomich; Ralph Mackinnon, Struy; Hugh Forbes, John Chisholm, Farley; George Tait.

Second Row: (left to right) Alexander Ross, John Chisholm, Imir; Donald MacKenzie, Wester Crochail; Theodore Campbell, Hughton; Pipemajor Lachlan Collie; James Fraser, Mauld (Captain); William MacKenzie, Wester Crochail; Duncan Scott, Cannich; Finlay Macrae, Eilan Aigas; Mr. Collie, Angus Fraser, Inshully, Roderick MacLennan, Fas-na-Kyle.

Third Row: (left to right) William Forbes, Struy; Donald Chisholm; Archibald Chisholm, Cannich; Captain Archibald Macrae Chisholm, James MacDonald, Cannich; Mr. MacPherson, Glen Affric Hotel; Donald MacDonald, Carnoch; Ewen MacDonald, Milness.

Front Row (left to right) Kenneth Moss, Tomich; Donald Macmillan, Kerrow; Alexander Chisholm, Craskaig; Alexander Chisholm, John Matheson; Duncan Chisholm, Runavraid, Donald Chisholm, Alexander Chisholm.

The late Archie Scott pointed out that his father Duncan Scott (second row) was 6 feet in height. This gives us some indication of the massive stature of those standing to the left of Duncan in the photograph - Willie MacKenzie from Wester Crochail and James Fraser of Mauld.

The Glen Urquhart men played a fine, combined game; and being as a rule, lighter and more active than their opponents, they were able to keep on the ball. Passing it rapidly from one another, their strokes were quick and sure, and throughout the game there was hardly a single miss. John Macdonald, Lewiston; John Ross and Finlay Fanning, Lochletter, played exceedingly well; while Andrew MacDonald, Balbeg; Donald Macdonald, sen., Balbeg; James Macdonald, Lewiston: and Ewen Macdonald, Lennie; also rendered splendid service. All the members of the team played a plucky game. The Strathglass men appeared throughout to act too much on the defensive. They undoubtedly played a fine saving game: but they stuck too close together to do good service against their opponents. Their play, however, was steady, and had several of the runs been well followed up, the result might have been different. Good service was rendered by Thomas MacGillivray, Wm. Mackenzie, Donald Cameron, Wm. Matheson and Ranald Mackinnon, while Donald Alexander and John Chisholm gave excellent support. The teams were directed - the Glen Urquhart Club by Captain John Fraser, Temple Pier; and the Strathglass Club by Captain John Fraser, Struy. Throughout the progress of the match the best feeling prevailed on both sides, and although two of the players had to retire from injuries, they were so slight that they were able to rejoin their comrades at the close. The following are the respective teams, a glance at which will show that the Glen Urquhart team, including the secretary, consist of fifteen members of the Clan Macdonald while the Strathglass team, including the secretary and president, was made of ten members of the Clan Chisholm:

Glen Urquhart team—Mr John Fraser, captain; Mr Andrew Macdonald, Balbeg; Mr Donald MacDonald, sen., Balbeg; Mr Donald Macdonald, Lewiston; Mr Hugh Mackenzie, Achtemarack, Drumnadrochit; Mr Finlay Fanning, Lochletter; Mr Peter John Macdonald, Balbeg; Mr Donald MacLean, Bearnock; Mr Ewen Macdonald, Balbeg; Mr Finlay Maclean, Upperton, Balnain, Mr John Macdonald, jun., Balbeg; Mr John MacDonald, Lewiston; Mr Mr Angus Macdonald, Lewiston; Mr Donald MacPhee, Milton; Mr Charles Macdonell, Kilmartin; Mr Alex. Cumming., Drumnadrochit; Mr John Ross, Lewiston; Mr Alex. Fraser, Achmony; Mr Alex. Macdonald, Bearnock; Mr Ewen Macdonald, Lennie, Mr John Macdonald, Balbeg, Mr D. D. Macdonald, secretary.

After the match the Glen Urquhart men, who had travelled to Inverness in the early morning, formed up, and headed by pipers, marched to the town, where hearty cheers were raised in their honour. As time was limited, the men proceeded direct to Muirtown, and returned home by the afternoon steamer, being congratulated on all sides on their victory. The Strathglass men, who had had a cold drive of 29 miles to Beauly in the morning, engaged rooms at the Caledonian Hotel, where they breakfasted before the match. At the close of the game, the men of the Cameron Highlanders marched with the Strathglass team, headed by three excellent pipers, back to the Caledonian Hotel, where they dined together, and all did ample justice to the hot and comfortable refreshments supplied by Mr Macfarlane. After dinner the Secretary of the Strathglass club explained to the team that they were indebted to Mrs Captain Chisholm of Glassburn, for the substantial and comfortable repast they had partaken of, as she was anxious they should dine together whether they won or lost. He begged to propose Mrs Captain Chisholm's health, with long life and happiness, which was drunk with enthusiastic cheering. Captain Chisholm replied and returned thanks. The team left Inverness by the 4pm train and drove up from Beauly Station in three brakes to their respective homes in Strathglass.

Reception of the News in Glen Urquhart

Immediately on the first goal being won by the Glen Urquhart team, the news was telegraphed to Drumnadrochit, where a large crowd had assembled to hear the result of the match, which was expected to be over by about 1.30pm. On receipt of the gratifying intelligence Mr Burgess, Banker, fired a cannon, and in this way the news of the victory was carried to every corner of the parish. As the steamer "Lochness," which conveyed the players from Inverness, appeared in sight at Temple Pier, hearty cheers were raised by the crowd which had assembled. At Drumnadrochit, the coaches were met by a large number of the country people, and the players enthusiastically welcomed. Telegrams were received at Drumnadrochit during the afternoon from natives of the glen in Glasgow and elsewhere inquiring as to the result, and congratulating the team on their success.

Another correspondent writes:-

A great ovation was waiting the Glen Urquhart team on their return home on Saturday night. The result of the game being wired beforehand, the young people and others joined together in giving hearty expressions to their feelings by piling bonfires at different places on the way up the glen. The first of these was on a circular hill to the west of Milton where the young people turned out in great force and cheered vociferously. Another bonfire was lit opposite Delshangie, and a third at a further point at Balnain.

[Glen Urquhart Rural Community Bulletin]

A fragment of the following appeared in Volume XLV of the Transactions of the Gaelic Society of Inverness, page 384. It is by John Fraser, Temple, who was captain of the Glenurquhart team which defeated Strathglass in February 1887. The last line of the fourth verse refers to the red caps worn along with blue jerseys by the Glenurquhart team. Strathglass wore white shirts and Glengarry bonnets.

Fhir a shiùbhlas air astar
A Srathghlais nam fear chòir,
Thoir mo bheannachd dha "Glassburn"
'S dha na gaisgaich bha còmhla ris.

Agus innis dhaibh mar a tha mi
Air mo chradh 's air mo leònadh,
O 'n chaill iad am blàir ud
Cha teid an tàmailt ri 'm bheò dhiom.

An ainm an Aigh ciod a thachair
Dha na Glasaich 's a' chòmhrag?
Chaill iad baileach an tapadh
Mun deach stad air a' chòmhstri.

Air m' fhirinn 's ann shaoil leam
'S bha mi daonnan an dòchas
Nach robh 'n leth-bhreachd ri fhaotainn
Ann an taobh so de 'n Roinn-Eòrpa.

Mo sheachd nàir' is mo mhasladh
Cha bheag an cachdan e dhomh-sa,
Luchd mo dhùthch' bhith dol dhachaidh
Gus an dad ach an deò annt'.

Ged a cluith iad le diorras
Airson a' cheud ghreis dhe' 'n chonnspaid
Thug na h-Urchadnaich chrionda
An cliù cho iosal 's a dh' fhòghnas.

Ach 's e gu tur rinn mo chiùrradh
Mo luchd-dhùthcha 's luchd m' eòlas
A bha da uair air an rùsgadh
Dheth na chliù so bu nòs dhaibh.

Tha e thìom dhoibh o 'n uair so
Stad dheth 'n uaills' is an teòmachd
'S a chaidh gun Dulan thoir uapa
Do'n "Churrachd Ruadh" fhad' 's beò iad

Faodaidh "Glassburn' bhith sgrìo(bh)ag'
'S am bi e sgìth le cuid bòluich.
Bha e gòrach a rìreadh
Dhol a' slimeadh 's an dòigh so.

Ach cha bhreugnaich e fhìrinn
Ged a sgrìobhadh e "volumes"
Oir tha buaidh le làn chinnteas
Aig Braigh a' Ghlinn' 's tha mi pròiseil.

It is not known who composed this luinneag which appeared in the "Scottish Highlander" some time after the game.
Kilmartin is Captain Alasdair Campbell of Kilmartin who was in charge of the Glenurquhart team.

'S ann a Urchadainn so shuas
Thainig oirnn na seòid bha luath,
Cluich air camag mar bu dual
'S a choisinn buaidh 's gach aite.

Chunnaic mise sealladh réidh
Nuair a choinnich iad ri chéil',
H-uile fear dhiubh ruith 's a leum
Cho 1uath ri féidh na fàsach.

'S ann an sud a bha na laoich—
Na Dòmhnullaich a Innse-braoin—
Cuir na Glasaich air an druim
H-uile taobh mar b' fhearr leo.

Bha "Kilmartin" uasal, fial,
Mar bu dual do chinnidh riamh,
Thug e deoch dhoibh agus biadh
'S tha beannachd Dhia 's gach ait' air.

Ghabh Caiptein Friseil an command
'S e cho duineil air an ceann,
'S cluicheadh e ri fear a bh' ann
O cheann gu ceann do 'n phairce.

'S e dol an aghaidh Caiptein airm
A Srath-ghlais le daoine garg,
Bu choltach iad ri sluagh gun seilbh
'S a' "churrachd dhearg" toir bàrr orr'.

SIOSAL AIR AN CEANN

The luinneag was replied to by the following one, also anonymous.

Urchadnaich ghreannaich, ruaidh,
Na tog do cheann cho airde suas,
Cha chuir sibh 'n còmhnuidh oirnn ruaig
Ged fhuair sibh buaidh an tràth ud.

Na bitheadh 'gar mhealladh fein
An duil gun d' rinn sibh gniomh bha treun,
'S e annaibh slaodairean gun fheum
Gràisg de bhallaich thàilleir.

Air an lionadh suas le pròis—
Is olc a thig e do bhur seòrs',
'S gun cuireadh pioghaid thar an sgòr.
Dà fhichead 's a dhà dhiubh.

Ach bha na Glasaich riamh gun bheum
Ghreanmhor, fearail, uasal, gleusd',
An cath gu robh iad neartmhor, treun
Cuir casg' gu grad air nàmhaid.

'S mar thig a' Gheamhradh rithist mu cuairt
Le còta sneachd is reòthadh chruaidh,
Cluicheas iad camag mar bu dual
'S gheibh iad buaidh air 's gach ait'.

*Le Caiptein Siosal air an ceann**
A toirt dhoibh misneachd anns gach am,
Duin' uasal eireachdail, neo-ghann
Air nach eil cearb na fàillinn.

*Captain A. M. Chisholm of Glassburn, a well-known Gael who had served in the Black Watch, led Strathglass whose team captain was John Fraser, Struy.

[Transactions of the Gaelic Society of Inverness, XLVIII, pages 342 - 345.]

Captain Archibald Macra Chisholm of Glasssburn.
First Chief of Camanachd Association, 1893-1897.

A' CHURACHD RUADH

air fonn: "Gabhaidh sin an rathad mòr

Caithidh sinn a' Churachd Ruadh,
Cluithidh sinn an caigeann cruaidh,
Buinnidh sinn do Ghleann nam buadh,
Bheir sinn buaidh mar b'àbhaist.

Morisnich an gion's an gruaim,
'S iomadh gaisge tha riu fuaight',
Cha tig faisg do'n Churachd Ruadh,
Bheir i buaidh's gach àite.

Fir Srath Ghlais fo chaiptean airm,
O chionn fad' an cleachdamh dearbht',
Fir nach tais - na gaisgich gharg,
A' Churachd Dhearg thug bàrr orr'.

Feachd o'n Chaiplich 's taic a' chuain,
Aird is Afraic's fad mu'n cuairt -
Daoine tapaidh's dreachmhor tuar,
A' Churachd Ruadh gun nàir iad'.

'N Inbhirnis is lìonmhor sluagh,
'M bi cluith's cleas a deas is tuath,
Cha bu cheist nach toir i buaidh,
Nithear luaidh's gach àit' oirr'.

Ealant', eangach, greannmhor, gleusd',
Cumail teann ri rachdan rèidh -
Sluagh gun mheang toir hip-ho-rè,
Churachd fhèin a b' annsa.

[Courier Inbhirnis, Màirt, 1888.]

An unknown group, venue also unknown. Courtesy of Roddy MacLennan, Inverness.

THE RENAISSANCE

After the middle of the nineteenth century interest in the ancient game was practically confined to the glens of Lochaber, Strathglass and Badenoch. From them alone could any revival be looked for. Fortunately, there were not wanting patriotic Highlanders in these districts who were willing and able to fan the dying embers into flame. The first outstanding figure of the period is undoubtedly that of Captain Chisholm of Glassburn – a name that will be remembered as long as the game is played. Realising that all future progress depended on the formation and promulgation of an authoritative code of laws, he set to work and drew up "The Constitution, Rules and Regulations of the Strathglass Shinty club," published in the year 1880. This, as far as the present writer is aware, is the earliest printed constitution of the kind.

Though lack of space forbids us to quote from it at length, there are two rules to which attention may be drawn, as providing a contrast to modern usage. "Rule 8 – The ball, if caught in the air, may be thrown or run with even through the hails (and the person running must be caught and not tripped up by club or feet, but whenever caught, must throw the ball or drop it), or it may be thrown from one to another as long as it does not touch the ground. Rule 10 – It is against the rules of the game to lift and throw the ball during a match."

The method of scoring was this: – Twenty-five points were allowed for a hail, and if the ball was driven across the goal-line or over the bar, one point was counted.

The Code of Rules was republished in 1888, with considerable emendations and additional improvements. As John Macdonald, Esq. (of the Keppoch family, grandson of the famous "Long John"), had actively collaborated in the vision, this "book of the words" was quickly adopted, not only in the North East, but also in the South-West, and became basic root from which all subsequent regulations were evolved. Curiously enough, neither in the Constitution of 1880, nor its revised successor of 1888, nor in the Rules of "The Inverness Town and Country Club" (no date), is any mention made the number of players which should compose a team.

In a letter received from Mr. Macdonald (presently residing in South Africa) light is thrown on the point. "Then we began to play with twenty-one a-side, and on a field 300 by 200 yards: the idea being to give plenty of players and full scope settling personal disputes without interfering with the progress of the play!"

Probably one of the most bitterly contested matches of that period, and one which did much to awaken the slumbering interest in the northern districts, was that played Inverness in February 1887, between teams represent Strathglass and Glen-Urquhart. The former were led Chisholm of Glassburn in person, and the latter by Campbell of Kilmartin. The contest was fast and fierce from the outset; the only hail scored was obtained by the Glenurquhart men a few minutes from the close of the play, and, needles say, became afterwards a subject of much controversy.

Another great encounter was that staged at Dalchoille in Badenoch, between Brae-Lochaber and the combined forces of Kingussie, Newtonmore and Laggan. It is worthy of record, because it was probably the last occasion on which a hair ball was used. Such is the information furnished to the writer by Mr. John Macdonald, who captained the Lochaber side. "The hair ball was supplied by the Badenoch men and used in the first half of the match. In the second played with a ball cased in leather; the core had been made by me and covered by a local harness-maker under my instructions. Its superiority was so manifest that the hair ball was never used again. The match ended in a draw. Years afterwards, whilst I was driving through Newtonmore, a man engaged in cabbage-planting observed me, and brandishing the head of a caman that he was using in his work, exclaimed, "That's the club you broke over Sandy Ban at Dalchoille, you Brae-Lochaber murderer." Needless to say, Sandy had been neither murdered nor otherwise damaged (at any rate, to speak of), as it was his club that I hit."

John Macdonald and his younger brother, now Colonel A. W. Macdonald of Blarour, were at that date resident at Keppoch, and doing much to restore the game to new vigour in their neighbourhood. To the latter's guidance, during 20 years as president of the Camanachd Association, Shinty owes much of its present strong and sound position in the Highlands.

From this time onwards the names of stalwarts, who have taken up the fiery cross and rallied to the cause, became more numerous; but to name these individually and to describe their work in detail would expand this booklet beyond its originally assigned limits.

By the autumn of 1892 a host of clubs had come into existence. Besides those of Strathglass, Brae-Lochaber, Kingussie, Newtonmore and Glen-Urquhart already mentioned, there were those of Glencoe, Ballachulish, Insch, Vale of Laroch, Vale of Leven, Dunally, Ardkinglas, Lochgoilhead, Dalmally, Oban, Bunawe, Strachur, Furnace, Inveraray, Kiltarlity, Inverness, Grantown, Strathpeffer, Alvie, Glasgow Cowal, Aberdeen University, Edinburgh University, Edinburgh Camanachd, London Scottish, London and Northern Counties, to which Beauly, Glenmoriston, Fort-Augustus, Invergarry, Spean-Bridge and others were soon added.

In the spring of 1893 the number of matches played in the various parts of the Highlands surprises us to-day; it astonishes us the more when we recall the limited facilities for transport of those days, and the fact that a Shinty meeting did not necessarily come to an end with the game itself.

A match played between the Kingussie and Glasgow Cowal clubs on April 3rd of the same year was described as one of the finest exhibitions of the game ever seen. It formed a culminating point in the renaissance. It aroused such intense and widespread interest that a general meeting of all supporters of the game was convoked at Kingussie in the following October.

At this memorable meeting it was definitely resolved, on the motion of Mr. John Macdonald, to form a Camanachd Association. Captain Chisholm of Glassburn was named as first Chief – a fitting tribute to his popularity. Just as happy was the selection of the first President in the person of Simon Lord Lovat, one of the keenest wielders of the caman in the North.

Not long afterwards the Association decided to institute the Challenge Trophy, to which the championship of the year is attached, and around which so many spirited contests have waged.

The Camanachd Association Challenge Trophy

Since that time the Camanachd Association has been recognised throughout the land as the supreme authority in the conduct of the game. No one can deny that its influence has been beneficial, inasmuch as it has succeeded in stabilising play on sound and sporting lines.

But important as the results have been which its officials have achieved, there are others of whose labours in the same direction much might be written. There are the numerous minor Associations – such as the Glasgow Celtic, Mactavish etc.—who have done yeoman service in encouraging competition in their respective districts. There are also the countless individuals, men and women, large-hearted and self-sacrificing who have grudged neither time nor labour to advance the interests of the national pastime. In the various towns and villages, glens and straths, they are still to be found; the highest in rank and the lowliest, each and all deeming it at once a duty and an honour to carry on the ancient tradition of their forefathers.

What is there in this Club-ball that it should exercise such a fascination on the Scottish Highlands? To the reader, who has perused these pages, a partial answer has doubtless already suggested itself. The Gael is by nature conservative.

"Lean gu dlùth ri cliù do Shinnsir,"
(Cleave fast to thy fathers' fame)

is a refrain which has come echoing down through the ages.

Yet that is but putting the question further back. Why did our forefathers adopt this pastime in preference to any other ?

In the ultimate analysis the only answer is, because it is an athletic exercise so eminently suited to the requirements of the Gael.

Camanachd calls for gifts, physical and mental, of no mean order. Naturally it is no pastime for weaklings or degenerates; nor is it an exercise wherein the slow-witted or dullards will be found to shine. It makes demand on stamina, on soundness of wind and limb, on brain as well as muscle, on prowess, on manliness and on courage, for which in few other games will a parallel be found.

It calls into play practically all the chief muscles of the human body; it requires quickness of eye and sureness of aim; it demands both rapidity and coolness of judgment; and, above all, it calls for perfect control of temper.

A finished caman-wielder must, therefore, be a first-class athlete. Ability to deal lightning strokes on the ball at so many different angles on the ground, in the air, whilst speeding over the turf, as well as whilst stationary; the free play of each and every muscle; the easy poise of the body on fleet ye steady feet—these are some of the qualities that one looks for in a first-class player, and these are the qualities which make such a one a picture not only of force and strength, but also of perfect grace and carriage.

[Ninian MacDonald, Shinty. A Short History, 1932, pages 92-98.]

"Of prefect grace and carriage........"

THAT SENSE OF HIGHLAND IDENTITY

During the nineteenth century the immediacy or locality of community related to a sense of direct, common, concern for a way of life for different groups of people. The notion of community was often contrasted with more formal forms of social organisation such as state, society or nation. Forms of sport contributed to a sense of community and identity in Argyllshire and other West Coast communities during the Victoriamn period. The passion which the socialist and nationalist land reformer John Murdoch had for shinty in the mid 1880s resulted from Murdoch's belief that shinty contributed to a sense of Highland identity and Celtic culture. On the one hand, it has to be argued that forms of sport, play and recreation in many West Coast communities actively contributed to a sense of community and nation. On the other hand it is more dificult to explain which nation or which expresssion or image of the nation games such as shinty were talking to; Scottish, British, Highland or Celtic? People identify with community as they do nation but the irony is of course that nationalism in the late twentieth century is probably the gravedigger of many nation-states and communities.

*[Hamish Telfer, "Play, customs and popular culture of West Coast communites, 1840-1900",
in Scottish Sport in the making of the Nation (ed Grant Jarvie and Graham Walker), London, 1994, page 123.]*

Nor was shinty just a casual pursuit, in John Murdoch's opinion. Like a later generation of Irish nationalists and revolutionaries who were nurtured in the Gaelic Athletic Association and who saw in hurling, Ireland's version of shinty, and explicit assertion of their country's claim to separateness, Murdoch always believed that Highland sports were an integral part of that sense of Highland identity which he strove continually to reinforce. Shinty matches were reported in the Highlander for reasons identical to those which lay behind the paper's coverage of efforts to rescue Gaelic tradition from oblivion. Everything which contributed to Highland distinctiveness, John Murdoch considered, deserved to be promoted and encouraged.

Coming home from school on Saturdays, we had quite a field day at Tràigh an Luig at Shinty playing. This was one of the best fields possible for the game and the players were good. My great delight was to play at this game; and soon I became not only a good player but came to be recognised as such.

Shortly before I got home there was a New Year gathering for a shinty match. The 'chiefs' were John Francis Cambpell and Colin Campbell, Balnaby, who was very often with the young laird. I remember I was the first person called by John Francis. Whether this had anything to do with what I am going to notice or not, I do not know. But there were famous players on the ground, among them David Crawford. David and I were on opposite sides and, even in a scramble with him, I justified the selection made by my chief. This did not go down well with David whose temper had not been improved with the drams which were going in the morning. So he made at me and when nothing else would do, he raised the club to strike me. I, however, kept my temper, siezed him, by the wrists and held him. And trying to pacify him, I said, 'Of course you are better than I am.' But Finlay MacArthur, hearing my protestations of inferiority, came forward and protested in his turn that I had proved in the play that I was better than my assailant. The story of the scuffle got abroad and it put a feather in my cap.

These reminiscences are in striking contrast with the present state of things along that part of the country. Tràigh an Luig is silent under the feet of catle. And the small farms from which the keen shinty players of these days came are consolidated into the large farms.

[James Hunter, For the people's cause: From the Writings of John Murdoch, Edinburgh, 1986, pages 14, 51-52.]

John Murdoch, 1818-1903

THURSO SANDS

Shinty on Thurso Sands

We were present the other evening at the Glasgow Caithness Gathering and we were delighted to hear the Chairman, Rev Dr Walter Ross Taylor refer in regretful tones to the decay of "knotty" in his native country. On New Year's Day when he was young, a hundred lads would take part in a shinty match on Thurso Sands. This year the sands were deserted. "Knotty" was a manly game, and developed healthy bodies and strong muscles, and he thought it was a matter for serious consideration if the young men of Thurso who did not now engage in this splendid pastime were physically as strong as the past generation who benefited by this exercise. He feared they were not, and hoped that the youth of Caithness would waken up and revive this old and delightful game. The Dr's remarks were loudly applauded, and we trust they will have due effect in the proper quarter.

[Celtic Monthly, November 1892, Volume 1, page 80.]

Caithness coast near Dunnet Head

YE NEVER HEAR O' KNOTTY NOO

Ye never hear o' Knotty noo,
The game is never seen
And yet we played it everyday,
Upon the village green,
The crofters 'gainst the villagers,
At dinner time we'd play
And up and doon the green we'd race,
Till the bell called us away.

So wrote the poet some ninety years ago, taking a nostalgic look back to his boyhood. Today memories of the game have receded even further, remembered only by old men from tales told by their grandfathers. The history of this game goes back long into time, it precedes football, hockey, shinty, and possibly golf. An early report comes from the Church Records of Olrig Parish. "Olrig, December 30th, 1705 it was related that there was several children in Murkle seen the previous Sunday playing at the knottie, such as C – – S, his son J. S – –, his son A. S – –, and his son S – –. The Session considered this an effect of bad education in that these men suffered their children rather to prophane the Sabbath than take them to church with them. Therefore they ordered the parents of those children should be cited to the next Session, and that they bring their children along."

"Olrig January 13th 1706 - The parents cited appeared at the next meeting, some of them brought their children with them, and others declared their children not above six years of age, and that it was altogether without their knowledge that they were so exercised that day. Upon their children should not be found at like exercise again, they were dismissed."

The game was also played at Halkirk and Westerdale where the sticks were turning shaws. There are also records of it being played until late in last century on Dunnet Links. There was also and annual game on Old New Year's Day on the sands at Reay at the end of the last century where any kind of stick, even umbrellas were used, the game being accompanied by much drinking and very often ending in fights.It was in the fishing villages, however, that the game seems to have reached its apogee. The sticks and clubs were hazel wands cut from the bushes along the burns, and the 'ball' the cork float of a herring net.

In Lybster, almost the most prominent herring fishing port on the Moray Firth last century, the game was played between local teams and teams from the Lewismen who came over to man the boats during the fishing season. According to a local historian as many as a hundred players a side would take part. Obviously these games would only be possible when on shore winds kept their fleet in harbour. At other times the game was pursued with gay abandon by the schools as the following extract from the Free Church School Logbook in October 1875 records. "In the afternoon several boys who continued to play their game of Knotty half an hour after the hour of opening were shut out for the rest of the day and hindered the work inside by noisy demonstrations without." Next day the demonstrators were punished summarily and severely.

In 1922 the old and honourable game was revived from limbo by the Lybster Branch of The National Lifeboat Institution was part of their fund raising exercise at the harbour. A local writer who, his tongue firmly in his cheek, drafted a set of more modern rules which he attributed to a well known Divine of the last century. A competition was arranged on the Harbour Green, advertised as The Knotty World Championships. Eight teams, four local, two from Findhorn and two fronm Stromness brought the game gloriously back to life. The final was between Lybster Tars and the Findhorn Furies, resulting in a narrow win by the home team. it is now hoped that the event will become an annual contest and Knotty will become known to a new generation of spectators.

The Exiles Spectacle: the Highlanders at play - mid-nineteen century

A HIGHLANDER LOOKS BACK

At the age of eight years I witnessed an unforgettable scene, the funeral of Old Cluny, Chief of the Clan Chattan. Cluny died on 11th January, 1885, and was laid to rest on the following Saturday, 17th January, in the family burial ground overlooking the river Spey and the mountains which were so dear to his heart. It was a somewhat cold winter day with a slight covering of snow. A very large crowd of people including women and children, not only from Laggan but many other parishes, and representatives of the greatest historical Highland families assembled to pay their last respects to a great man of whom it could truly be said: he was the last of the Jacobite Chiefs.

It was a memorable scene when, after an appropriate service, the coffin was raised and firstly carried shoulder high by a detachment from Cluny's old regiment, the 42nd Black Watch Royal Highlanders, and afterwards by employees and the general public, preceded by the Black Watch pipers with muffled drums, also my father and my brother John with their bagpipes, playing in turn the solemn notes of "The Lament", as they wended their way along the avenue. On the coffin lay the Chief's Glengarry bonnet with eagle feather, his sword and the old green banner with its tattered but honoured stains from many a battlefield.

My father played the last lament as the cortege entered the burial place, and never will I forget it as he struck up "The Lament for the Harp Tree", as fine a piobaireachd as ever was composed, and, as the coffin was reverently lowered, he changed into "MacCrimmon's Lament". "Cha till, cha till mi tuilleadh an cogadh no sìth, cha till mi tuilleadh". "I'll return, I'll return no more, in war or peace, I'll return, no never". With the strains of the piobaireachd lingering in their ears clansmen and friends, many in tears, left the mortal remains of their venerable chief sleeping, who, as a proprietor and laird, knew his people, lived with them, and spoke their language, the Gaelic, which speaks to the Highlander as no other language can.

Cluny Macpherson was 81 years of age and occupied the castle and lands of his ancestors for nearly 70 years, having succeeded his father as Chief of the clan in the year 1817.

In the beautiful glen of Sherrabeg, when I was about 12 years old, I saw and took part in the junior shinty team. The battle for honour was waged between the North and South side of the River Spey. The men from the North side were captained by that delightful gentleman farmer, Mr Donald MacKillop, Blargie, and the team from the South side by Mr Gilbert, factor for Sir John Ramsden, a shinty enthusiast to the backbone. The younger generation contest comprised the lads from the Gergask and Kinlochlaggan schools and were captained by a lad Macrae and myself.

Angus Macpherson, 1877-1976.

On a cold winter's morning with snow on the ground, the horse hair balls were set in motion, the caman or shinty stick was thrown in the air between the opposing captains and caught in the descent, then hand over hand the caman was gripped and the one who last could swing the caman round his head three times without losing his grip won the choice of hail or goal to play to. My father was on the field to cheer the teams to victory and when the sound of his bagpipes echoed through the Pass of Corrieyairick there never was a finer Balaclava fought; many of the seniors played in their stockinged feet; cuts and bruises were the order of the day; no referees, but catch as catch can, and beat your opponent at any cost.

After an hour and a half of strenuous action the battle ended all square with one goal each. Tempers were forgotten, first-aid applied, and then all marched, to the tune of "Highland Laddie", to the farm steading at Sherrabeg where a team of willing ladies had hot coffee ready for us and a plentiful supply of bread and cheese, and of course for those who cared to indulge a bountiful supply of the 'wine of the country', which in those days could be bought for 2/6 per bottle. Some of the "bodachs" (old men) may have had difficulty in their homeward trek, but what mattered, it was a day to be remembered, and a time when Laggan could produce men of calibre and strength who knew nothing of present day illnesses, who never saw a dentist, and preserved their natural teeth in many ceases to a ripe old age – four score years and more.

Writing of the grand old game of shinty brings to mind the annual Cluny Ball play. This was one of the great events of the year when all comers were welcomed by the Chief and his Lady. The Castle Party headed by the family Piper, marched to the scene of the contest. All who brought a caman were expected to take part in the game. Jackets were laid down for goal-posts at the full length of the field – a very long one with no out of touch line, and no referee, but the Chief shouting in pure Gaelic to encourage his own chosen team, in opposition to that of one chosen by a neighbouring proprietor. After the game was over the time-honoured custom was resorted to, and who could ever forget the after-speeches from the worthies of the Glen – Charlie Oag and his contemporaries. Since those far-off days, I have played shinty in most of the crack teams including the Kingussie team, and in finals and in semi-final matches. In the year 1889 (I think it was) the until-then unconquerable Kingussie team fell to the gallant men of Ballachulish, Argyll, by the one and only goal. I shall never concede that we Kingussie men were truly beaten for the match was decided by what would be today an infringement of shinty rules. Otherwise the result would have been different and at least a draw. I shall, however, think of the men of Argyll as gentlemen and true sportsmen; few are now left to tell the tale of that great match fought on the battle-field of North Inch at Perth.

Cluny MacPherson. (Courtesy of Jack Richmond)

CUIMHNEACHAN NA H-OIGE
(MEMORIES OF YOUTH)
BY
ANGUS MACPHERSON

I.

Tha na monaidhean cho rìoghail
Cur fàilt' agus mulad orm
Na beanntan a dhìrich mi
A nuair bha mi òg:
Na fàsaichean cho lionmhor
Ga 'n fhagail cho cianail
'S na osnaidhean g'am phianadh
Is iarguinn g'am leòn.

II.

Tha na gaisgaich air falbh
O'n àit' anns an d'rugadh mi
S 'na fèidh deanamh spòrs
Anns gach clachan 's lòn;
Cha chluinnear an òigridh
Ri ceòl agus mireag
No na seann daoine cridheil
Càirdeil is còir.

III.

Tha gach (eas) agus alltan
Ri ceòl agus dannsamh
Cur na mo chuimhne
Na balaich s'na seòid
An tigh 's an deachaidh m'àrach
A nise na fhàsach
'S a' Phìobaireachd cho àluinn
Air a càradh fo'n fhòid.

IV

Mo chreach 's mo dhìobhal
Nach d'fhuair na daoine dìleas,
Na fàrdaichean grianach
'S am fearann mar bu chòir;
Cha bhi na fèidh a' rànaich
An diugh anns na gàraidhean
Far am b'àbhaist do na fearaibh
An deoch slàinte a bhi 'g òl.

V

Ach thig lath agus ceartas
Do na Ghàidheil ghlan, ghasda,
'S cha iad air am fuadach
Air son airgiod no òr;
Bithidh na fèidh air an sgiùrsadh
Ri mullaichean Druim Uachdar,
A 'nuair a thilleas na daoin' usisle
Gu glinn ghorm an òig.

VI

Deadh shoraidh agus slàinte dhuit
Sgìre Lagan na gruagach,
Far an tric a ghabh mi cuairt
Le na caileagan òg
A nuair a thig ceann mo làithean
'S an cadal nach fàg mi,
B' e mo dhùrachd bhi air m' fhàgail
'S a' chlachan nan còir.

(LAGGAN)

[Angus Macpherson, A Highlander looks back, Oban, n.d., pages 15, 20 and 22.]

194

The Boys of the Eilan   **March**   **J. W. MacGregor**

CLUIDH-BHALL AN T-SLÈIBH

(Oran na Camanachd)

Eisdibh gus an cluinn sibh naigheachd
Listen till you hear the news
Sann mu dheighinn na camanachd
It is about the camanachd
'S ioma' baiteal chruaidh chaidh chluidh san t-sneachd
Many a hard battle was played
O shean le 'ur sinnsearachd
in the snow of old by our ancestors.

Coisir/Chorus

Sios e! Suas e! a mhàin! san àird e!
Up with it! Down with it! Up in the air!
"Thuirlich e" is "Thadhail e"
"It went for a bye" and "it went for a goal"
Tha na cluidheadairean fhàthast anns an t-Sleibh
There are still players in the Sliabh
Cho math 's chaidh riamh air Eilean
as ever went on an island.

Chorus

Bha gillean gasda feadh nan croitean
There were fine boys among the crofts
Do dhaoine a b'àbhaist ar còmhnadh
of men who used to be our help,
Mac a'phearsain luath, 's Ceannadaidh cruaidh,
Swift MacPherson and hardy Kennedy
agus Seonaidh Mòr san t-Sròine
And big John of Strone.

196

Chorus

Nuair chluinneas sinn gaoth air an Eilan
When we hear wind on the Eilan,
Se shèideas milis ann ar cluais
How sweet it blows in our ears.
Cha chluinn sibh guth nuair thig an Nollaig
You will not hear a word when Christmas comes
Ach "Am bheil thu ullaimh a dhol Suas?".
But "are you ready to go up?"

Chorus

Thun àite far an robh iomadh baiteal
To the place where there was many a battle
Eadar gaisgeach deas is tuath
between heroes north and south.
'S far an robh an còmhnuidh balaich sgairteal
And where there were always forceful lads
Làidir, tapaidh agus cruaidh.
Strong, courageous and hardy.

Chorus

Rao'l, 's Ailean, Eòghann is Calum,
Ronald, Allan, Ewen and Calum
Donnach, Lachluinn 's Alasdair luath,
Duncan, Lachlan and Alasdair the swift.
Anndra, Aonghas, Dòmhnull is Iain
Andrew, Angus, Donald and Iain.
Clann nan Catan is Mhic Dhòmhnuill Ruaidh
Cattanachs and sons of Donald Ruadh.

Cumaidh sinn suas ar cluidhe-ioman
We will keep up the caman play,
Cluidh is grinn a tha fo'n ghrèin
The finest game under the sun.
Se chuireas aighear 's sunnd air ghillean
It is what puts high spirits and cheers in boys.
a'ruith 'sa mireadh, danns' is leum.
Running, frisking, dancing, jumping.

Chorus

Nuair thig oirnn fuachd a' gheamhraidh
When cold comes on us in winter
Sneachd air beanntan, 's gaoth o tuath,
Snow on mountains and wind from the north.
Sann bhitheas na gillean òg san àm sin
The young boys will be at that time
Ag iomain-ball le camain cruaidh.
Driving a ball with a hard clubs.

Chorus

Bithidh a'chloinn bheag nuair ghabhas iad buinn,
The little children when they take over from us
Glèidh' criomag maide le ceanna crom
Will be keeping a bit of stick with a bent head.
'S am bliadhn' neo dha, 's iad bhitheas nan suinn,
And in a year or two, the brave fellows will be,
'S iad uile cruinn le deòin air Eilean.
All gathered together on the Eilean.

[Badenoch Record, December 21, 1935.]

198

David Anderson, Kingussie and captain of Scotland.

NOTHING IS MORE CONDUCIVE

In order to fully enjoy life one must have good health; and nothing is more conducive to soundness of constitution than vigorous outdoor exercise in games of skill, requiring a sharp eye, steady hand, cool judgement, and, I may add, good temper. Cricket, Tennis, Bowls, Golf &c., all have their votaries, but the game which has taken the most wonderful hold on the British public within recent times is Football - so much so that it has elbowed at least one other competitor almost entirely out of the field, viz: - Shinty - which some people who ought to know are old-fashioned and out-spoken enough to maintain is the better game of the two; and certainly, to my taste, a match at Camanachd between two teams of picked players, is, as a spectator display, far more entertaining that a game at Football - be it Rugby or Association.

In the past, say up until the "forties", no game was more generally played throughout Scotland - from Solway to Pentland Firth - than Shinty. In the Southern districts, where it was usually "Knotty" or "Hummy", it has almost disappeared. The Highlands are now considered the nursery of the game; and although many of our large schools (notably Glenalmond and Loretto) play the game under the name of "Hockey," and the Universities of Edinburgh and Aberdeen have each got their Camanachd Club, yet it is to the Northern Counties we must look for any extensive fostering of this pastime. Argyllshire is doing well and Inverness-shire too; but I fear that further north other forms of recreation have usurped the place which rightfully belongs to this characteristically Scottish game. In Sutherland and Caithness it was not kept up as it might be. At one time Durness was famous for its great Shinty Gatherings, which eclipsed even the "Orduighean"; and in every village and district the New Year's day Shinty match was an annual institution. Have Caithness-men forgotten the good old times on Dunnett sands, when they waged earnest warfare at "Knotty", headed by their lairds - Traill of Ratter and Sinclair of Freswick? Why is this grand old national game allowed to die out in such places as Helmsdale, Brora, Golspie, Dornoch, Lairg, Bonar, not to speak of Tongue, Farr, Assynt, &c.?

To the cities of the South is due the credit of reviving the interest in Camanachd which we have at the present day. The Edinburgh Club is, we believe, the Premier Shinty Club of the World, for at the time it was formed - in 1869 - there was no other Association of the kind in existence. From time immemorial, however, the game had been kept up there on New Year's day by patriotic Highlanders, who stoutly adhered to the customs of their fathers; and many a tough and hearty tussle we have witnessed in Queen's Park, where they used to play. The new idea of founding regular clubs was gradually followed in other places. Glasgow, London, Manchester, Alexandria, Greenock, Inveraray, each set the ball a-rolling and the contagion spread far and wide, till now there are upwards of two dozen bands of good men and true enrolled in Clubs duly constituted for the perpetuation of the old game. Many will be glad to hear that the Inveraray Club is coming up again; and some day we may look for another keen contest between them and their old rivals, the Glasgow Cowal, than which there is probably not a club in existence today that can put a better team on the field.

A pressing want of the day seems to be an assimilation of rules of play. The Shinty Association which was formed in Glasgow about 13 years ago, if not quite dead is at anyrate in abeyance; and many interested people think it or a similar institution should be revived, with the object of establishing uniformity of practice and rules, and of stimulating and popularising the game. There is no reason why such an institution could not be brought to bear the fruit expected from it if properly managed, and if a healthy, fair-spirited rivalry existed among the Clubs constituting it. This is a matter calling for immediate reformation : and I hope to see a conference held ere long between representatives of existing Clubs with a view to bringing about a clear understanding on various points of difference.

The existing Clubs are, so far as I can remember, as follows: - London and Northern Counties, London Scottish, Edinburgh Camanachd, Edinburgh University, Aberdeen University, Glasgow Cowal, Inveraray, Furnace, Strachur, Bunawe, Dalmally, Lochgoilhead, Ardkinglas, Dunally, Glencoe, Vale of Larroch, Brae-Lochaber, Glenurquhart, Strathglass, Kiltarlity, Inverness, Strathpeffer, Alvie, Insch, Kingussie, Newtonmore.

As it is intended to make this magazine a medium for imparting information interesting to all Camanachd players, it would be well if secretaries of the above Clubs, and of any other Club which I may have overlooked, should put themselves in communication with the Editor, who is anxious to give the game a "back".

A. Mackay Robson, 1892
[The Celtic Monthly, October 1892, Number 1, page 12.]

IS BINNE GLÒIR

Thathas ag amas air an rann a leanas gu math tric mar shàmhla de na seann làithean agus linn a dh'fhalbh, an co-cheangal ris a chamanachd ann an Alba agus Eireann. Chan eil an rann, ged tha, cho sean sin!

The following verse is often quoted when referring to the antiquity of shinty and hurling - usually in sentimental terms of a glorious past and bygone days. "When of old…" might well be the feeling, but the verse and its author were not lost in the mists of time. It was in fact composed by P.J. Devlin, an Irish journalist who wrote under the pen-name "Celt" in the Freeman's Journal (forerunner of the Irish Independent) in the first two decades of this century. Devlin was himself a hurler in the 1890s.

Is binne glòir mo chamain fhèin
na guth nan eun no ceòl nam bàrd;
's binne fuaim air bith fon ghrèin
na pòc air ghleus o liathroid àird.

More sweet the tone of my own stick
than voice of birds or music of bards;
and nothing, under sun, so sweetly sounds
as a smack with skill, on a lofty ball.

"Is binne glòir"

A SHINTY MATCH IN SUTHERLAND

CAMANACHD

Times have changed in the North of Sutherland, and with them the habits and customs of the people have undergone an alteration also. The amusements of the winter months are still indulged in, but not so heartily, I fear, as they were in the days of long ago. Shinty was a favourite game on the sands of Balnakeil o'er-shadowed by the fine baronial residence of the Lords of Reay, and on New Year's Day the game is still played. It may not prove uninteresting to the readers of the *Celtic Monthly* to describe a New Year's Day Match as it was played on these beautiful sands many years ago.

It is a fine clear morning, with a touch of frost in the air sufficiently keen to add zest to the exertions of the day. The players having arrived, the Shinty is thrown down, and boys, lads, and men play merrily for half-an-hour without drawing sides, like the first flourish of offence before beginning in earnest.

The crowd thickens, old men appear upon the ground, and young wives and maidens also, as spectators, come dressed in their best attire. A murmur goes round that it is time to begin; it gets louder and they collect in a group. The company having assembled, it was proposed and unanimously carried, that the game be commenced in earnest. Retiring to the middle of the sands, two persons are chosen to draw sides, and a club is tossed in the air for the first call. The chosen one standing out in the ring looks around for companion-at-arms, who modestly holds back until called by name, when he advances, not unconscious of the honour conferred on him, but with affected humility, perhaps finding fault with his principal for having made such a bad choice. His opponent next selects his man, and so proceed, at first cautiously, each party consult together as to whom they should choose. At times both call out a favourite player simultaneously, and then the battle wages long and loud. But they now get impatient, and the names are called out still faster, until none are left save a few half-grown boys too young to join the strife of heroes, and too old for entering the battle of the pigmies. A hole is then made in the sand, the men are seen stripping; shoes, stockings, bonnets, clothes are left in the custody of some daughter or fair favourite, or upon a sand hillock.

Two field marshals are appointed, who take their stations; the ball is tossed out of the hole, each man firmly grasps his club, each eye is on the alert, up it ascends, and then begins the fight of heroes. All else is forgotten, brother comes against brother, father against son, for their blood is up. Now they seem all in a knot, next instant they separate, they press in a body upon one end, and they then diverge like mountain streams; but though many they are one, for they have a common object, though only a piece of wood three inches in diameter. The fair ones, gentle and simple, group along the shore, while many a loving look is exchanged, no doubt stimulating some greater exertions. The running of one is beautiful, another's playing is awkward, that of a third is superb, of a fourth ludicrous. The masculine exhibition on that sea shore is really fine. What flashes from that young man's eyes as he strikes forward the ball! What a proud step after he has done it! What attitudes that field marshal puts himself into as the ball is deliberately fixed on a fulcrum of sand before him! Conscious of the gaze of a thousand eyes, he retreats a few steps, and measuring the object with the eye, clutches more firmly the club, and comes down with it in a circular sweep, hitting the ball beautifully, and following it with his eye as it rises into the clear blue sky. No rest being allowed, the ball is at times by mistake thrown into the sea, into which though the surge should be considerable, a dozen stalwart fellows leap, and even midst the breakers struggle for it. As a tribute to bravery, the one who finds it is permitted to strike without molestation, a sufficient reward, he considers, for his ducking.

But look at that group who support a fainting man. From an accidental stroke of the club on the temple of his skull is laid bare. He is deadly pale as they carry him out of the melee. Women also surround him, among whom is the young man's sweetheart. Pale and trembling, she takes the handkerchief off her neck, and binds it round his head. His eyes open; that look she gave him has acted like a cordial. The warm blood once more mantles his face, he says he is quite well, and wishes again to enter the melee, but is kept back by a beseeching look from the maiden, and the tears by which it backed have more weight with him than the remonstrances of a thousand tongues.

But we see another and a larger group, but it is difficult to wedge one's way into it. There is a ring and loud words, inside are two fellows with brawny arms, pale with anger, collaring one another, while others try to hold the determined fighters back.

"Let them alone," cries a sensible old man, and, left to themselves, they see what a ridiculous figure they cut; they look at each other, shake hands, and set off once more in their pursuit. Sometimes, however, they are not so easily separated, and blood flows ere they desist from fighting. But see that poor limping dog which had faithfully followed his master, and for his fidelity has got a broken leg. What has so suddenly dispersed that female group ?

The ball has effected this with as great expedition as a shell falling among a party of troopers. Off it goes, however; that handsome young fellow who eyed it intently had a design upon it, and now is his time, beautifully does he send it along, never missing, and as skilfully does he out-manoeuvre his adversary, who meets him; he waits, strikes it, and passes him. With the ball at his foot, a false step and all would be lost, for he is hotly pursued, the whole field being in full cry at his heels. But he knows his power, and reserves his strength to the last. Forward he goes, only now pursued by two or three, and, out-distancing all, he is cheered by his own party, while the opposition only sullenly growl. Reaching now the goal, he strikes the ball against the rock, while a triumphant hail rises from a hundred voices, and meets him gratefully as again he draws breath. By this time it is almost dark, and as each youth, weary with the day's exercise, returns home in the gloaming, he looks out for the girl he loves best, and engages her as his partner for the evening dance.

[London - Robina Findlater.]

Ag amharc air ais

Air tulaich ghuirm ri taobh na tràigh,
Fodh sgàil tlàth nan creagan lom;
Tha m'inntinn mar gum biodh i snàmh,
Ag èisdeachd gàirich throm nan tonn.

'S mi cuimhneachadh nam bliadhn' a thriall,
Mar bhruadar diomhanach nach till,
'S mo chàirdean lionmhor, gràdhach, fial,
Tha cnàmh a 'n diomhaireachd na cill.

Cò bheir an sgeula dhuinn air ais,
No 'm bi sinn glaiste uainn gu bràth?
Am faic sinn tuilleadh gnùis am mais',
A phaisgeadh ann an glaic a' bhàis?

An cluinn sinn tuilleadh cainnt am beòil,
A sheòladh sinn le 'n còmhradh glic?
An caidil iad a chaoidh fodh 'n fhòid,
An dorchadas a bhròin fodh 'n lic?

An lean an saoghal-so gu bràth,
A bàrcadh air 'us dheth an t-sluaigh!
'S 'g an iomairt mar na tuinn air tràigh,
An ùine gheàrr a bhios an cuairt.

Tha linn an deadhaidh linn gun tàmh,
Mar abhuinn làn a' ruith do 'n chuan,
'S mar lusan maoth a thig fo bhlàth,
'S a bhàsaicheas 'n uair 'thig am fuachd.

Tha caochladh sgriobht' air gnùis gach nì,
'S cha bhuain' an righ no 'n duine bochd;
An glòir 's an ionmhais cha toir sìth,
'S iad aig a chrìch gun bhrìgh, gun toirt.

Ach tha ar dùil ri tìr as fheàrr,
Far am bheil fois don ànrach sgìth;
Far nach bi dealachadh gu bràth,
'S far nach tig bròn no plàigh gar claoidh.

Ach fàgaidh sinn e aig an Triath,
Am breitheamh ceart nach fiar a' chòir,
'Thug dhuinn ar tùs, 's dha 'n aithn' ar crìoch,
'S a bhios gu suthainn siorruidh beò.

N. MacLeòid.

[Celtic Monthly, June 1894, Volume 2, pages 167-168.]

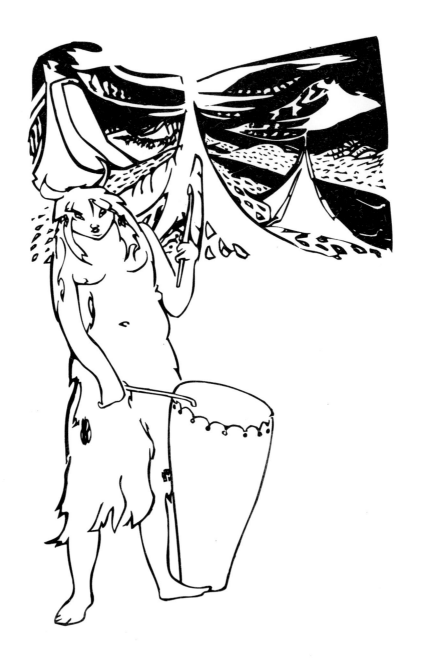

A SPECTRE ARBITER: A NEW YEAR SHINTY STORY

From time immemorial the game of *camanachd*, or shinty has been observed in the Highlands on Christmas and New Year's Day, and it is a sport which is usually keenly contested and greatly enjoyed by rich and poor, young and old, on these days still. The annual days too, were, and are still, observed as days of feasting and general joviality. The advent of Christmas and New Year were, therefore, eagerly longed for by all the classes of people. In olden times the laird and his vassal, the tenant, tradesman, and cottar joined issue in this annual sport. These were the "good old times". The people met one another on New Year's day with the salutation "Bliadhna Mhath ùr dhuibh" (a good New Year to you), and was answered - "Mar sin dhuibh-se 's pailteas dhuibh" (I wish you the same, and plenty of them). Every district or township - sometimes several townships joined together - sent its contingent to the place appointed for the shinty match. Two men of equal calibre were chosen as captains, or leaders, and they made up their teams thus. Each of them, time about in succession, called his favourite player to his side from the crowd until the teams were formed. After a few other characteristic preliminaries they entered the lists with the *camans* (clubs). The games, which were begun with Highland spirit, were continued with the same enthusiasm till nightfall. As numerous kegs of whisky, rum, or gin were on the ground, many a hearty shake of the hand was given throughout the day, and many a big glass was emptied - with, "*Air do shlàinte, charaid, 'do dheagh bhliadhna ùr*" (Your good health, friend, and a good New Year) - at those invigorating gatherings. But much of this is now, alas! a thing of the past.

In no part of the Highlands, perhaps, was the sport of shinty more heartily enjoyed than in South Uist. Every township sent its contingent (from the beardless youth to the grey-haired sage) to the several machairs on Christmas and New Year's Day. The machairs of Benbecula, Iochdar, Howmore, Dalibrog, Kilpheder, and Smerclate, were peculiarly adapted for this famous recreation. On these machairs the skill and capacities of the contending parties could be, and were, displayed to full advantage.

At one of these *camanachds*, on the machair of Dalibrog, on a New Year's day some years ago, a dispute arose as to the team which gained the most hails. The contention at length assumed such proportions that the captains were about to decide the point by an appeal to strength. This would of course involve both teams, which in the end might prove very serious. Several of the more peacefully disposed persons on both sides did their utmost to pacify and persuade the captains to cease the contention, and part, as usual, on friendly terms; but all to no purpose. One of the captains, whom we shall call John, a strong, powerful, man, was about to strike his opponent with his club, when he chanced to cast a glance along the strand, which the elevated spot on which they stood overlooked, and was surprised to see a tall, well-built man, in dark attire, coming towards him at a quick walking pace. Immediately the man saw that John noticed him he beckoned on him to go to him to the strand. John at once drew his companions' attention to the approaching person, and also told them that he had beckoned on him to go to him. But as they all failed to see any object whatever at the spot indicated by John, they were seized with terror, and left for their respective homes, believing the person seen by John was none other than the Evil Spirit, who appeared on the scene on account of the disturbance. Some remarkable impulse seems to have been conveyed by John by the stranger's beckoning, for he immediately felt an irresistible desire to obey the call - to go to the man, and he did so. On approaching the stranger, John noticed that he glided towards him - that his feet did not even touch or move any of the small pebbles over which he came. Though he was as brave and courageous as he was powerful, John now began to tremble with fear, for he never saw the man before. He had a military bearing, and a bold, unearthly aspect. If John entertained any rambling thoughts as to who the stranger was, they were soon set at rest by being informed that the person had come from the world of spirits to prevent him (John) from ending the New Year's day in the unseemly manner which he was so determined upon. The man, when in life, whom the spectre represented, was, it was said, closely related to John's family. The spectre then told John that as he had to act as arbiter in the quarrel, he (John) must meet him in such a place the following evening, and every evening afterwards which he (the spectre) might appoint, on pain of some dire evil befalling him (John), if he disobeyed.

What passed between John and the spectre at the many conferences they afterwards had no one ever heard, for John kept it firmly secret. Their meetings, however, were so numerous and unpleasant that John was heartily sick of them, and yet he was constrained by some mysterious influence to attend them. To escape, if possible, those disagreeable conferences, and thus get some measure of peace, John at length removed to another part of the island, but that, alas, made no difference - the spectre discovered him the very next evening, and exercised the same control over him as he had done in the place he had left.

The only thing John revealed that the spectre told him in all his intercourse with him after the first evening was, that he would die in a place which was the a mossy waste, without house or hut from end to end. Some years after the ghost told him this, John, without any reference to what the spectre had said - indeed he had no recollection of it at the time - went to the pace mentioned, built a house there, and died in it at a ripe age. We are assured that the same ghost has spoken to different people on various occasions on South Uist.

We have suppressed the names of persons and places for certain reasons; but have no doubt our South Uist readers will readily recognise them.

We now conclude our story by wishing the *Celtic Monthly* a long and prosperous career, and our readers a happy New Year, with many of them.

A. B. McLennan, Lochboisdale
[Celtic Monthly Volume 1 November, 1892, page 62.]

Glasgow Cowal:
John Sinclair, Duncan Martin, William Robinson, Peter Campbell (1)
Hugh MacCorquodale, Peter Campbell (2), Daniel Turner, Thomas Scott, Cameron Henderson
John MacKay (Editor, Celtic Monthly), President, Donald MacCorquodale, Umpire
Duncan Morrison, Dr Archibald Campbell, Archibald Campbell, John MacCorquodale

KINGUSSIE V COWAL, APRIL 3, 1893

At Ruthven when the sun was high
The Cowal came forth to do or die,
And wild and fierce their battle cry
As the ball went rolling rapidly.

But Ruthven showed another sight
when, in the low and fading light
Kingussie, crushed by southern might
Lay prone on Highland scenery.

By rush and dribble Cowal made
On Kingussie's goal a deadly raid,
And yet the lads were not dismayed
'Midst all the dreadful revelry.

Then shook the ground with thunders riven
As through the goal the ball was driven
And louder than the bolts of heaven
Cheers rent the April canopy.

But louder still the cheering grew,
As "P.K." had it all but through
And down the wing swift "P.G." flew
To raise the number rapidly.

The combat deepens - on ye brave
Who rush to shoot and then to save;
Strathbungo's banners proudly wave,
O'er Cowal's glorious victory.

And as the thunderous cheering rolls,
Cowal retires with one good goal
Kingussie falls, yet dauntless souls
And full of warlike chivalry.

Fair D. he hung his auburn head,
And soft was the gallant Captain's tread,
As they in silence swiftly sped
The scene of Badenoch's misery.

[The Oban Times, June 1, 1895.]

Following the flying ball: David Borthwick, Kingussie and Scotland, 1993

NOT AN ORCHID

An English View of Shinty

Camanachd is not an orchid; nor is it a biological eccentricity, nor the latest freak of pathological nomenclature. It is a recreation. In Scotland there are three games which can best claim to be native to the soil - golf, curling and shinty - and the greatest of these is shinty, whereof the Gaelic name is camanachd.

The Badminton Library is practically dumb on the subject of shinty. Mr Andrew Lang, who knows the North fairly well, has never been once observed to allude to the game; and a caman , or shinty-club, could conceal its identity in a London shop window for months. Even in Scotland, until you get above the Isle of Bute and the fair city of Perth, camanachd has dropped into oblivion, and football holds the field. Yet fifty years ago it was the craze of Caledonian youth, and practically the only recreation whereat he could, with athletic abandon, bark his shins and black his eyes.

England, today, has an innocent, innocuous apology for camanachd in the game of hockey, and the hurling clubs of the Gaelic organisations in Ireland play a game, which in a measure, approximates to it; but shinty - real shinty, robust, rollicking, three-star shinty, so to speak - is becoming yearly more limited in the area of its popularity, and even in the comparatively small field into which it is being crowded, it is losing many of the more striking features which made it pre-eminently the outdoor sport of the fiery, fleet-footed Celt.

To the game of shinty there go two implements - the club or caman and the ball. Of old time, the club was , and to some extent is still, in the more primitive parts of the North, a carefully selected young oak tree, whereof the thickest end has been heated with fire and bent to a curve, which it is made to retain at first by means of thongs. When it is considered to have been long enough bound to retain its shape without the thongs, these are removed, and the club is, in a rude way, ready for use, having a hook at the end of its shaft like the bend of a golf club. Experience has taught however, that nature does not, somehow, very frequently create oaklings of the most convenient form for camans, and Science meets her half-way by selecting a straight shaft or bas of hazel or ash, and a cas or foot of oak, and joining the two together by splicing, or what in the elegant parlance of the modern Highlander is described as "wupping" with rosined cord. In this wise, plus some trimming with a knife, is a shinty made. It is an elegant weapon, graceful to wield, and of delightful capacity for hacking an opponent's head, or elevating his knee-cap.

The ball, till recent years, was a small sphericle of hard wood, dextrously cut out with a knife or turned on a lathe. A little larger than a golf ball, and somewhat less than a cricket ball, it was admirably adapted for propulsion by a smart blow from the cas of a caman, and even after the resistance of a 200ft drive through the air had been overcome, its effect on an in intervening optic or falange was astonishing. But the weak spirit of self-protection which permeates Scotland in these latter days has now entirely substituted a leather ball with a cork core for the old wooden pill, and has reduced the interest and excitement of the game fifty per cent.

The object of each team of players, as in football, is to drive the ball between its opponent's goalposts and score as many points as possible. Up till recent years the word "hails" was used to designate the points thus gained, but the inevitable craze for modernising things made shinty players use the term "goals", which is not half so expressive.

In the more barbaric counties north of the Highland line the game is still played with an unlimited number of players on either side. Parish plays against parish and clan against clan, and, with occasional pauses for alcoholic refreshments the players have been known of a New Year to recreate themselves this way for six or seven hours on end. Thereafter they usually dispute regarding the number of "hails" won and lost, and the subsequent proceedings take a sanguine hue.

But, even in the manner of playing the game, insidious innovations are having their way, and a ridiculously new-fangled "Shinty" Association, has framed rules limiting teams to twelve-a-side, and the duration of the game to ninety minutes. There are even some absurd restrictions on the player's liberty to trip up an opponent or hack him over the head in the enthusiastic spirit of the traditional game. If these rules were rigorously insisted upon, Shinty might as well give place to Draughts or The Minister's Cat.

There are also umpires and referees and other embroideries under the new laws, but they are extraordinary umpires and referees who are not amenable to the reasoning of a partisan crowd of parishioners with convenient a plenitude of "divotts" to throw. In spite of this modernising, however, the hardy old game languishes, as we have indicated, even in the North. The Inverness and Oban newspapers are the vehicles of much defiant challenging between existing shinty combinations, and some of the letters to the editors suggest in an alarming way scenes of ensanguined struggle. But the old ardour has, in reality, cooled down, and to challenge in the Argyll country, now the proud national supremacy of Inveraray or Furness, would probably have no fatal results.

There is a challenge cup somewhere; to be contended for, at least it figures in print frequently enough, but its exact whereabouts is never very obvious, and it has been insinuated that it is merely a mythical piece of plate, a Celtic figure of speech without even the capacity for holding a "wee hauf". A proposal has been set on foot to send a shinty combination to Chicago to show the Americans one face of British athletics of no recent institution, yet with no less exciting features than the all absorbing baseball game in these States. It might interest the American pure and simple - if such exists - but it would have, perhaps, little novelty for the Scotch aliens of the North-West of America, who, it is said, retain the old game of camanachd with all its pristine verve. And it is, indeed, perhaps on the alien Scot more than on the native land that the survival of the game may depend in the future. He plays it on the Banks of the Red River and the Fraser; there is at least one Camanachd Club at the Cape, and the breezy expanse of Wimbledon Common periodically finds the London Celt following the flying ball.

[Inverness Courier, May 12, 1893.]

KINGUSSIE 2 COWAL 0: FIRST CAMANACHD CUP FINAL

The draft of rules prepared by the secretary in connection with the proposed trophy were revised by the committee and adopted at a meeting in Inverness on Thursday, 17th October 1895. The secretary was instructed to send a copy of the proposed rules for the trophy to all known shinty clubs throughout the country, whether associated or not, along with a circular calling a meeting of the Association for 16th November and an intimation that entries for the competition would be received up to 12th November. The secretary was also asked to apply by public advertisement for subscriptions in the Inverness Courier, Northern Chronicle, Elgin Courant, Oban Times and People's Journal and was authorized to receive and acknowledge all sums for that object on behalf of the committee.

The rules for the competition, after revision and slight amendment, were duly approved at a general meeting on Saturday, 16th November in Inverness. It was also resolved that, because of the difficulty involved in visiting Portree, the Skye club would play competition games on the mainland on ground to be arranged by the trophy committee which would be composed of one representative from each competing club, five to form a quorum. Meetings of this committee were to be held at Kingussie unless otherwise arranged.

Mr Duncan Macpherson, Gun and Fishing Tackle Maker, Drummond Street, Inverness, had sent a letter asking the Association to accept a hickory caman to be presented to the captain of the trophy winning team. The caman was gratefully accepted and Mr Macpherson thanked. This presentation of a silver mounted caman by Mr Macpherson became an annual feature at these meetings and his nephew Mr John Macpherson, who had a long connection with the Inverness Club and with the Association, continued the custom.

For the purpose of dividing the country into playing districts and balloting for the first round of the competition, the committee met at Kingussie on Friday, 29th November, 1895. The result of the balloting was as follows.

Northern District, Rogart v Inverness, Caberfeidh v Beauly, Lovat v Nairn. Portree, a bye. **Central District**, Newtonmore v Grantown, Alvie v Laggan, Kingussie v Insh. **Western District**, Glengarry v Spean Bridge, Brae Lochaber v Ballachulish. **Southern District**, London Camanachd v Glasgow Cowal.

The first mentioned club in each case had choice of ground and ties were to be played on or before 10th January.

The various rounds having been played, the final tie of the Camanachd Cup took place at Inverness on 25th April, 1896.

[Extracted from Shinty!, Inverness, 1993.]

KINGUSSIE V GLASGOW COWAL

Great interest was centred in the match which was played in Inverness on Saturday. The occasion was the final match of the Camanachd Cup competition - a competition which has been the means of raising the flagging interest in the fine old Highland pastime of shinty. The contending teams were the Kingussie and Glasgow Cowal, two brilliant exponents of the game, and the contest might be fitly termed a fight between the North and South. The Cowal Club came North with a terrorising name, but it was quite on the card that the Badenoch warriors would grimly fight for the honour that was at stake. Thanks to the energy of Mr Campbell, Secretary of the Association, who carried out all the arrangements, the park at Needlefield, where the match was played, was put into good condition for the game. The day was practically observed as a holiday in Kingussie, and the special train which conveyed the team to Inverness brought over 400 persons desiring to see the contest. From strath and glen ardent enthusiasts flocked into Inverness, the streets of which contained an unwonted number of wearers of kilt and knickerbocker. The Glasgow team arrived on Friday night to be in trim for the contest. The weather seemed in a smiling mood, but just before the match began, it grew murky, and a drizzling rain fell which rendered the playing pitch a bit slippery. Notwithstanding the charge of a shilling, crowds flocked to the match, and there must have been about 1000 persons present. The money drawn at the gate reached the sum of £41. As the teams lined up on the field, the crowd anxiously weighed up their physical abilities. The Cowal team looked a smart, wiry, well-built lot. Their opponents are heavier, and look as if possessed of more stamina and grit. On the whole, from outward physical appearance, there is little to choose between the teams.

— by ROD CAMPBELL —
— CIRCA 1905 —

— KINGUSSIE SHINTY CLUB —

Roddy Campbell composed this march for Kingussie Shinty Club circa 1905. It saved me composing a march for a great shinty team.

The following were the teams:- Kingussie: Goal, John Campbell; backs, J. Campbell and A. Macpherson; half-backs, A. Gibson, Dallas, and Pullar; forwards, Grant, Cumming, Robertson, Campbell, and Ross (captain).

Cowal: W. Robinson; backs, P. Campbell and D. Martin; half-backs, Dun. Morrison and John Macinnes; centres, D. Robinson, A. Campbell, and A.B. Ferguson; forwards, Peter Macinnes, Thomas Scott (captain), J. McCorquodale, and A. Crawford.

The ball has been thrown up by Referee Macgillivray, and the commotion around the ropes is hushed. The Cowal start well, but Gibson of Kingussie strikes the ball towards Cowal territory. Back it comes with unerring accuracy, and Cowal has the first bye. The Kingussie team looked unsettled and, taking advantage of this, the Glaswegians are playing well; their striking is sharp and sure, and Tom Scott plants a fine shot, but Campbell saves with a timely stroke. Still the Cowal players keep the ball in Kingussie territory. Again and again Dallas of Kingussie, by most determined and really brilliant play, averts danger, and frustrates his opponents, who are essaying for hails. Matters look as if Cowal will score, but their forwards are a bit lax, and are often outplayed by Kingussie defence. The game opens out to some extent. The Badenoch men are beginning to play to some purpose and with more method. The forwards are getting more of the ball, and, encouraged by the slogans of their enthusiastic supporters, who are as demonstrative as Highlanders ought to be, they play up and make the acquaintance of the Cowal custodier. The Cowal still look the more likely to score, but the Kingussie defence seems impregnable, and the Kingussie forwards, no doubt inspired by the brilliant play of their own defence, re-awaken to a sense of their responsibility, and, by powerful striking, rush into their opponents' territory. Pullar, Gibson and Dallas stand out prominently. The characteristics of the play of the teams were most diverse. The men of the hills - Kingussie - fought in the most impetuous manner. Their striking was vigorous and determined. The city men - the Cowal - hit sharp and sure, and their players up till now, at any rate, with more finish than their opponents. The play was carried with unabated vigour from side to side, and from goal to goal. Ultimately, with a dash and impetuosity that was well nigh irresistible, the men from Badenoch press their opponents, and Ross has the satisfaction of scoring the first goal for Kingussie, after seventeen minutes' play. On resuming, the Cowal came away beautifully, and in a twinkling a rare shot flies directly over the Kingussie uprights. The Glasgow men assault most severely, and it does surprise many that they do not score. A. Macpherson and Johnnie Campbell are ever to the fore, and defy the best efforts of the Cowal players to score. The Badenoch men are now asserting themselves more strongly, and on pressing they are again dangerously near scoring. The back division are plying their camans to some purpose, and are sending the ball well in. A. Campbell snaps the ball, and by a scorching shot scores the second hail for Kingussie, amid the loud and prolonged demonstrations of the spectators. Nothing succeeds like success, and it would seem as if Kingussie were really to be masters of the situation, as they hurried away for more hails. The Cowal again assert themselves. The tall, lanky centre is undoubtedly as finished and competent a player as any on the field, and by his work the team makes progress. Again the weakness of the forwards is seen, and the two Kingussie backs find no difficulty in keeping their goal clear until half-time is called.

Resuming, the Cowal made a fine effort to reduce their opponents' score. By clear, sharp, timely striking, their forwards, who are clustering about the vicinity of the Kingussie uprights, receive likely chances but are thwarted, or send the ball bye. The players are not only using their clubs, some are adepts at accurate stopping with hand and feet, and this lends some variety to the play. The Kingussie fly away. A. Ross catching the ball in the air, deftly sends a shot for the Cowal uprights, but it passes over the bar. The pace did not slacken. It was wonderful how the players maintained the high rate of speed and energy required. The ball was carried from one hailpost to another. A. Macpherson was working with much power for the Kingussie team, his powerful striking being of immense service. Fouls were awarded both sides, but it gave neither any advantage. Cowal look like scoring, and are worthy of a point on play, but their forwards cannot cope with the Kingussie defence. We thought that this was owing to the fact that some of the centre players lay too far back when pressing. Kingussie had also opportunities of scoring, but they also failed to register another point. Towards the close of the game, Cowal made a plucky effort to score, but the wary Kingussie defenders were not caught napping, and amidst intense excitement, Kingussie carried away victory, and won the championship. The scores were - KINGUSSIE, 2 hails; GLASGOW COWAL, 0.

The victory of the Kingussie team was a very popular one. The team left Inverness by train at 7pm and was accompanied by a large contingent of supporters. The engine was gaily decorated with Macpherson tartan ribbons, and the engine driver and fireman had donned the Kingussie jerseys. The train steamed out of the station amidst the loud cheers of a large number of persons who were on the platform. On their return, the players were accorded an ovation, pipers playing lively airs and youths carrying lighted torches, assembling at the station, and marching through the town, with bonfires lit above the burgh.

[Inverness Courier, April 28, 1896.]

MARCH:-

— by W^M M. M^{AC}DONALD —
— INVERNESS —

— THE BUGHT —

I composed this tune for the finest shinty pitch and stadium in Scotland. This is the home ground of Inverness Shinty Club.

ORDERLINESS AND GOOD TASTE

Our Canadian letter

HIGHLAND SPORTS

In Summer our Societies take a rest. Meetings are suspended and business is forgotten in the general cessation that prevails. But the warmth of summer sunshine is not sufficient to keep the Canadian Highlander off the field of sport. The arena is changed from the platform and hall to the green sward, where the bagpipes are heard cheering on the shinty players, providing music for the skilled dancer, or in martial strain striving for a prize in keen competition. The Highland games of Canada are noted events. Their fame is well known in Scotland and all over this vast continent. Beginning with the 24th May, the Queen's birthday, which is loyally observed here as a statutory holiday, gatherings take place almost every week until October. They are conducted by societies at suitable points of locality, are extensively advertised, and are as a rule very popular. In connection with them a class of

PROFESSIONAL ATHLETES

has grown up, and the same dancers and pipers follow the circuit of the games, living on the proceeds. This is the one and only regrettable feature of otherwise really good and useful assemblies; but public opinion is gradually bearing an influence against professionalism and in favour of good amateur work, and the result will be a great improvement in the near future. The best piper need not be a professional in the sense of making his living by the money prizes he wins at twenty gatherings in the season. He may be contented to take a medal, or a set of pipes, or some other prize than money, and so maintain a higher ideal than the mercenary one. The same with the dancer, the sprinter, the hammerer, and the competitor in the strength feats generally. The programme at these gatherings vary but little from that of the gatherings in the Highlands. There are entries in Highland dances, bagpiping, Highland costume, putting the stone, tossing the caber, vaulting, jumping, &c. Occasionally there is a game of quoits, bowling on the green, a game of shinty always popular, and the inevitable tug-of-war, a veritable exhibition of skill and muscular strength over which there is usually a fierce contest and much excitement.

There are in Canada many first-class competitors in the various events above named, and it is a real pleasure to witness the proceedings at many of the large gatherings.

AMONG PIPERS,

the few who possess high merit as players are a credit to their race and calling, and indeed the same may be said of those who rank high in the other lines of competition. On the whole the result of the Highland gathering is good. The national sentiment is stimulated, and the best phases of our national character are the more easily reached and cultivated because of the manly exercises and the games of the old home being kept alive. The gatherings, as a rule, are conducted with the utmost respect to orderliness and good taste, and the impression left on the mind is one of pleasure when the evening closes the proceedings.

Sgian Dubh, Toronto, July, 1893
[Celtic Monthly, July, 1893, page 166.]

CAPE BRETON REPRISE

Farewell to Nova Scotia, your golden girls and a' that
Who showed us hospitality, stole our shorts and a' that
For a' that and a' that, it's coming yet for a' that
That shinty players the world o'er shall brothers be for a' that.

We showed you how to play the game, without ice and a' that
You showed us what our kilts were for, exposed our pride and a' that
For a' that and a' that, it's coming yet for a' that
The bonnie lassies pinched our clothes, spoke of love and a' that.

We emptied the Moosehead brewery, had lobster feeds and a' that
Missed Cape Breton's Cabot Trail because of hangovers and a' that
For a' that and a' that, it's coming yet for a' that
That Donnie speaks Canadian and Jan just loves her Comfort.

We've called collect and run up debts, had a nice day and a' that
Guess who used the Hilton, the Sheraton and a' that
For a' that and a' that, it's coming yet for a' that
That Hugh Dan and his merry men, will sober be and a' that.

We packed the Hof and Privateers, drunk them dry and a' that
Shooters, light and rum and coke, we drammed all day and a' that
For a' that and a' that, it's coming yet for a' that
And now it's back to Scottish beer, bloody work and a' that.

*(Composed by Anne-Marie Middleton, on the occasion of Skye Camanachd
and Kingussie re-introducing shinty to Nova Scotia and Cape Breton after
an absence of 100 years, in July, 1991.)*

DONALD CAMPBELL, THE DROVER

One of the most interesting historical anecdotes uncovered in the research for the Camanachd Association's centenary volume SHINTY!, was the story of Donald Campbell, the Drover.

He was team captain of Furnace Excelsiors shinty Club about 100 years ago and, by most accounts, the foremost player in the Furnace area at the time.

The nickname may possibly have arisen from the style of his play or from the way he captained his team; it was certainly not related to his occupation - he was a steamboat pilot on the Firth of Clyde with The Caledonian Steam Packet Company Ltd.

Furnace Excelsiors, circa 1893. Donald Campbell, The Drover is seated at the centre of the group.

THE KILT SHALL BE INDISPENSABLE

In view of the revival of the interest in shinty (is it a feature of the Celtic renaissance?), a revival which is not confined to the Highlands, but extends to London and elsewhere, I intend to offer a series of brief sketches of the more important of our shinty clubs, with groups, so far as available, of their past or present teams. It is but fitting that the Cuideachd Camanachd Dhuneideann should form the subject of this opening sketch; for, in addition to being the champion of the Shinty League of the capital, it has the proud distinction of being the oldest organised shinty club in existence.

Founded in 1870, it owes its origin to the late Mr Cattanach, Mr. P. Cameron of Corrycoillie, and other enthusiastic Celts, in their endeavours to prevent the apparent decline of the ancient national game. By reason of the willing support rendered by many Highlanders resident in Edinburgh and elsewhere, the club has flourished and prospered, and its membership role has included many famous names. Among those who have been actively connected with the organisation may be mentioned the late Eneas Macdonell of Morar, the late Sheriff Nicolson, Sheriff Mackechnie, Mr. A. V. Smith Sligo of Inzievar; Mr. Pat Cameron and his late brother George; Messrs. R. Menzies, S.S.C.; A. R. Forbes, Register House; A. N. MacAulay of the Clan Cameron Association. The honorary members of the club include the Earl of Rosebery, Sir Lewis MacIver, Sir James Russell, Professor McKinnon, Mr. Horatio R. Macrae of Clunes, and Mr. Theodore Napier.

The present chief, who occupies the central position in the accompanying group of the League Championship team, is Mr. A. Mackay Robson, one of the club's original and most enthusiastic members. On his left is the chieftain, Mr. Alexander Kennedy, a Badenoch player who has had a place in the team since 1876; while on the right of the chief the vice-chieftain, Mr. A. McBean, another son of Badenoch.

The past and present membership includes representatives from all parts of the Highlands, from Sutherland to Kintyre, and from Banff to the Western Isles. The present team is largely composed of natives of Badenoch, a district where the game has always retained its popularity. Members from the famous shinty districts of Cowal, Inveraray, and Lochaber have also contributed largely to the success of the club, while not a few of the younger players have received their training in Edinburgh itself.

Among its great rivals - Glasgow Cowal, the Glasgow Camanachd, Glasgow Ossian, Furnace, Kingussie, Aberdeen University, London Camanachd, Vale of Leven, and Glencoe Clubs - the Edinburgh Camanachd has always maintained an honourable place, while it has survived the waning of several one-time powerful combinations, of which the two last named are instances. For some years it has held the championship of the Edinburgh Shinty League; and although not one of the original members of the new Camanachd Association, it has of late been affiliated with that body for the promotion of the best interests of the game.

Two important functions rank as red-letter days on the calendar of the club each season - the game at the Highland Society's gathering and the match on New Year's Day. The bye-laws ordain that, at the latter meeting, "the kilt shall be indispensable." The club possesses no private ground, but the generosity of the Town Council has obviated any necessity for procuring this, as a shinty ground has been set apart by the City Fathers for the use of the Edinburgh clubs in order to promote an interest in the game, and the favour is much appreciated.

As a social institution, also, the club has an honoured place in the Capital of Scotland, and merits all the support which may be accorded it by Celts in and around Midlothian. The present secretary is Mr. Donald Macleod, Edinburgh, in whose hands the club will lose none of its ancient prestige.

R.T.H.
[The Scots Pictorial, January 16,1899, page 425.]

Edinburgh Camanachd. (Scots Pictorial, January 16, 1899.)

BRAG NAN CAMAN

Air madain Diluain, tràth sa Bhliadhn Ur 1894, chluinte brag nan caman air Traigh Ard-Thong beagan mhiltean a-mach a Steòrnabhagh. Bha Club Camanachd Steòrnabhaigh a'cluich an aghaidh sgioba de thàillearan a'bhaile.

A rèir an Ross-Shire Journal b'e deagh gheam a bh'ann agus nochd na h-uidhir de dhaoine ga choimhead. An deidh leth-cheud mionaid, agus iad a'call 5-0, ghèill na tàillearan is thìll a'chuideachd air fad dhan bhaile ann an deagh shunnd.

Ma tha e na annas gu robh iomain air stèidh cho laidir ann an Leòdhas bho chionn ceud bliadhna, is gu robh club oifigeil ann an Steòrnabhagh, se an t-annas buileach gu robh dusan tàillear sa bhaile a b'urrainn cluich! Ach tha ainmean an dà sgioba an sud an dubh san geal sa phàipear.

Chan e gum bu chòir dha a bhith na iongnadh gu robh iomain a cheart cho cumanta sna h-eileanan uair a bh'ann - is chan eil cho fior fhada bhuaithe - is a bha e air tir-mor. Thig thu fhathast air criomagan eachdraidh is beul-aithris a tha ga dhearbhadh.

Bho chionn dà bhliadhna bha mi a'bruidhinn ri bodach a Uige Leòdhais a bha a'sreab ris a cheud. Cho-luath sa bha an sgoil a sgaoileadh bhiodh e fhèin 's a cho-aoisean ag iomain air tràighean Uige gach latha anns na bliadhnaichean roimhn Cheud Chogadh. B'ann a clàran barraille, neo fiodh sam bith a thigeadh air a'chladach, a bhiodh iad a'gearradh nan caman.

Ann am Muile, bha cuimhne aig Seonaidh Simpson nach maireann air a bhith a'cluich aig àm na Bliadhn Uire air Tràigh Chalgaraidh anns na bliadhnaichean eadar an dà chogadh. Chruinnicheadh iad an sin, sean is òg, is chluicheadh iad uile gus an trèigeadh iad a rèir an t-seann chleachdaidh, gun riaghailt is gun rèiteire.

Neo Mgr Iain Moireasdan nach maireann, "Father Rocket" mar a theirte ris. Chuala mi naidheachd aige-san mu fhear a chaidh a bhàthadh air an t-snàmh ann am fear dhe na lochain beaga, dubha ud a tha cho lionmhor ann an Uibhist a Deas. Bha e a'fiachainn ri faighinn a-mach gu eilean am meadhan an locha, son caman a bhuain a preas seilich a bha a'fàs ann. Cha robh fiodh ro phailt son camain ann an Uibhist.

A dh'aindeoin sin lean an iomain ann gus an linn seo fhèin. Ann an Leabhar Bliadhna an Iomain 1974-75 gheibhear cunntas air a gheam mu dheireadh ann an Uibhist a Tuath ann an 1907 son a chupa a thug an t-uachdaran, Sir John Campbell-Orde, seachad ann an 1895. Tha e coltach gun robh an cuthach air sgioba Shollais a chionn is gun do cheannaich sgioba an Taobh-Siar camain ceart air tir-mòr!

Ach ma bha iomain cho beothail ann an Leodhas is ann an Uibhist nuair a bha an dùsgadh mòr ann bho chionn ceud bliadhna, ciamar nach do dh'fhàs e mar thachair feadh a chòrr dhen Ghàidhealtachd?

Tha mi cinnteach gu bheil adhbhar neo dha ann, ach is neònach nach e astar mara duiligheadas siubhail cuid mhòr dhe. B'ann air eiginn a chùm na Sgitheanaich a'dol is gun iad ach leth-mhile a tir-mor, anns na làithean ud a bha saoghal an iomain a'cuartachadh air Cupa a'Chamanachd agus Cupa MhicTaibheis. Bha sin do-dheanta ann an Leòdhas neo an Uidhist; bha iad buileach air na h-iomaill.

Tuigear cuideachd, ann an linn roimh dhrochaidean neo cabhasairean, gu robh e duilich an geam a bhrosnachadh taobh staigh Uibhist fhein. Ach de mu Leòdhas le sluagh mòr; ciamar a sgap ball-coise an sin is nach do sgap an iomain?

Balaich ga thoirt dhachaidh bho dheas, far an robh iad na bu trice air àrainn ball-coise an an cuideachd luchd-iomain? Am fasan a b'ùire a'sgapadh a-mach bho Ghalldachd baile Steòrnabhaigh, a dhaindeoin deagh rùn 1894? Is neònach nach robh measgachadh adhbharan ann.

Ann an cuid de dh'eileanan dh'fhàs an sluagh òg tuilleadh is gann is sgapte son sgioba de sheòrsa sam bith a chumail a'dol. Shaoilinn gur e sin a thachair ann am Muile, far an robh boillsgeadh beothachaidh san iomain airson bliadhna neo dha an deidh a'Cheud Chogaidh.

Agus an diugh, is ceanglaichean siubhail a'sior fhàs nas luaithe is nas pailte - am faic sinn dùsgadh as ùr anns na h-eileanan?

Tha e doirbh a bhith ro dhòchasach ann an suidheachadh far a bheil seann fhriamhaichean a'gheama air crionadh chun na h-ire is gum bheilear a'meas ball-coise mar an dualchas agus iomain mar an coigreach.

Ach bha sgioba de dh'òigridh an Eilein Sgitheanaich am Beinn-na-fadhla aig deireadh an t-samhraidh a'cluich an aghaidh sgioba òigridh an sin. Cò aig a tha fios, lath-eigin.....

Màrtainn Dòmhnullach

FROM STORNOWAY TO THE SAHARA

Shinty and Stornoway go together much as snow and the Sahara do. And yet in January 1894 Stornoway shinty club defeated as 12-man select from the tailors of the town 5-0 in a challenge match on Tong sands!

At the time shinty was much more common in the islands than is realised nowadays and in many of them it lingered well into this century. In the years up to World War 1 the school-children of Uig, Lewis, regularly played on the sands with camain (sticks) made out of barrel staves. In the inter-war years traditional new year games, involving the whole community, were still played on the vast beach of Calgary in Mull.

South Uist folklore records the tragic drowning of a young man as he swam to the wooded island in a loch to cut a caman. The Shinty Yearbook of 1974-75 records the memories of a parcticipant in the North Uist Challenge Cup Final of 1907.

So why did shinty die out in these areas? Isolation and transportation difficulties were certainly a major factor. The Minch effectively denied island teams the chance to compete in mainland-based competitions.

The southward drift of the young in search of work also played a part, especially in sparsely populated islands like Mull. But why did football oust shinty in relatively populous Lewis?

Did returning islanders bring it home from the central belt, or did it simply become the fashionable game in anglicised Stornoway after that brief flirtation with shinty in 1894?

Whatever the case, once gone it is difficult to revive. But a team of Skye children visited Benbecula to play the local kids last summer. A portent for the future perhaps?

[Martin MacDonald, Shinty Yearbook, 1994-95.]

TIUGAINN A DH'IOMAIN

Mas deidheadh tòiseachadh air gèam camanachd, bha an dà cheann-stoc, a' tighinn ri chèile agus rachadh an t-òran a sheinn mar a leanas. Tha grunn eiseamplairean ann dhen òran. Sann a Ceap Breatunn a thànaig an tè seo.

Iomain a chamain.

Dè an caman?

Caman iubhair.

Dè an t-iubhair?

Iubhair adhar.

Dè an t-adhar?

Adhar eun.

Dè an t-eun?

Eun nidein.

Dè an neidein?

Nidean phreilleach.

Dè am preilleach?

Preilleach eich.

Dè an t-each?

Each mòr blàr buidhe.

Dè am buidhe?

Buidhe ghorm.

Dè an gorm?

Gorm na mara.

Dè mhuir?

Muir eisg.

Dè an t-iasg?

Iasg dubhain.

Dè an dubhan?

Dubhan airgid.

Dè an t-airgead?

Airgead a ghoid mise a ciste mo sheanmhair, ma dhinnseas tusa do dhuine a chunna tu riamh bheir mise ort-e, bheir mise ort e.

COME TO PLAY SHINTY

Before a game of shinty started, it was the custom in many areas to take part in a short ceremony, inviting the assembled players to take part. The song exists in various versions. This one was recorded in Cape Breton, Nova Scotia.

Come to play.

To play what?

To play shinty.

What shinty?

A shinty of yew.

What yew?

A yew of the air.

What air?

Air of birds.

What bird?

Bird of a nest.

What nest?

Nest of hair.

What hair?

Horse hair.

What horse?

A big, white-blazoned, yellow horse.

What yellow?

Bluish yellow.

What blue?

Blue of the sea.

What sea?

Sea of fish.

What fish?

Fish of a hook.

What hook?

A silver hook.

What silver?

Silver I stole from the big yellow chest of my grandmother. If you tell anyone you ever saw, I'll beat you for it. I'll beat you for it!

[John L. Campbell, Songs remembered in exile, 1990, pages 80-81.]

THE CROOKED ASH

The crooked ash
Crooked sapling I grew o'er the bend of a stream
'longside big brothers tall and straight
Haunt of young truants with crippled camans
Ah, in each hungering eye I read my fate.
When I came of age - twas one windy night
A young "guest" with a gapped-tooth saw and soap
With conquest as his mad right crept by;
Around his waist a ragged rope
He cut me down the barefoot whelp
His soapy saw it made no noise
And he hummed to himself in the dead of the night
'Sure as Schoolmaster says: "Boys will be boys".
Dismembered in a vacant wheel-less hearse
I was butchered, God help me, planed and planed
No more to be choir-loft for linnet and finch
Or to rejoice with the eels when it rained.
Next I lashed an oul' ball to left and to right
Rebellious on soft wet threadbare grass
("Too damn heavy" from my freckled devil's limb)
mercy, 'planed' again with broken glass!
Ah, splinters showered the sky that torrid noon
Not mine, oh no, but from big brother ash!
When the long whistle shrills to the end of the fray
(How a bouchal revels in a man's rugged part?)
O bashed, bloodied, blessed crooked ash
Long, long will you reign in a hurler's heart!

(Michael "Brud" White)

Trinity College, Dublin, Hurley Team 1880. The sticks obviously are not of the broad tradition and would be suitable only for playing the ball on the ground.

Sean Keating. The Tipperaray Hurler. 20th century. Oil on Canvas. Hugh Lane Municipal Gallery of Modern Art, Dublin.

A HURLER'S PRAYER

Grant me, O Lord, a hurler's skill
with strength of arm and speed of limb,
Unerring eye for the flying ball
And courage to match then what ere befall.
May my aim be steady, my stroke be true,
My actions many, my misses few;
And no matter what way the game may go
May I part in friendship with every foe.
When the final whistle for me is blown
And I stand at last at God's judgement throne,
May the great Referee when He calls my name,
Say "You hurled like a man;
you played the game".

John "Kaid" McLean

INVERARAY BOYS

Let them sing about their Bonnie Mary,
And the days of Auld Lang Syne,
But gi'e me the boys of Inveraray,
From the shores of dark Loch Fyne,
Where they leave the cradle, soon as they're able
To chase the Shinty Ball,
To play the game - to win more fame,
To vanquish one and all.

They had seen the gallant lads of Furnace,
Who had won renown before,
For these good neighbours had crowned their labours,
By defeating Newtonmore.
Then it was hinted on famous Winterton,
The boys would do the same,
And truth to tell—in two years, well
They hadn't lost a game !

They went from victory to victory,
From success to success,
Till the Cup they covet, they took from Lovat,
'Way up in Inverness.
"Then let 'em all come" said good King Malcolm,
Our boys will not look back.
But will uphold—the game of old,
For the yellow and the black.

It excited-delighted Lochfyneside,
The doughty deeds they had done,
And there was reason, 'cos in one season

Three senior Cups were won.
In that lot is, of course the Scottish,
The Celtic and the Dunn,
But sad to say-one passed away,
The Dunn! alas! is " Done."

They are wiry, fiery, energetic,
Their play fast, crisp and keen,
they beat Furnace, Oban, Kyles Athletic,
And the dashing, clashing "Spean."
As they kept scoring - for ever soaring,
And always aiming high,
They went right up for the Celtic Cup,
And brought it from the Skye.

[J. Kaid MacLean, Book of Remembrance, 1939, pages 32-33.]

NEWTONMORE

Lovers of Camanachd, look towards Badenoch,
Watch the lads donned in Red, White and Blue,
Go on the field to play, Camans to wield, till they
Bring the Cup back to the shores of Craigdhu.

CHORUS:

They are the Scottish Champions,
Gallant Newtonmore,
And when they play at Camanachd,
Keep your eye on Johnnie Cattanach,
And by Jove you're bound to see him score,
For he learned to play by the banks of Spey,
In Bonnie Newtonmore.

Twice though they qualified, Kyles their aims nullified,
The Cup was transported to Bute's rugged shore,
Yet restless it slumbered, its days there were numbered,
It sighed for Badenoch, its loved home of yore.

CHORUS

Argyllshire was cheering when Furnace appearing,
Tried to oust the boys from Craigdhu,
But playing with science, their password " Defiance,"
They ousted Lochfyne by five goals to two.

CHORUS

[Kaid MacLean, Book of Remembrance, 1939, page 42.]

THE FURNACE SHINTY SONG

Furnace, 1923

Good old Harry do not tarry, hasten o'er the brine,
And drop me by the Quarry on the shores of dark Lochfyne.
From there I shall not wander, nor shall I ever stray
When I met with Dr Campbell and the boys who won the day.

Chorus:
The grand old game of camanachd our fathers played of yore
How can he claim his father's name who can't his fame uphold?
With neatness, fleetness, stamina and keenness to the fore
The grand old game of camanachd shall live for evermore.

In the first round old Oban found that they were on the run
And after all they saw the ball and that was all they won.
Ballachulish sons with their great guns were next held in the trap
The Furnace boys caused a great surprise with an easy going "nap".

The country cheered when Kyles appeared to damp the Furnace roar
But there inspired the Furnace fired and four times did they score.
T'was very sad if Kyles were had and with their great success
The boys went forth up to the north to win at Inverness.

Now let us sup we've won the cup, we've vanquished Newtonmore
With sterling play they won the day we'll toast them o'er and o'er.
They've heads with sense in their defence I just record the fact
In all their ties with many byes they kept their goal intact.

(J. Kaid MacLean.)

THE NEW YORK HIGHLANDERS

We have started a shinty club here named the New York Highlanders Shinty Club and have adopted a red and green jersey. We have very fine grounds and a brilliant lot of players. We have introduced American ideas to our training system. Chief among our players are John Fyfe, of Demerara fame; Gregor Moir, Carr Bridge; Louis Fraser, Laggan; and Angus MacPherson also a son of Laggan and universally acknowledged not only to be one of the most expert shinty players that left the shores of Scotland, but was also in the very forefront of pipers and dancers. He can easily lay claim to be the greatest piper and most graceful dancer in all America. The aim of the promoters of the new club is to keep alive in the land of their adoption the game which in their youth, afforded them such delight, and which in some measure at least gave them that grit and pluck which are essential in fighting the stern battle of life."

[Kingussie Record, May 2, 1903.]

SCARCELY SUITED TO PETTICOATS

SPORTS AND PASTIMES

Shinty

SHINTY is very plainly growing in popularity. Under its various names it is steadily gaining ground in England, Scotland, and Ireland. In London great interest is at present being taken in the return International match, which takes place on the 19th of this month. In the Highlands the game has been taken up by lairds and tenants, and if it once goes to the Badenoch district the chances are that we shall find golf taking a back seat in popular estimation for once in a while. A year or two ago the enmity between the Kingussie and Newtonmore regions over the matter was deadly, but now that the game has extended its dominions, there is a likelihoood of a Badenoch union against the world. In Inverness the ladies have taken to the game, and, though it is scarcely an exercise suited to petticoats, the ladies of the Highland capital make fairly good play.

[The Scots Pictorial, April 20, 1897.]

THE LITTLEJOHN ALBUM

Roger Hutchinson on Sport

Who won the Littlejohn Vase this year? I ask because a couple of telephone calls to usually reliable informants could not enlighten me.

The result of this venerable contest was not reported, that I noticed, in the local or in the national press. Why is the Littlejohn Vase competition so ignored?

I suspect, because it is played for by students, outwith the immediate auspices of the Camanch Association. But the Littlejohn Vase is one of the oldest shinty trophies available (and is therefore, by definition, one of the oldest sports trophies in Scotland). And it has a fascinating history.

Alexander Littlejohn was a Londoner of Scottish origins who made a small fortune in the City at the end of the 19th century.

He used some of his money to buy the Invercharron Estate in Easter Ross (and thenceforward called himself Littlejohn of Invercharron) and a good deal of the rest of his fortune in pursuing a fascination with classical civilisations.

He appears to have submerged himself in the study of four such civilisations — the Greeks, Romans, Etruscans . . . and the Celts. It was undoubtedly his interest in the latter which made him take notice of the

shinty players of Aberdeen University (shinty had been played in an organised form at Aberdeen Uni since at least 1861).

In 1905 Alexander Littlejohn approached the Aberdeen University Athletic Club and offered them a "challenge vase" to be used "particularly for continuing the interest in the Ancient Celtic Game of Shinty".

The AUAC naturally accepted this stockbroker's friendly offer, but when the trophy arrived they were stunned.

It was a sensational piece of work. The Littlejohn Vase was modelled in silver on a fourth-century BC sculpted container, an Etruscan vase, which had been found in 1770 in a lake at Pontinello, Italy (and which is now, I am told, in the Burrell Collection, Glasgow).

Aberdeen's new trophy was — as any captain who has since held it aloft will attest — an amazing, ornamental quaich set upon a stately plinth. It was accompanied by a leather-bound volume, adorned with gold leaf and tartan inset, which outlined in medieval calligraphy the history of the game of shinty, and articles of the deed of gift. This remarkable manuscript remains under lock and key in the Queen Mother library, Aberdeen.

But the cup itself was taken into the light of day. Generously, the students of Aberdeen decided that they could not keep such a spectacle to themselves, and so they opened a competition between the three Scottish university shinty teams in 1906.

Glasgow won the Littlejohn Vase in that first year, and since then it has passed around the campuses, accumulating a hoard of great stories and some fine displays of shinty. Some of the greatest shinty players in Scotland have held the Littlejohn Vase, and some of the worst. It has made riotous journeys from north to south and south to north passed through the unsteady hands of many a jubilant young man, and yet remained intact. It is a remarkable trophy.

And I don't know who presently holds it. Why? Will somebody please tell me.

From the West Highland Free Press, June 14, 1991.

There are few shinty trophies as attractive and with such an interesting history as the Littlejohn Challenge Vase, played for by the Universities. Relatively few people, in fact, have seen the magnificent cup, and its appearance in the Association's travelling exhibition added much to a hugely impressive collection of silverware.

Even fewer people have seen the Littlejohn Album which accompanied the trophy when donated to Aberdeen University by Mr Alexander Littlejohn of Invercharron. It is a beautifully produced, and ornate piece of work - hand-worked monograms on fine vellum - and it is normally kept under lock and key in the vaults of the University.

A copy is held however by the Gaelic Society of Inverness in the Public Library, Farraline Park, Inverness.

(See also the colour section for the magnificent title page on the album).

The Littlejohn of Invercharron Challenge Vase

a reduced Copy in Silver of

The Warwick Vase.

This Vase was found in 1770 during excavations carried on in the bed of a small lake called Pantanello overlooking the Vale of Tempe near Tivoli sixteen miles from Rome. How it came there is not known. Hadrians villa was occupied by the Ostro-Gothic king Totila 540 AD when he laid siege to Rome, and the Vase may have been cast into the lake to save it from the invaders. The villa was finished about 138 A·D but this work is of an earlier date and is attributed to Lysippus of Sicyon, a Greek artist of the 4th century B.C. when the noble severity of Phidias was replaced by the elegant style.

The Vase is of white marble and is circular in form. It is 5ft 6in high and 5ft 8in in diameter at the lip, and is placed on a square pedestal of modern construction. The handles are formed of pairs of vine stems, the smaller branches of which twine round the upper lip and with drooping bunches of grapes form a symmetrical frieze. The lower rim is covered by two tiger or panther skins, of which the heads and the forepaws adorn the sides of the Vase while the hind legs interlace and hang down between the handles. Arranged along the tiger skins are several heads, all except one being those of Sileni, or male attendants of Bacchus and the single exception being a faun or Bacchante. Between the heads are thyrsi or bacchic staves twined round with ivy and vine shoots and litui, or augural wands, used in taking omens

The capacity of the Vase is 163 gallons.

(Warwick Castle and its Earls).

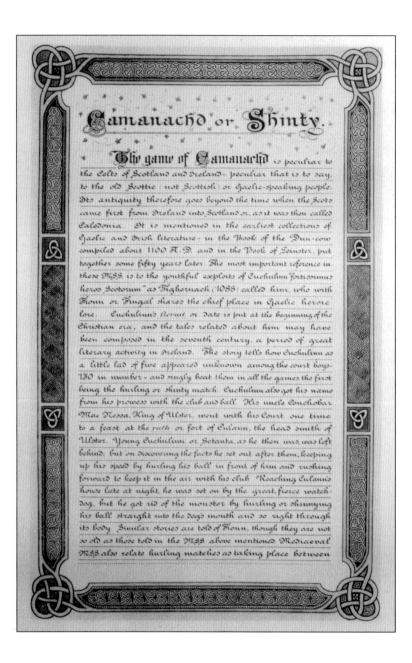

Camanachd or Shinty.

The game of Camanachd is peculiar to the Celts of Scotland and Ireland - peculiar that is to say, to the old Scottic (not Scottish) or Gaelic-speaking people. Its antiquity therefore goes beyond the time when the Scots came first from Ireland into Scotland or, as it was then called Caledonia. It is mentioned in the earliest collections of Gaelic and Irish literature - in the Book of the Dun-cow compiled about 1100 A.D. and in the Book of Leinster, put together some fifty years later. The most important reference in these MSS is to the youthful exploits of Cuchulinn "fortissimus heros Scotorum" as Tighernach (1088) called him, who with Fionn or Fingal shares the chief place in Gaelic heroic lore. Cuchulinn's floruit or date is put at the beginning of the Christian era, and the tales related about him may have been composed in the seventh century, a period of great literary activity in Ireland. The story tells how Cuchulinn as a little lad of five appeared unknown among the court boys - 150 in number - and singly beat them in all the games the first being the hurling or shinty match. Cuchulinn also got his name from his prowess with the club and ball. His uncle Conchobar Mac Nessa, King of Ulster, went with his Court one time to a feast at the rath or fort of Culann, the head smith of Ulster. Young Cuchulinn or Setanta, as he then was, was left behind; but on discovering the facts he set out after them, keeping up his speed by hurling his ball in front of him and rushing forward to keep it in the air with his club. Reaching Culann's house late at night, he was set on by the great, fierce watch-dog, but he got rid of the monster by hurling or shinnying his ball straight into the dog's mouth and so right through its body. Similar stories are told of Fionn, though they are not so old as those told in the MSS. above mentioned. Mediaeval MSS also relate hurling matches as taking place between

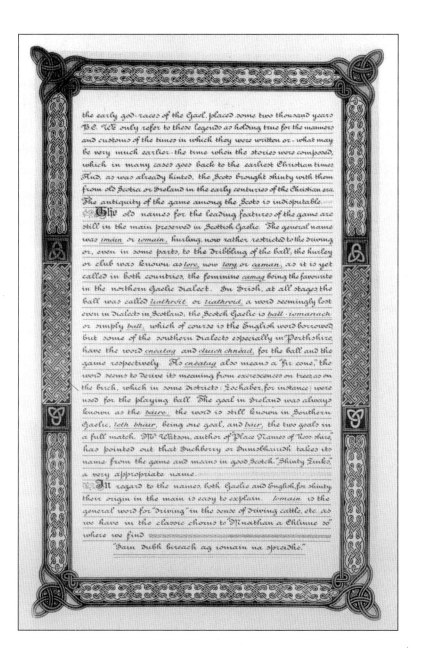

the early god-races of the Gael, placed some two thousand years B.C. We only refer to these legends as holding true for the manners and customs of the times in which they were written or - what may be very much earlier - the time when the stories were composed, which in many cases goes back to the earliest Christian times. And, as was already hinted, the Scots brought shinty with them from old Scotia or Ireland in the early centuries of the Christian era. The antiquity of the game among the Scots is indisputable.

The old names for the leading features of the game are still in the main preserved in Scottish Gaelic. The general name was *imain* or *iomain*, hurling, now rather restricted to the driving or, even in some parts, to the dribbling of the ball; the hurley or club was known as *lorg*, now *lorg* or *caman*, as it is yet called in both countries, the feminine *camag* being the favourite in the northern Gaelic dialect. In Irish, at all stages the ball was called *liathroit*, or *liathroid*, a word seemingly lost even in dialects in Scotland; the Scotch Gaelic is *ball-iomanach* or simply *ball*, which of course is the English word borrowed; but some of the southern dialects especially in Perthshire, have the word *cndatag* and *cluich chnéad*, for the ball and the game respectively. As *cndatag* also means a "fir cone," the word seems to derive its meaning from excrescences on trees, as on the birch, which in some districts (Lochaber, for instance) were used for the playing ball. The goal in Ireland was always known as the *baire*, the word is still known in Southern Gaelic, *leth bhàir*, being one goal, and *bàir*, the two goals in a full match. Mr Watson, author of *Place Names of Ross-shire*, has pointed out that Suchberry or Innisbhainidh takes its name from the game and means in good Scotch "Shinty Links," a very appropriate name.

In regard to the names, both Gaelic and English, for shinty, their origin in the main is easy to explain. *Iomain* is the general word for "driving" in the sense of driving cattle, etc. as we have in the classic chorus to "Mnathan a Chinne só" where we find

"Sam dubh breach ag iomain na spréidhe."

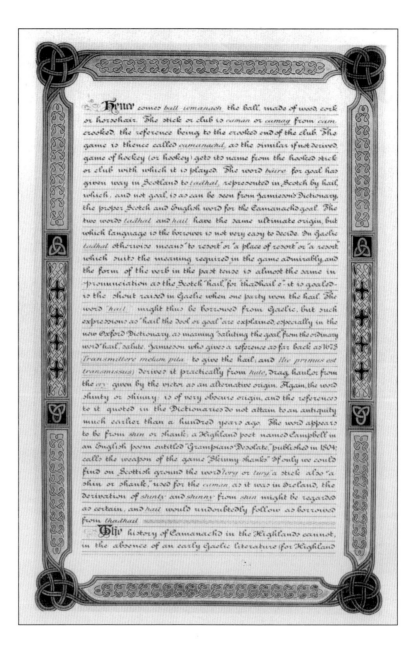

HENCE comes *ball iomanach* the ball, made of wood, cork or horsehair. The stick or club is *caman* or *camag* from *cam* crooked, the reference being to the crooked end of the club. The game is thence called *camanachd*, as the similar if not derived game of hockey (or hockey) gets its name from the hooked stick or club with which it is played. The word *bàire* for goal has given way in Scotland to *tadhal*, represented in Scotch by hail, which, and not goal, is as can be seen from Jamieson's Dictionary, the proper Scotch and English word for the Camanachd goal. The two words *tadhal* and *hail* have the same ultimate origin, but which language is the borrower is not very easy to decide. In Gaelic *tadhal* otherwise means "to resort" or "a place of resort" or "a resort", which suits the meaning required in the game admirably, and the form of the verb in the past tense is almost the same in pronunciation as the Scotch "hail," for "thadhail e" it is goaled—is the shout raised in Gaelic when one party won the hail. The word "hail" might thus be borrowed from Gaelic, but such expressions as "hail the dool or goal" are explained, especially in the new Oxford Dictionary, as meaning "saluting the goal," from the ordinary word "hail," salute. Jamieson who gives a reference as far back as 1673 (*Transmittere meam pila* to give the hail; and *ille primus est transmissus*) derives it practically from *hale*, drag, haul, or from the *cry* given by the victor as an alternative origin. Again, the word *shinty* or *shinny*, is of very obscure origin, and the references to it quoted in the Dictionaries do not attain to an antiquity much earlier than a hundred years ago. The word appears to be from *shin* or *shank*, a Highland poet named Campbell in an English poem entitled "Grampians Desolate," published in 1804, calls the weapon of the game "Skinny shanks." If only we could find on Scottish ground the word *cry* or *cuig*, a stick also "a shin or shank," used for the *caman*, as it was in Ireland, the derivation of *shinty* and *shinny* from *shin* might be regarded as certain, and *hail* would undoubtedly follow as borrowed from *thadhail*

THE history of Camanachd in the Highlands cannot, in the absence of an early Gaelic literature (for Highland

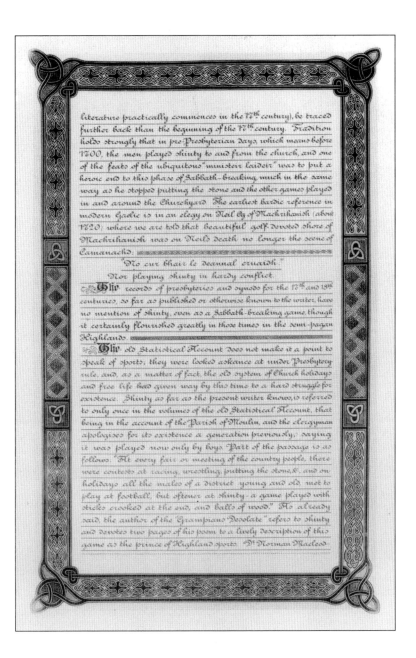

literature practically commences in the 17th century), be traced further back than the beginning of the 17th century. Tradition holds strongly that in pre-Presbyterian days, which means before 1700, the men played shinty to and from the church, and one of the feats of the ubiquitous "minister leader" was to put a heroic end to this phase of Sabbath-breaking, much in the same way as he stopped putting the stone and the other games played in and around the Churchyard. The earliest bardic reference in modern Gaelic is in an elegy on Neil Og of Machrihanish (about 1720) where we are told that beautiful golf-devoted shore of Machrihanish was on Neil's death no longer the scene of Camanachd:

"No cur bhair le deannal cruaidh."

Nor playing shinty in hardy conflict.

The records of presbyteries and synods for the 17th and 18th centuries, so far as published or otherwise known to the writer, have no mention of shinty, even as a Sabbath-breaking game, though it certainly flourished greatly in those times in the semi-pagan Highlands.

The old Statistical Account does not make it a point to speak of sports; they were looked askance at under Presbytery rule, and, as a matter of fact, the old system of Church holidays and free life had given way by this time to a hard struggle for existence. Shinty as far as the present writer knows, is referred to only once in the volumes of the old Statistical Account, that being in the account of the Parish of Moulin, and the clergyman apologises for its existence a generation previously, saying it was played now only by boys. Part of the passage is as follows: "At every fair or meeting of the country people, there were contests at racing, wrestling, putting the stone, &, and on holidays all the males of a district young and old, met to play at football, but oftener at shinty - a game played with sticks crooked at the end, and balls of wood." As already said, the author of the "Grampians Desolate" refers to shinty and devotes two pages of his poem to a lively description of this game as the prince of Highland sports. Dr Norman Macleod

251

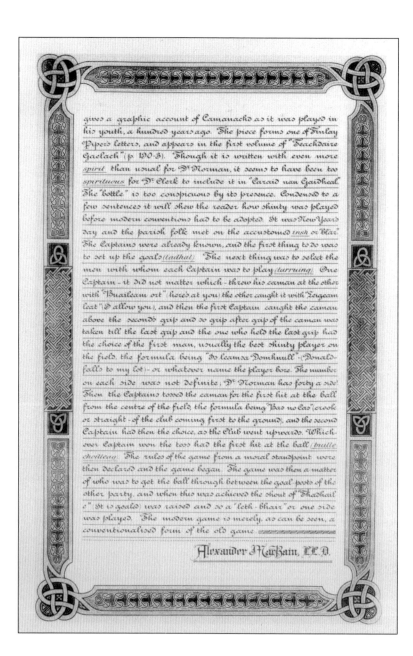

gives a graphic account of Camanachd as it was played in his youth, a hundred years ago. The piece forms one of Finlay Piper's letters, and appears in the first volume of "Teachdaire Gaelach" (p. 190-3). Though it is written with even more *spirit* than usual for Dr Norman, it seems to have been too *spirituous* for Dr Clerk to include it in "Caraid nan Gaidheal". The "bottle" is too conspicuous by its presence. Condensed to a few sentences it will shew the reader how shinty was played before modern conventions had to be adopted. It was New Year's day and the parish folk met on the accustomed *insh* or *blàr*. The Captains were already known, and the first thing to do was to set up the goals *(tadhal)*. The next thing was to select the men with whom each Captain was to play *(turruing)*. One Captain - it did not matter which - threw his caman at the other with "Buaileam ort" (here's at you) the other caught it with "Leigeam leat" (I allow you), and then the first Captain caught the caman above the second's grip and so grip after grip of the caman was taken till the last grip and the one who held the last grip had the choice of the first man, usually the best shinty player on the field, the formula being "Is leamsa Domhnull" - (Donald falls to my lot) - or whatever name the player bore. The number on each side was not definite; Dr Norman has forty a side. Then the Captains tossed the caman for the first hit at the ball from the centre of the field, the formula being "Bas no cas" (crook or straight - of the club coming first to the ground), and the second Captain had then the choice, as the Club went upwards. Which ever Captain won the toss had the first hit at the ball *(buille choilleag)*. The rules of the game from a moral standpoint were then declared and the game began. The game was then a matter of who was to get the ball through between the goal-posts of the other party, and when this was achieved the shout of "Shadhail e" (It is goaled) was raised and so a "leth-bhair" or one side was played. The modern game is merely, as can be seen, a conventionalised form of the old game.

Alexander MacBain, LL.D.

An ingenious caman:
From the F. J. Bigger Collection, Belfast City Library.

AN INGENIOUS CAMAN

Iomain or Camanachd, shinty, is a favourite game. Equal sides are picked, the object of the game being to score as many goals as possible. Stones are used for goals - the ball may be of wood, hard wound worsted, or of hair, peat, or other available material, while the 'caman' is a bent stick of wood or a large tangle. In these islands people have to be ingenious and to make the best of the materials they have.

"As Uist is barren of trees, a tangle caman is nearly as common as a wooden one. Another ingenious caman is made of a large piece of canvas bent with both ends caught in the hand. It is very effective. The Uist boys used to be, and in some places still are, very proficient at the game, the main qualities necessary for an ideal 'iomain' player being speed and dexterity."

[Alexander Morrison, "Uist Games", Celtic Review Vol IV, April, 1908.]

AN NOLLAIG MHÒR AGUS AN NOLLAIG BHEAG:
TWO NOLLAIG DAYS ON ISLAY

New Year Day was called Làth Nollaig in Islay. Formerly there were two Nollaig days. One was on the 25th December, and was called the Nollaig Mhòr. It was not much observed by the people. The other was on the 13th January, and was called Nollaig Bheag. This was the popular New Year Day among the people generally. It commenced with Twelve O'clock of the night before. First-footing was generally indulged in, and as it was considered an honour to be the first visitor to a friend's house in the New Year, there was a great rush immediately after midnight by the first-footers. Of course they generally did not know each other's plans, and several parties often enough met at the same house. The first-footer brought a Bottle of Whisky with him, and where accompanied with a friend, or it might be two, or even three, each might have a bottle. The inmates had to be treated to the contents of each Bottle, of course, and they returned the compliment in "a dram from my bottle", accompanied with bread and cheese.....

After breakfast, shinty players began to gather on the various places where shinty games were in the habit of being played. Balinaby Machair was one of the most famous of these shinty fields. On this field there were vast crowds of players usually, cheered on by six or seven pipers, who played on the field the whole day, and in the presence of Mr. Campbell of Islay, and the Laird of Balinaby, both in full Highland dress. Balinaby's men played against Shawfield's men, and the contest was often keen and carried on with great spirit. D. D. remembers to have seen two men, one, McNiven, and the other McLauchlain, take part in one of these contests. They were both old and grey-haired at the time, but were recognised as distinguished players. So keen was the contest on the occasion that they divested themselves of nearly every article of clothing, their feet were bare, and they had napkins tied round their head, while they were wet with perspiration. While the shinty play was going on, others amused themselves in groups dancing to the music of the pipes. In the evening Balls were held. Men and lads clubbed, each paying 6d which admitted himself and a partner.

....A good shinty (stick) was very important and men went sometimes great distances for a good one. D. D. and a companion went with moonlight, after their day's work, across Lochguirm from Balinaby to Foreland wood in quest of shinties.

[Maclagan Mss page 277 From Donald Dewar, labourer, Port Charlotte, Islay, in Tocher 24, page 327.]

THE CLOUDS OF WAR

The clouds of war were lowering as the Beauly Camanachd Club celebrated their 1913 Camanachd Cup success. In 1914 the Great War broke out and as loyal Territorials Alastair and Donald Paterson enlisted and joined up with the 4th Camerons and were soon embarked to the continent. The retreat from Mons and the Marne, the Aisne and the Somme settled into 'trench warfare'. Alastair rose to the rank of Lieutenant and Donald earned his stripes as corporal piper. Whether "going over the top" or directly "into advance", the risks were more or less the same and the outcome for all none could predict. Alastair died of wounds received early in action at Festubert's ford of death and Donald later on in the same battle.

On the 9th March 1915, H. Rawlinson, Lieut. General commanding IV Corps had issued the following communique - "The attack which we are about to undertake is of the first importance to the allied cause. The army and nation are watching the result, and Sir John French is confident that every individual in the IV Corps will do his duty and inflict a crushing defeat on the German VII Corp which is opposed to us", and at some hour after the 16th March 1915 there is no doubt but both Alastair and Donald Paterson played their parts supremely at that final venue as they did on Kingussie's Shinty Field two years before.

The sorting out of papers fron the old "family chest" often yields varied "pearls". It was so with Anne-Mary Paterson, on a day while engaged in this fascinating pursuit when "a small piece of paper, yellowed with age dropped to the floor". Perusal of this apparent 'scrap of paper' revealed it as a pipe tune called 'The Beauly Shinty Club' and was probably composed by Donald in honour of the Camanachd victory of 1913. Donald Paterson's bloodstained pipes and plaid-clasp along with a fragment of material were returned to Beauly. The pipes are now the proud possession of cousin Duncan MacGillivray a talented piper and composer who has edited the tune to meet the play of present times.

"They shall not grow old, as we that are left grow old ..."

[Roddy MacKinnon, Beauly Camanachd centenary, 1992, pages 66-67.]

The Beauly Shinty Club

March

D. Paterson
C. 1913

The Beauly Shinty Club

NO NEED OF SANITORIA

For several reasons the game of camanachd has not of late years increased in favour with Highlanders as it ought to. While the most lukewarm of us are now growing proud of our Gaelic, few indeed have yet realised that in shinty we have a game that, as a winter pastime, is superior to any other. Cricket in summer, shinty in winter, and golf all the year round, for those who can no longer play shinty, afford ideal exercise and physical training from the cradle to the grave. As a means of physical development I claim for shinty the highest place. Cricket, shinty and golf would do more preventative work against consumption among us than many dream of. Without a doubt we would have no need of sanatoria. If an earnest worker doubts this assertion, let him start a shinty club in a country district or village and watch the results. Clumsy, top heavy, slouching lads speedily grow alert and active, quick of eye and nimble of foot, new blood in their pulses, and fresh thoughts in their brains. I have watched these desirable results with the greatest delight. Why, there is hardly a shinty player in Scotland but volunteered for service during the South African War. All Gaels should support a game of which they have every reason to be proud.

[Shinty: Historical and Traditional, TGSI Vol XXX pages 52-53.]

"alert and active, quick of eye and nimble of foot". Stephen Borthwick, Kingussie and Scotland.

AN APPROPRIATE OCCUPATION FOR FALLEN ANGELS

There is a fascination to many people, of whom the present writer is one, in the study of traditional stories with the view of arriving at some conclusion as to their probable origin, says Mr. David McRitchie in the "Scotsman". Of such stories, not the least fascinating are those which relate to the Blue Men (Na Fir Gorma). Certain beliefs regarding those people have been passed to us by a former minister of Tiree, John Gregorson Campbell, who obtained some of his information from a native of Skye. "The fallen angels were driven out of Paradise in three divisions; one became the Fairies on the land, one the Blue Men in the sea, and one the Nimble Men (Fir Chlis), i.e., the Northern Streamers, or Merry Dancers, in the sky".

The Blue Men seem to be specially associated with the sea, and more particularly with the water of the Minch. "The channel between Lewis and the Shant Isles (Na h-Eileanan siant, the charmed islands) is called the 'Stream of the Blue Men' (Struth nam Fear Gorm). A ship, passing through it, came upon a blue coloured man sleeping on the waters. He was taken on board, and, being though of mortal race, strong twine was coiled round and round from his feet to his shoulders, till it seemed impossible for him ot struggle, or move foot or arm.. The ship had not gone far when two men were observed coming after it on the waters. One of them was heard to say, 'Duncan will be one man,' to which the other replied, 'Farquhar will be two.' On hearing this, the man, who had been so securely tied, sprang to his feet, broke his bonds like spider threads, jumped overboard, and made off with the two friends who had been coming to his rescue. "It is not easy to regard Duncan, Farquhar, and their unnamed friend in the light of fallen angels, but such is the story."

There is a hint of a more ethereal connection in the account communicated to me by the late Neil Macleod, a well known Gaelic poet, and author of Clàrsach an Doire (1883). Born at Glendale, Duirinish, Skye, he was a son of Donald Macleod, the famous Skye bard.

"According to promise," writes Neil Macleod, "I am jotting down a few remarks regarding 'the Blue Men'. About the middle of the Minch, between Skye and Uist, the sea runs like a stream. The current is called Sruth nam Fear Gorm, ''The Blue Men's Stream''. Tradition has it that on clear moonlight nights the Blue Men could be seen playing a lively game of shinty. The fishermen thought it a good omen to see the Blue Men playing their game." In this too brief account the scene of the game of shinty is not definitely given, but the aquatic character assigned to the players could lead one to infer that the game was something in the nature of water polo. On the other hand, the locus may have been anywhere on the coast of Skye or one of the smaller islands. Shinty playing, however, whether on land or on sea, does not seem to be an appropriate occupation for fallen angels. The one feature of Neil Macleod's reminiscence that has a celestial suggestion is his statement that the appearance of those azure shinty players was welcomed by the fishermen as a good omen. Here it is not unlikely that the Fir Gorma were confused or identified with that other division of the fallen angels known as the Fir Chlis (otherwise Fir Chlisneach), or Nimble Men, and that the "clear moonlight nights" were really those nights on which the Aurora Borealis was most in evidence; the shinty players being merely a West Highland conception equivalent to the Merry Dancers of Lowland Scotland. The main objection to this interpretation is that, whereas the northern lights, personified as cerulean shinty players, were hailed with delight as the harbingers of a good time coming, they were elsewhere (in spite of thir joyous name the Merry Dancers) dreaded as a portent of impending disaster.

"All night long the northern streamers
Shot across the trembling sky:
Fearful lights that never beckon
Save when kings or heroes die."

These speculations are based on the assumption that the Blue Men are merely the creation of fancy. The question has, however, another aspect. There are many traditions which have a basis in fact, although an element of unreality has gathered round them in the course of time. In some cases the accretions are so numerous and so fanciful that they almost or altogether obscure the kernel of truth which is their origin. But it is still possible to discern the main source of the Gaelic traditions of the Blue Men.

[The Badenoch Record, August 19, 1922]

HANGING ONTO THEIR PANTS

The annual picnic of the Lewis Society of Duluth, Minn., was held this year at Dan Mahoney's summer estate on the North Shore Road, about 20 miles from Duluth, a beautiful site overlooking and bordering Lake Superior. A bus was chartered from the Street Railway Co., and those who had no automobiles took advantage of the bus service.

There were about 100 people present, and among the outside guests were Mr. John MacLeod, and daughter Annabella, who motored from Seattle, Washington. Mrs. MacLeod (nee Mary Macaulay) was born in the Island of Bernera, Uig, and is a sister of Mr. Angus G. Macaulay, cashier of the Duluth Street Railway Co. Her daughter Annabella is one of the foremost soprano singers of the West, and before taking up residence in Seattle was a popular soloist in the city of Duluth; she is equally at home in her rendition of Gaelic songs, and credits Mr. John H. Matheson of Duluth, for having taught her her first Gaelic song, "An Cluinn thu' Leannan". Other visitors included Mr. Donald MacLennan, jun., and two sons, Donald and John, also Mr. Donald MacLennan, of Raymer, Valtos, Uig, and Mr. Neinhauser, all from Minneapolis, Minn.

Mr. Alex. G. MacKnight, an honorary member of the Society, one of the most patriotic and beloved Scotsmen in America, was sadly missed, having left Duluth some months ago for Washington, D. C. as Assistant Attorney to Donald Richberg, Chief Councillor for the National Recovery Administration. This has to do with governing codes in the various industries in the United States. We as a Society, are mightily proud that one of our members has been appointed to one of the most important offices of our present Government in Washington, and was certainly deserving of the honour.

The Sports

The day was an ideal one for sports; the older folk enjoyed bowling on the beautiful lawn in front of the house, and in the afternoon came the races for the children, and other games for the ladies; to recall memories of bygone school days in Lewis, the men folks played a game of buttons, or as we used to say, "cluich air na puttanan," and some of the "bodachs" were hanging onto their pants before the game was over, much to the amusement of the ladies. But the real titbit of the day was a game of "Giomman" on a field adjacent to the house.

It was first of all arranged that the battle was to be between the "Uigeachs" and the "Shiarachs," but it was decided to pick sides; Donald MacLennan, the noted "Cherrag," and Alex. MacRae, of Miavaig, Uig, were chosen captains. Heroes of many a hard fought game on the sands of Reef and Valtos, those two men of Uig faced each other. The ball was placed and covered over with earth in a little hole: they threw their camans up in the air to see who would win the toss, and the

"Cherrag" as usual, was the lucky one. Then came the usual challenge from the "Cherrag" to Alick Sheumais, his rival captain. "Bual am port" and the answer "Leigan Leat" was given as in the days of yore, when we had no "bròg na bonaid," ag ioman air traigh Valtos. Finally sides were picked, the "ballaich" lined up, the whistle blew, and the battle was on; and believe you me, mate, it was no child's play: some of those fellows were using golf clubs, walking sticks, barrel staves, and what not, and one was lucky to miss their wild swings, and not get his head knocked off. First one side, then the other, had the advantage and occasionally in the middle of a scrimmage down would go half a dozen "bodachs" in a heap.

"A Whale of a Game"

The "Cherrag" was playing "a whale of a game," as he could hit with either hand, and all at once, when Donald would change the caman from one hand to another, up would go the howl "Seàs do thullaich, a Cherrag." Our Uig friends are familiar with this one, and his old school chums understand what it was all about. It was not very long after the game started that the "Cherrag" let go a drive, and the first "hail" or "hiley" as we term it in Uig, was registered. Not to be denied the other side rallied, and in a few minutes the score was tied. This did not sit very well with the "Cherrag," and he came back with a vengeance and scored four "hileys" in quick succession, - "Nach be phlàigh e." So ended the game five "hileys" to one, and the end of a perfect day. We wish to say that on the field were four "boys" who all played "Giomman" on the sands of Uig, all schoolmates, viz. Alex MacRae, Miavaig; John H. Matheson, Valtos; Norman A. Matheson, and Donald E. MacLennan, both Raymer, Valtos, Uig. After the game we all congregated at the "Cabin," and sang several Gaelic songs, concluding with the following verse -

> "'S iomadh ceum a shiubhail sinn,
> Bho bha sinn òg le chèile,
> Nuair bha sinn 'g ioman air an tràigh,'
> 'S gùn trusgan oirnn ach fèile."

Our best thanks go to the ladies for serving a lovely supper on the lawn. God bless them.

So ended this hectic and pleasant outing. Aboard the bus Gaelic songs were sung all the way home, and a hilarious time was had by all.

> "From the dim sheiling of the misty island
> Mountains divide us and a waste of seas:
> But still the blood is strong, the heart is Highland,
> And we in dreams behold the Hebrides".

J. H.M.
[Stornoway Gazette, September 28, 1934.]

A MEMORABLE GAME

Tailteann Games...School children parade before the 1924 Games in Croke Park.

THE SHINTY MATCH
SCOTTISH PLAYERS WIN SHINTY MATCH
Shinty v Hurling
Scotland best in thrilling struggle
Scotland 2 goals; Ireland 1 goal.

The visit of a Scottish Shinty team to Croke Park, where they met an Irish hurling team on Saturday, aroused considerable interest. The game was followed with rapt attention by a huge crowd, and at times enthusiasm reached a high pitch. Scotland were victorious after a fast and strenuous, but thoroughly sportsmanlike game.

The last occasion on which a shinty team visited Dublin was in 1897, when the Cowal Shinty Club played the Celtic Hurling Club at Jones' Road. Mr Michael Cusack, founder and first President of the G.A.A., was referee.

The first change noticeable in the game when compared with our national pastime of hurling was the difference in goal posts and methods of scoring. The "net" is much narrower than the hurling goal, but higher, and points, as in hurling, are not counted. Tha Irish caman is broader and much more useful in ovehead play; the shinty stick is capable of greater accuracy on the ground. Handling the ball is not permitted in shinty.

The difference in style was at once apparent. The Irishmen, used to clean, open hurling, were somewhat non-plussed at the beginning by the brilliant groundwork of their opponents.

The handicap was particularly evident in the forward line, where, with the possible exception of Garret Howard and Gleeson, both Limerick men, the Irish representatives were outplayed.

BRILLIANT DEFENCE

In defence and at midfield the hurlers were supreme, and many a time when the Highlanders swarmed round our goal our hearts were in our mouths until Murnane or Dirwan, or "Builder" Walsh, or Jack Darey - a magnificent quartette - rushed in to drive the ball back to their forward line.

It was fully fifteen minutes before the Irishmen accommodated themselves to the swift ground play of their opponents. Henceforward, they could do everything but score.

Play was in progress for twenty minutes when Weir intercepted a flying shot from Nicolson, and with wonderful dexterity curled it past Mahoney into the Irish net. It was the only score of the first half.

NOVEL METHODS

A chapter of missed chances by our forwards followed, and when the ball went within reach of the Scottish custodian he returned it with some of the wizardry which we are accustomed to associate with Tom Daly, the University College keeper.

In the first half Garrett Howard and Gleeson tested MacFadyen with shots from every angle but he was unbeatable. His methods of pucking out, too, evoked considerable amusement, but proved quite as effective as the high drive from the Irish end. Placing the ball carefully, and measuring his stroke as in golf, he invariably sent it well over the half-way line.

A slight re-arranegment in the Irish half back line brought a change of fortune after the resumption. Mick Darcy, who was playing instead of Mattie Power, the brilliant Kilkenny left winger, sent a long pass to Gleeson. With a rapid glance towards the Scottish goal, the Limerick man sent the ball past MacFadyen for the equaliser against tremendous cheering.

CONFLICT OF GIANTS

"Builder" Walsh and Hugh Nicolson were then seen in an exciting duel for possession which ended in the advantage of the Faugh and All Ireland player.

The Highlanders were again active round the Irish goal, and a brilliant piece of combined play by the whole forward line was finished by Greenshields beating O'Mahony and giving Scotland the lead once more.

Fast, high class play characterised the closing stages and the long whistle found Scotland winners of a memorable game by two goals to one.

The referee was Mr J. Kaid MacLean, picturesquley attired in the Highland tartan.

The teams were as follows:

Scotland - D. McLachlan (Argyle), capt., W. Armstrong (Kyles), vice-capt., D. MacFadyen (Kyles), Alex. MacDonald (Glasgow University), A. MacLean (Skye), H. MacGregor (Brae Lochaber), John Gemmell (Cowal), Allan McFadyen (Kyles), Hugh Nicolson (Skye), Andrew Nicolson (Kyles), D. Weir (Kyles), W. Greenshields (Kyles). Substitutes: Colin Murchison (Skye), D. Campbell (Furness). Neil MacCallum (Furness).

So painstaking were the Selection Committee that for each man picked a player was selected for the same position as a reserve. The individual members selected have been prominent in League and championship games for some years.

Ireland - J. Mahony (Galway), goal; D. Murnane (Limerick), full-back: J. Darcy (Tipperary), right back; M. Dirwan (Galway), left back; D. Rine (Cork) left half; James Walsh (Dublin), right half; James Humphries (Limerick), mid-field; B. Gibbs (Galway), right wing; M. Power (Kilkenny), left wing; Hayes (Tipperary) and Howard (Dublin), forwards.

The match thus ended in a victory for the visitors. It was a popular victory, and thus came to close an event whcih will live for many a year in the memories of all of us.

[Irish Independent, August 4, 1924.]

267

THE SHINTY REFEREE

O sure I'm not sea-faring
But I'll tell you how I felt
When we went o'er to Erin
To meet our brother Celt.
Ach, the boat she started tossing
When Dick Cameron said to me
"Twill be a divil o' a crossing
For the Shinty Referee!"

But sure we're all together
From the castle and the plough
The shamrock and the heather
They are intermingled now.
Long may they be in harmony
And rivalry prevail
To show the world our flags unfurled
And we are Clann nan Gaidheal.

But that blooming Irish Ocean
Sure she neither ebbs nor flows
She set me right in motion
From my head down to my toes
Till the big and little fishes
Came up in turns to see
And gave their grateful wishes
To the Shinty Referee!

No longer are we troubling
About the grand old game
Since we have seen in Dublin
Both countries play the same
Those camans told of days of old
Of muscle, brawn and brain
So let us strive to keep alive
Our grand old fathers' game.

As for differentiation
I would never ever dream
Agin Ireland as a nation
We had an ideal team
Yet Ireland said about the Kaid
Our humble Referee
"Twas such as him with heart and limb
that set old Ireland free!"

John Kaid MacLean
("while lunching with the boys who were victorious in Dublin, 1924".)

SHINTY IN THE WESTERN ISLES

Contrary to what many in the shinty circles believe, this worthy game was once played in the Western Isles. Although it is some years now since the districts and townships in the Islands challenged each other, shinty was once more popular than football, which has now taken over as the main game; in fact, shinty was the only game played in Uist at the beginning of the century.

The method of play varied throughout the islands and, indeed, from township to township. From the information received, it appears that the game played in Uist was not unlike that played today; it was also more organised in Uist than in Lewis and Harris. For formal games the Uist teams were selected from specific districts and consisted of twelve players, whereas the Lewis games were just one township against another and the number of players in the team depended on how many men were present at the time of the game.

The sticks used were home-made. In Uist the "bas" was cut from a small patch of woodland at Balranald and spliced to the "Cas." In Lewis the stick was often obtained from driftwood; but sometimes the branch of a tree, usually willow, was shaped to take the desired form; in fact, if there was some trouble in achieving the correct shape a sheep's horn was attached to the end of the stick! The Lewis stick was one-sided like a hockey stick as opposed to the typical two-sided caman. The one-handed game seems to have been played in Lewis from time immemorial to the 1st World War. Balls were generally made from gutta-percha although it is known that the Lewis men sometimes used rubber balls and often had to make their own of thread wound round and round and then sewn all over to keep it tight and hard.

Shinty was played on the machair on whatever area was available. Often, in Uist, games were played well into the night and shinty was played by moonlight. The purpose of the game was to get the ball to the furtherest extreme of the opponent's land. It is known of one game that was played on a "pitch" two miles long! Rules were virtually non-existent but deliberate hitting of an opponent was penalised by suspension. The game lasted for at least 2 hours but often for much longer.

Shinty was played mainly in the winter. Sometimes one hundred players plus spectators turned up for practice matches. The most important game of the year, and that which meant to the island shinty followers what the Camanachd Cup final means to us, was held on New Year's Day. On this day every year all the men and boys in the district met and tried to prove that their district was better than the others. Tradition tells of the prowess of a certain man, MacPhail, playing for Sollas, Uist, who gathered the ball from the thow-up and such was his speed and skill that he dribbled the ball over the other team's (Westside), boundary lines with the West-side men in vain pursuit. And this game was played on the aforementioned two mile "pitch".

In one of the villages in Lewis, Back, on New Year's Day, the opponents from either end of the village met on a field at the half-way mark and battled it out until one team had defeated the other. Apparently, the same team won every year as they had the better sticks which were made from branches stolen from the trees on Lord Leverhulme's estate!

The last shinty final to be played in North Uist took place in 1907 at Sollas. The story of it was told by the only surviving member of the 2 teams, Mr Lachlan MacQuien, Tigharry, North Uist, now aged 93. Sollas and West-side were the two teams taking part and they played for the "North Uist Shinty Challenge Cup" presented by Sir John Campbell-Orde, a North Uist landowner, in 1895. As walking was the only means of transport the West-side team had to go on foot to Sollas, nine miles away. Dr. MacKenzie was the West-side's team manager and Sir John Campbell-Orde was the Sollas manager. Capt. MacDonald, Balranald was the referee. To distinguish the teams West-side wore red sashes. The field was 200 yds X 200 yds.

The West-side team was equipped with mainland shinty sticks brought to Uist, probably from Inverness, by one of the team, Roderick MacDonald, who worked in Portree and who travelled to Uist to play for the West-side team in the final. These were excellent sticks too, according to Mr MacQuien far superior to the local ones, many of which splintered in the ensuing play. The Sollas team protested at the introduction of these new "weapons" and there was quite a dispute before the game eventually got under way.

The game started at a furious pace but the West-side team, with the new sticks, soon took the initiative and forced the Sollas team on to the defensive. Sollas adopted 'defence in depth' tactics mounting only sporadic attacking raids on their opponents goal. So well did the Sollas team defend that at half-time the score was 0-0 but on the resumption the Sollas defence was pierced and the final score was 4 - 0 in favour of the West-side. The Sollas supporters, who had brought their pipes with them, were disappointed on this occasion.

There were quite a few star-performers in both teams but from what has been heard from other sources, the man who told us the story of this game, Mr. MacQuien, was one of the best players in Uist in his day.

It is very sad that this great game has died in the islands after being played there for years but it is to be hoped that the embers of interest in the great traditions of their forefathers are still there, that these will soon again be kindled by the appropriate encouragement from Shinty's official governing body, that enthusiasm and interest of the youth of these areas will be thus revived and that the 'crack of the ash' will once again resound on the machairs of the Western Isles.

[D. R. MacDonald and Liz MacInnes, Shinty Yearbook, 1974-75.]

CAMANACHD GUR ROGHADH SPÒRS E

Camanachd gur roghadh spòrs e
Am a'gheamhraidh is tùs an earraich
Mach 'san achadh 's gillean greannmhor
An deagh ghleus ri cluich cho annamh,
Nach camanachd bu dual d'ar sinnsir,
Ag iomain bhall air Là Callainn,
C'àit 'eil coimeas ris 's an Eòrpa,
H-uile fear cho eudmhor ealamh
Dol g' a dhubhlan bhuidhinn tadhail.

[Angus Morrison, Dàin is Oran, 1930, page 101.]

SPÒRS ANNS NA HEARADH

Spòrs

Nuair a bha sinn òg bhiodh sinn ag iomain ach cha bhiodh againn ach àrca lìon-sgadain agus caman air a ghearradh à craoibh. Bhitheamaid cuideachd a'deanamh luingisean le fiodh agus a cur crann is seòl orra. Se sin an cur seachad a bh'againn.

Games

When we were young we used to play shinty, but we had only a cork from a herring net, and a caman cut from a tree. We also made boats from wood, and put a mast and a sail on them. That was the pastime that we had.

[Dòmhnall Shàm, Horgabosd, (Donald MacDonald, Horgabost) in Croft History, Isle of Harris, Volume 1.]

Am Machair. Borve, South Harris   *Eòlas*

BU CHRIDHEIL AR DUAN

Chunnaic mi 'n uair 's bu luath sinn, Ailein
Air ghluasad far am biodh ceòl,
Cha chuireadh oirnn smuairean uair a chaithris
Air luadh neo banais 'nar n-òig';
Bu chridheil ar duan an uair na Callainn
'S mo luaidh na fir nach eil beò,
A bheireadh dhuinn duais bho fhuaim nan caman
Gu luath 's a' ghloin' air a bhòrd.

[Alasdair MacDonald ("Am Painter Mòr"), Inverness County, Cape Breton Island.]

AIR MACHAIR AN DÙIN

Gillean mo rùin air machair an Dùin -
'S e seo a' Bhliadhn' Ur thug sòlas dhuinn.

Gillean mo ghràidh a thàinig thar sàil -
Bha Alasdair, Eardsaidh 's Dòmhnall ann.

Air m'uilinn san leabaidh 's mi 'n dèidh dhol a chadal,
Chuala mi Challaig is chòrd i rium.

Gillean mo chridhe-sa, sheinneadh an fhidheall -
B'e miann a' chloinn-nighean bhith còmhla riu.

'S e Maighstir Bòid a bha air an ceann
Is cumaidh e teann sa chòmhrag iad.

Iain beag à Port-Rìgh na ghille cho grinn,
Is cumaidh e strì nan Dòmhnallach.

[Bho Dòmhnall Ruadh Choruna, 1995, duilleag xxix, ged nach e Dòmhnall fhèin a rinn na rannan seo.]

AN IOMAIN AN EIGE

HM: O, bhiodh iad ag iomain a seo, tha fhios agad, riamh suas gu tha mi cinndeach, cha chreid mise nach e nineteen twenty-five no six a chunna mise an iomain mu dheireadh air an tràigh.

DAM: Is bha sibh fhèin ag iomain?

HM: Bha mi shios a latha sin gun teagamh ach cha deach mòran iomanach a dheanamh. Chuir iad na camain an dàrna taobh agus fhuair iad ball-coise. Se raghainnich an fheadhainn òga.

DAM: Seadh. Ach 's ann air an tràigh - a Lathaig?

HM: Tràigh Lathaig shios a sin, 's ann. Ach nuair a bha mi nam bhalach a' dol dhan sgoil 's sinn.... o, suas a chuile car, agus even dha na trì bhliadhnaichean an deidh a' cheud chogaidh, bhiodh iomain glè mhath ann. Bhiodh a chuile duine 'san eilean a' cruinneachadh a dhionnsaigh na tràghad. Agus gheibheadh tu, tha mi cinndeach, cruinn air fad iad, suas mu mhiadhoin latha, mun dà uair dheug.

Bha 'n uairsin dithis de ghillean òga, dh'fhaodte suas mu fhichead bliadhna no sin, air an cur amach gus na daoine roinn. Agus mar a bha roinn air a dheanamh, bha 'n dà ghille bha seo a'seasamh mu choinneamh a chèile is bha an còrr dhen t-sluagh mun cuairt daibh, no cruinn, is an dà ghille mu choinneamh a chèile. Is thilgeadh an darna fear an caman a dh'ionnsaigh an fhir eile 's bha e ga ghlacadh mu mhiadhoin na luirge, dh'fhaodte agus bha iad sin ag obrachadh suas air....lurg a'chamain suas gus a' mhullach. Is ga be cò aige bha 'n dòrn mu dheireadh sann aige-san a bha a'cheud taghadh. Agus bha 'fear sin gun teagamh a' taghadh an t-iomanaich a b'fheàrr a bha e smaointinn a bha cruinn agus bha 'n duine bha seo dol a null 's a' seasamh ri thaobh. Bha sin an ath fhear a' taghadh an ath duine. Bha iad a' taghadh nan daoine mar a b'fheàrr a bha iad a' smaointinn a bha iad air an iomain gus a robh a chuile duine bha cruinn air a roinn amach leth mar leth air gach taobh.

'S an uairsin an dithis ghillean seo, a rinn a' roinn, bha iad a sin a' tilgeil nan caman os an cionn 's bha na camain a' tuiteam air an tràigh, agus mar a chanamaide anns an iomain, "a' bheulag" agus "a' chùlag". A' bheulag 'nuair a bha thu a' bualadh leis a làimh dheis gu h-ìseal air a' chaman, agus a' chulag 'nuair a bha thu a' bualadh leis a' làimh cheàrr gu h-ìseal air a' chaman. Ach 'se 'bheulag a bha cunntas agus ma..... laigh an caman agadsa air an tràigh 's a' bheulag a' cur gu tuath, sin an taobh air am bitheadh tu. Agus ma laigh caman an fhir eile 's a' bheulag a' cur gu deas.... sin an taobh a bhiodh esan 's a chuid dhaoine 'cur a chionn 's ann cur a tuath agus a deas a bha 'n tràigh a'ruith. (Dh'fhaodte gu robh i rud beag ris an ear-thuath no ris an iar-dheas ach 'se glè bheag co-dhiubh.) Ach dh'fhaodadh e air uairean tachairt gun tuiteadh an dà chaman an aon rathad. Dh'fheumadh iad an uairsin a bhith air an tilgeil a rithist aca is dh'fhaodte gu feumte an tilgeil dha no trì a dh'uairean mus faighte an dà chaman a' cur an aghaidh a chèile. Agus an uairsin ma bha an caman agadsa leis a' bheulag a' cur gu tuath, bha thu dol an taobh a deas. Bha 'n fheadhainn eile dol an taobh a tuath. Agus bha 'nuairsin na coilleagan air an cur suas: 'se "choilleag" a chanamaide ris. Mar a chanas iad as a' Bheurla, goal.

DAM: O seadh, ach bh aon rud a bha sibh a' ràdha: dè bha iad a' ràdha 'nuair a bha iad.....?

HM: O, 'nuair a bha iad a' roinn nan daoine..... A' fear a fhuair an dòrn mu dheireadh, 's ann aige bha cheud taghadh 's bha e.... Chanadh e, "Buail am port" [Buaileam ort?]. "Ligidh mi leat", chanadh a' fear eile. Agus a' fear aig a robh 'n dòrn mu dheireadh, mar thubhairt mi, bha e a' taghadh a'cheud duine.

Ach co-dhiubh bha na coilleagan air an cur amach, tè air an taobh a deas is tè air an taobh a tuath agus 'se mu dhusan troigh a leud a chuireadh iad unnta. Agus gheibheadh iad spideagan de chlachan, an fheadhainn a bhiodh air an taobh a deas, thall ann am bun Abhainn na Caime, agus an fheadhainn a bh'air a' cheann a tuath, gheibheadh iad a bhos an ceann Daoibhinn, gheibheadh iad clachan ann a sin.

DAM: Agus dè an t-astar a bha eadar an dà cheann?

HM: Cha robh tomhas sònraichte air a chur a mach idir, a Dhòmhnaill Eardsaidh. Cha robh.

DM: Ach dè an t-astar a bhiodh....?

HM: O laochain, bhitheadh tha mi cinndeach suas dh'fhaodte ri dà cheud slat. O tha mi cinnd-... tha mi smaointinn gum bitheadh....Whisper [probably Hugh's brother Angus]: Còrr.

HM: Agus, co-dhiubh, mar a thuirt mi cheana, thòisicheadh an iomain suas, dh'fhaodte, ma mhiadhoin latha agus, och, chumadh iad orra suas gum biodh e trì uairean feasgar, nas lugha na chuireadh a' làn car de mhoill orra no stad. Ach chunna mi iad a' cluich agus gun mhòran is leud trì no ceithir a shlatan aca dhen tràigh: a' mhuir-làn, tha fhios agad, 'nuair a bhiodh e suas mun a' mhuir-lan.

DAM: Is cha robh cus riaghailtean a'dol, tha mi cinndeach?....

HM: O cha robh riaghailtean idir ann, o cha robh riaghailtean ceart aca, gun teagamh sam bith, cha robh.

Agus co-dhiubh, ri mo chuimhne-sa, 'se Latha Nollag, 's latha na Bliadhn' Uire is Latha nan Trì Rìghrean, 'se sin na trì latha tha cuimhn' agam-s' air am biodh daoine a' dol a dh'iomain sios. Ach an ginealach a bha romham, agus ginealaich eile roimhe sin, bha àsan a' tòiseachadh Latha Samhna. Bhiodh latha Samhna aca, Latha Fèill Amharast agus Latha Nollag 's latha Bliadhn' Uire is Latha nan Trì Rìgh. Bhiodh na còig latha aca agus bhon a 'se Latha nan Trì Rìgh a' latha fo dheireadh a bhiodh aca dhen iomain, nan ligeadh a' làn leotha e, bhiodh iad shios gus am biodh an oidhche air tuiteam 's na rionnagan air an adhar mun tigeadh iad dhachaidh, agus bhiodh iad cho sgìth is nach toireadh iad am bainne a spàin 'nuair a thigeadh iad dhachaidh.

DAM: Ach bhiodh iad uaireannan ag òl mus d'rachadh iad ann?

HM: Bhiodh iad ag òl mu rachadh iad ann gun teagamh agus cha b'ann gu math a bhiodh sin air uairean cuideachd.

DAM: Agus 's ann timchioll nan taighean a bhiodh iad, an ann?

HM: O 's ann: o bhiodh iad a' dol mun cuairt chun nan taighean, 's ann, mu rachadh iad a dh'ionnsaigh na tràghad. Gun teagamh, gun teagamh 'sam bith 's dh'fhaodadh nach biodh sin a'cuideachadh ghnothachainean air uaireannan. Bhiodh feadhainn, a reir a' nàdur a bh'aca, bhiodh iad na bu chaise is na.... b'fhasa leotha, dh'fhaodte, aimhreit a dheanamh air thàillibh gu robh iad a'gabhail dhramachan is sin. Chan e gu faca mise mòran aimhreit riamh ann, ach chan e nach biodh a leithid ann gun teagamh rom latha-sa. O bhitheadh.

DAM: Agus co-mheud a dh'dhaodadh a bhith air gach taobh?

HM: O h-uile.... bhathas a' deanamh dà leth orr'.....

O laochain, tha mi cinndeach, tha mi cinndeach gu faca mi suas, dh'fhaodte, còig duine fichead no suas gu deich duine fichead air gach taobh.

DAM: Nis bha sibh a' ràdha rium gu faca sibh aon bhodach ann turus. Dè 'n aois a bha e?

HM: O bha e suas ri.... Mun cheithir fichead agus bha e gun ròine air ach a bhriogais 's a leine. Tha cuimnhn' agam glè mhath air. Bha latha briagha grianach ann gun teagamh. O bha, Gilleasba' mac Iain 'ic Aonghuis. Bha e ceithir fichead bliadhna tha mi cinndeach. Agus a' latha bha seo - Latha Bliadhn Uire, tha cuimhn' agam, glè mhath air an tràigh:....cha robh ròin air ach a bhriogais 's a lèine. Agus tha cuimhn' agam fhathast, 's ann a' cur a nunn gu deas a bha e, a nunn a dh'ionnsaigh na Caimeadh a bha e. Agus bhuail cuid-eigineach am ball thall on taobh thall, agus chunnaig e e tighinn agus sheòl am ball on a' ....a' falbh ro àrd, mu àirde uchd agus sheas e agus chuir e mach uchd agus 's ann mar sin a stad a 'm ball....A, 'n duine bochd, agus tha mi a' smaointinn gun chaochail e 'n ath shamhradh a rithist.

DAM: Agus rachadh aige air beagan ruith a dheanamh?

HM: O rachadh. Dheanadh e beagan ruith agus bha e cheart cho togarach deònach as an iomain ri duin' òg, ri gill' òg... Bha. Agus romh, uel, rom latha-sa co-dhiubh, bhoidh iad a'cuir dhiubh am brògan. Bhiodh iad cas-ruisgte agus a' sneachda 's a' reothadh air an tràigh. Bhitheadh.

DAM: Agus rud eile bha sibh ag innse dhomh mun a' choilleig a bha seo. Niste....'nuair a thigeadh am ball eadar na clachan?......

HM: O bha e 'nuairsin a staigh.

DAM: Is dè theireadh iad ris a sin?...

HM: O se leth-chluich, cha chreid mi, a chanadh iad ris a sin. 'Nuair a rachadh e staigh dà uair se cluich. Bha cluich air an dàrna taobh ma chuir an taobh a bha thall, ma chuir iad dà uair troimh 'n choilleig air an taobh eile, bha cluich orra. Mas e aon uair a chuir iad thromh 'n choilleig i, 'se leth-chluich a bh'ann. Agus 'nuair a rachadh e seachad air taobh..... taobh a deas neo ceàrr na coilleig 's ann tuathal a bha i: chaidh e tuathal, chaidh am ball tuathal. Agus tha fhios agad....

DAM: Ged a rachadh e taobh seach taobh?

HM: Taobh seach taobh, taobh seach taobh: bha e 'n uairsin bha e tuathal agus an fheadhainn a bha 'cur a dh'ionnsaigh na coilleig sin chan fhaodadh iad a dhol na b'fhaide, gun teagamh sam bith, chan fhaodadh iad a dhol na b'fhaide na 'choilleag fhèin. 'Nuair a chaidh am ball seachad 'se 'fear a bha 'glèidheadh na coilleig a bha falbh an uairsin a dh'fhaighinn a' bhuill, ach chan fhaodadh e thoirt air adhart na b'fhaide na choilleag, gun teagamh sam bith.

DAM: Air neo dh'fhaodadh iad a bhith 'na....?

HM: O dh'fhaodadh iad a bhith, dh'fhaodadh iad a bhith na charaibh an uairsin, ach cha toireadh e uair sam bith air n-adhart air a' choilleig i - am ball. Agus glè thric 'se fear a bhiodh math air buille, a bhuaileadh buille math sgoinneil, a bhiodh aca a' glèidheadh na coilleig.

DAM: Is dh'fheuchadh esan an uairsin a'bhuille?

HM: Dh'fheuchadh esan a'bhuille 'n uairsin 's chuireadh e 'm ball a null pìos math an taobh eile. Agus bha iad an uairsin, bha iad as a dheidh a rithist an dà thaobh.

DAM: Agus dè seòrsa buill a bh'aca?

HM: Bha cnuachd de fhreumhach challtuinn.....

DAM: Is ciamar a bha iad a'toir cumadh air?

HM: O bhiodh iad ga shnaidheadh le sgithinn an toiseachd agus an uairsin bhiodh iad ag obair air ga shuathadh 's ga dheanamh mìn le rusp no eighe. Agus chluinninn... rud eile chual mi iad ag ràdhainn, gus a dheanamh na bu ruighne is nach sgoilteadh e as a chèile leis na buillean...ga ghoil ann am poit de dh'uisge air an teine..... Bha. Is thèid mise 'n urras buille dhe na buill ud gu fairicheadh tu i.

DAM: 'S cha robh còmhdach sam bith timchioll air?

HM: Cha robh còmhdach ach a' chnag chruaidh fhiodha, cha robh.

DAM: Agus na camain a niste?

HM: O na camain, gam buain a's a' choillidh. Bhiodh calltuinn is leamhan is darach is seileach is beithe 's a chuile seòrsa deanadh caman. ...Bha 'm beithe na chaman grinn aotram ach bha e uamhasach furasda bhristeadh. Agus bha leamhan, dheanadh e caman grinn (?cuideachd a bhiodh glè?) aotram. Agus gun teagamh an darach, tha fhios gur e caman bu chruaidhe is bu treasa is a b'fhaide a sheasadh dhiubh air fad, ach glè thric bhiodh dèireach ann. Bhiodh dèireach a' dol suas thromh lurg a chamain, dol tromh d'làmhan, leis a' bhall fhiodha, tha fhios agad. Bha bhuille cho cruaidh eadar am ball fiodha agus an caman daraich. Agus sin agad rud a chuala mi iad ag ràdhainn ach cha do dh'fhiosraich mi fhìn riamh e: nan cuireadh tu toll no dha le gimleid chaol thromh lurg a' chamain nach ruigeadh an dèireach thu idir.

DAM: Agus a faca sibh fhèin camain air an tolladh?

HM: Chunnaig uair no dha.

DAM: Agus a robh iad.... a' slisneadh a' chamain no toir cumadh 'sam bith air.....?

HM: O gun teagamh bha, an caman air a shliseadh. Agus, tha fhios agad, bha roinn mhòr dhiubh 'ann air an lùbadh a bha iad - air an cur ann an laghainn. 'S ann, 's ann.

DAM: Seadh, Ciamar a bha iad a' deanamh seo?

HM: Bha, laochain, ga chur a's an teine - an teine mhònadh. Chuireadh tu mu, suas mu throigh.... Dh'fhaodte gur e slat dhìreach a bh'agad, dh'fhaodte mu cheithir troighean no sin de leamhan no de dharach. Gun teagamh gheibheadh tu a' leamhan uaireannan, dh'fhaodte, 's an cromadh nàdurra ann cuideachd. Ach, mar bu trice, chan fhaigheadh tu ach lorg - mar a chanadh iad - lorg dhìreach - dh'fhaodte mu cheithir troighean a dh'fhad is sin. Agus bha thu 'ga chur, an ceann trom dhi gun teagamh, an ceann ìseal, a's an teine..... mu throigh no sin suas bhon cheann ìseal dhi agus a' ghriosach 's na h-èibhleagan mòna mun cuairt da. Ach dh'fheumadh tu 'n aire thoirt nach loisgeadh tu 'fiodh.... Bha 'rùsg gun teagamh 'sam bith a'losgadh air falbh gu math, ach dh'fheumadh tu 'n aire thoirt: bha e glè bhuailteach gun tachradh e gu loisgeadh tu 'fhiodh fhèin. Agus 'nuair a bha thu sin ga chur a's a' laghainn gus a lùbadh, ma loisg thu 'fiodh, sgàineadh a' fiodh, tha fhios agad. Ach an fheadhainn a bha math air na camain a dheanamh is sin,..... bhiodh iad na faireachadh daonnan 's cha leigeadh iad leis a' mhaide losgadh. Agus 'nuair a chuireadh iad a's a' laghainn mar seo e, lùbadh iad e cho bòidheach sa chunna tu riamh. Agus ma bha, nise, 'n teasachadh ceart aige air fhaighinn 'sa' losgadh ..... dh'fhagadh tu, o, dh'fhaodte tri latha no sin a's a' laghainn e 's bheireadh tu as e agus dh'fhuiricheadh a' chumadh sin air.

DAM: Robh thu ga cheangal 'nuair a bha.....?

HM: O bha, bha. O.....dh'fheumadh tu 'cheangal. Cha robh àite no inneal sònraichte aca mar sin mar laghainn ann. Dh'fhaodte nam biodh fàradh no rud dhen t-seòrsa sin agus gun teagamh, tha fhios agad..... tha (?rungaichean) an fhàraidh, tha iad tuilleadh is farsaing bho chèile. Co-dhiubh, nan cuireadh tu pìos de bhòrd eile tarsuinn agus gun deanadh tu cumhang e, dheanadh thu 'n t-àite cumhang dh'fhaodte mu thrì òirlich no mar sin, agus a chur a staigh ann a sin agus a lùbadh agus a cheangal le ròpan, an ceann.... a'leth eile dheth... suas mu mhiadhain, a' lorg a bha seo 's i air a lùbadh agad, dh'fhàgadh tu ann a sin i airson dh'fhaodte trì latha 's bheireadh tu as i, 's bha cumadh cho bòidheach 's sa chunna tu riamh air. Bha e sin, fhios agad, air a shliseadh...air a dheanamh trì-oiseineach.

DAM: Seadh...an ceann ìseal?

HM: An ceann ìseal, an ceann a bh'air a lùbadh.

DAM: Seadh agus dè..... robh ainm 'sam bith ac' air a' cheann a bha sin dhen a' chaman?

HM: Bha, bois a' chamain....a' bhois.

DAM: Agus dè bh'aca air a'.....?

HM: Lurga. 'Se a' lurga 's a' bhois...'se. An caman calltuinn, o mur a faigheadh tu gum biodh a'chumadh nàdurra air ga bhuain, cha robh e uamhasach furasda lùbadh idir. Cha lùbadh e idir cho bòidheach ris an darach 's ris an leamhan. 'Nuair a bhiodh darach is leamhan, fhios agad, air a lùbadh, dheanadh tu cearcall dheth is cha bhrist e.

DAM: Rud eile bha mi dol a dh'fhaighneachd dhuibh : dè cho àrd sa dh'fhaodadh am ball tighinn mus biodh e....? Dè cho àrd 's a thigeadh e 'nuair a bhiodh e cunntais airson... leth-chluichd?

HM: O tha, a Dhòmhnaill Eardsaidh, chan eil mise smaointinn gu robh e cunntas mur a robh e ruith air a' làr....

DAM: Dh'fheumadh e bhith ruith air......chan fhaodadh e bhith an àirde, chan fhaodadh e bhith troigh os cionn.....?

HM: A, uel, dh'fhaodte ged a bhiodh e òirlich no troigh no rud dhen t-seòrsa sin, ach tha fhios agad, fear a bhiodh cho àrd ri d'chruachan no ri d'ghualainn, cha chuala mi riamh iad 'ga chunntas mar goals.

DAM: O, bha rud eile bha sibh a' ràdha: cha robh na gillean òga a' faighinn..... a measg nan daoine eile idir?

HM: O, cha robh, na fir mhòra. Cha robh, cha robh: clann sgoile, gus am biodh tu suas ceithir deug, gus am biodh tu seachad air aois sgoile. Chan fhaigheadh tu measg na fear idir, chan fhaigheadh.

DAM: Agus a robh an uairsin iomain aca-san dhaibh fhèin?

HM: Iomain aca dhaibh fhèin, aig a' chloinn. Bha.....Bhitheadh iad thall eadar dà abhainn Lathaig eadar a' Chaim agus an abhainn thall glè thric, no dh'fhaodte bhos ann an Ceann (?Daoibhinn)....shios aig uamha Cheann

Daoibhinn, tràigh bheag ann a sin. 'S bhiodh iad ann a sin leotha fhèin... a chionn chan fhaigheadh iad buille co-dhiubh ged a.....nam biodh iad a measg an fheadhainn mhòra. Agus a rithist, leis a' bhall fhiodha, gu robh e cunnartach gu faodadh iad a bhith air an dochann. O, bhiodh, bhitheadh, bhitheadh: leis a' bhall agus leis na camain cuideachd. Och, bhitheadh, agus aimhreitean mu dheidhinn.....

DAM: 'S cha robh duine a' riaghladh na cluichd a Dhòmhnaill Eairdsidh. Cha robh. Cha robh.

DAM: Is chan fhaca sibh iomain an deaghaidh, dè thuirt sibh, nineteen......

HM: O tha mi smaointinn gur e twenty five... nineteen twenty five no twenty-six. Tha cuimhneam a bhith shios. Tha mi a'creidsinn gur e nineteen twenty-five fhèin a bh'ann....

DAM: 'S cha robh na gillean fhèin ag obair as a dheaghaidh sin?

HM: O bha feadhainn òga, o bha suas gu fichead bliadhna bha roinn... beagan ann dhiubh sin ach à chan eil fhiosam, cha robh 'n togairt no 'n deònaich aca ga h-ionnsaigh idir. Bha iad car a' tionndadh a-null ri ball-coise, 's ball-cosie shios 'sa latha bh'ann co-dhiubh 's cha deachaidh mòran iomanach a dhèanamh - glè bheag. Chaidh am ball-coise a thoirt air lom 's 's ann air a sin a chuir iad seachad a' latha. Cha robh mise riamh tuilleadh air tràigh as a dheaghainn sin 's chan eil mi a'smaointinn gun robh no duin' eile......

O, chan fhaca mi dithis dhiubh bualadh a chèile riamh rim chuimhne-sa air an tràigh - chan fhaca. Ach thachair e uair is uair rom latha-sa. Ach tha mi cinndeach gu robh na dramachan, math dh'fhaodte, a' dèanamh roinn dhe sin gun teagamh. Is a bharrachd air a sin tha daoin' ann, a Dhòmhnaill Eardsaidh, co-dhiùbh, tha, chan urrainn daibh cluich: chan urrainn, chan fhuiling iad sìon.... mòran a dhol nan aghaidh.... Agus chan e fear-cluich ceart a tha sin idir..... Duine nach fuiling rud a dhol na aghaidh, cho math ri rud a dhol leis, cha bu chòir dha a bhith cluich ann.

DAM: Cha bu chòir. Ach bha a h-uile duine a' cluich co-dhiùbh?

HM: A h-uile duine 'cluich a siod, bha, a h-uile duine cluich a siod.

[Tocher, School of Scottish Studies, No. 36-37, pages 364-378.]

THE BOYS OF THE EILAN

*(A song about Newtonmore's 1929 victory in the Camanachd Cup Final at Spean Bridge
when they defeated Kyles Athletic 5-3.)*

Chorus:

*Sing a song about camans and camanachd play,
And come let us all shout Hip-Hip-Hip-Hooray,
April the sixth was a glorious day,
For the brave Shinty boys of the Eilan.*

*On April the sixth, 1929,
A beautiful day, the weather was fine,
Three thousand spectators, stood round the line,
At Spean to witness the Final.*

*The goalman and backs and centres fought well,
And swift dashing forwards in play did excel,
Great was the cheer that rang through the Dell,
When they won back the Cup from the Kyles men.*

*In the annals of Shinty their name shall remain,
Right bravely they fought on the Lochaber plain,
And brought back the Cup to their own native vale,
Neath the shade of Craigdhu to the Eilan.*

*The gallant MacDonalds played bonnie and pure,
Budge and MacPhersons were steady and sure,
The Rosses and Cattanachs fought hard to secure,
The honour again for the Eilan.*

*Jim Guthrie in goal we will never forget,
For cool and successful he guarded the net,
Each dangerous onslaught with courage he met,
Defending the name of the Eilan.*

*Come now and give three cheers for the grand Committee,
And Hip-Hip-Hooray for the Dame Coig-na-Shee,
Also the trainer, I'm sure you'll agree,
They all did their best for the Eilan.*

One other name we esteem and regard,
Our great Highland sportsman, the Balavil Laird,
Since the days of his youth we have known him to be,
A true friend of the boys of the Eilan.

I will mention another, you know his address,
John MacPherson, the Sports, Inverness,
Beautiful camans he gave to express,
His love for the game and the Eilan.

Another MacPherson who is worthy of praise,
Loyal to Shinty he has been all his days,
With his Pibroch, songs, reels and Strathspeys,
You can hear his sweet lilt on the Eilan.

Captain J.D. MacPherson of Keppoch near Roy,
True to the village a Newtonmore boy,
There is naught in the World that gives him more joy,
Than helping the lads of the Eilan.

From a field so historic and famous of old,
Your grandsires, remember, were warriors bold,
Play up descendants, bred from that fold,
Ye sons of Banchor Eilan.

It's an old Highland pastime, may the game never die,
From the far London Scot, to the Island of Skye,
From the Braes of Lochaber, to where Islanders cry,
Eskma, feasgama agus Eilan.

The cradle of Shinty is Badenoch we know,
Where the game has been played since the Spey first did flow,
When winter appears in its mantle of snow,
It's "Hello are you going to the Eilan?"

Now strike up the music, sing, dance and rejoice,
Let the young and the old use their lungs and their voice,
And give ringing cheers for our own gallant boys,
The Camanachd lads of the Eilan.

ARGUMENTS AND YARNS

No fewer than five playing members of the Inverness shinty club are prisoners of war in Germany. Two of them have been able to send cheerful letters to Mr J.M. Buchan, hon. secretary of the club, telling him of their experiences in camp, and the fact that they have met several other Highland soldiers who were also shinty players. They are, as might be expected, badly off for camans, and ask that a supply might be sent through the Red Cross. Mr Iain MacKinnon, who was one of the leading players in the local team, writes from Stalag IX, C:

"...Since my previous note, our old camp has been split up, as you will observe, by the Kommando No. (51B). Seventeen of our old camp, practically all North country boys, have accompanied me to this, our new abode, and we were fortunate eneough to join another strong Highland contingent here, so that now the shinty arguments and yarns are more pronounced than ever.... The boys want me to ask if it would be possible to get a dozen or so clubs sent direct to our camp through the Red Cross. Being prisoners of war we can't go to the wood for "bherans"".

[Inverness Courier, March 24, 1942.]

Stalag 9C No 1401 shinty team. The camain were, apparently made from beech.

"On the turf, as under the turf, all men are equal"

ALL MEN ARE EQUAL

Yet, has this country any great reason to boast if she manages to produce a bruiser with a thicker skull than a negro's? Or need she pat herself on the back because she raises a race of men whose sole objective is to drive a piece of guttapercha further and straighter than other mortals? Only disastrous results can follow, if such mentality is encouraged. Yet games are of such excellent use not merely as recreation from strain, but also as safety-valves for the mischievous forces in human nature, directing thoughts from unhealthy tendencies and chastening the frame into symmetry and grace—that it would be most unfortunate if a place were not kept in them for people who can never aspire to professional proficiency.

That is the reason why we should rally round such forms of national sport as have not yet bowed the knee to Mammon. One of the outstanding features of Shinty is that throughout its lengthy history it has stoutly resisted anything that savoured, however faintly, of professionalism. Another is that it has always risen superior to class distinction. In Cricket we find "gentlemen" and "players" herded into opposite ends of a pavilion. In Football, Rugby is the code of the "gentlemen," and "Soccer" or "Northern Union" of the professional; golf and tennis are games which are not played below certain strata of society. But on the Shinty-field no social distinctions have ever obtained; from the chief to the lowest clansman each and all have vied in generous contention.

"On the turf as under the turf, all men are equal."

[Ninian MacDonald, Shinty. A Short History, pages 28-29.]

TOSS THINE ANTLERS, CABERFEIDH

Give ear, O Lords and ladies gay,
To this, my humble sporting lay.
A rousing camanachd display
You'll see, when Kyles and Cabers play.
Seventh April is the day,
Inveraray is the way;
Toss thine antlers, Caberfeidh.

Calum MacQueen is referee;
An Edinburgh University Blue is he,
Who knows the game like ABC.
He rules each match with firm decree;
Determined aye fair play to see,
No back-chat will permitted be.
Toss thine antlers, Caberfeidh.

Eight times champions are Kyles,
Against teams of many different styles.
No club on mainland or in Isles
Knows more of shinty's subtle wiles;
Shall Cabers come one-sixty miles
And beat them? Tighnabruaich smiles!
Toss thine antlers, Caberfeidh.

Though Nicolsons at last have gone
(Most worthy father, brother, son)
Donald MacFadyen carries on,
Of all hail-keepers Number One;
The forwards dribble, pass and run,
Then shoot with caman as with gun.
Toss thine antlers, Caberfeidh.
Many a time in days of yore

The final tie saw Newtonmore,
With Doctor Cattanach to the fore
Pile up the hails in mighty score,
Successive triumphs numbering four
E'en Kyles can boast but three, no more.
Toss thine antlers, Caberfeidh.

It seemed that history would re-tell
In 1934 as well,
For Kyles and Oban put their spell,
To sound the reigning champions' knell,
But, on Kingussie's famous Dell,
The pride of Badenoch shinty fell.
Toss thine antlers, Caberfeidh.

Let now Strathpeffer have its say
Their second final tie today;
Four years ago, their skies were grey,
They lost, near Oban's charming bay.
Now may they bask in Sol's bright ray;
Too often Kyles and Newtonmore held sway.
Toss thine antlers, Caberfeidh.

Though Kyles' great talent none ignore,
Mackenzie, Campbell, Cummings, more
Can carry Cabers to the fore,
And, when they hit the winning score,
A thousand yells will skyward soar,
A thousand throats will wildly roar:
"Caberfeidh"

(Eric Ros Birkett)

AN T-EARRACH

Air an raon fhada leathann
An ear-thuath air Port-righ,
Shuas air cùl a'bhaile,
Raon mor iomain na Bòrlainn,
Sgioba Sgoilearan Phort-righ:

Gillean mu shia-diag 's mu sheach-diag,
Iad uile deante is sgairteil,
Cruadalach agus tapaidh,
Sgitheanaich, Ratharsaich, agus fear dhiu
Leòdhasach mòr, socair laidir.

Latha o chionn lethchiad bliadhna,
Latha grianach ciùin,
Gun snaithnean ceòtha air a' Chuilthion
No air claigeann a' Stòir.

Ach an diugh ceò eile
Air raon mòr na Bòrlainn,
Ceò na làthaichean a dh'fhalbh
Ciar thar na h-òigridh a chaill an òige
Is ochdnar dhen dha-dhiag marbh.

Chaill iad uile an òige
S i'n toiseach mar linn eile,
Ach an ceann dà bhliadhna
Borb le cunnartan a'chogaidh,
Le tinneas, leòintean agus bàs,
a shearg flùraichean na h-àbhaist
Ged a thàrr a'mhòr-chuid as.

On the long wide field
North-east of Portree,
Up behind the village,
The big Home Farm shinty field,
The Portree school team:

Boys about sixteen and seventeen,
All well-made and full of vigour,
Hardy and courageous, from Skye and Raasay, and one,
Big, strong and gentle from Lewis.

A day fifty years ago,
A calm sunny day,
Without a thread of mist on the Cuillins
Or on the skull of the Storr.

But today another mist
On the big Home Farm field,
Mist of the days that have gone,
Dim over the youth who have lost their youth,
And eight of the twelve dead.

They all lost their youth,
Which was at first like another generation,
But before two years ended
Barbarous with the dangers of war,
Sickness, wounds and death,
Which withered the flowers of the customary,
Though the majority survived.

Am bliadhna tha buidheann eile
A cheart cho gleusda 'n Sgoil Phort-righ,
A cheart cho calma ris an sgioba
A bha san t-strì air raon na Bòrlainn
Mun do bharc an leth-cheud bliadhna
Air an linn laidir ud de dh'òigridh.

(Somhairle MacGill-Eain)

This year there is another band
Quite as skilled in the School of Portree,
Quite as hardy as the team
That stood on the Home Farm field,
before the fifty years surged
On that strong generation of the young.

Sorley Maclean.
Spring 1937

Edinburgh University 1929-30, Littlejohn Vase winners. Somhairle MacIll-Eain (Sorley Maclean) is seated to the far left, middle row.

KNOCKIE

The South-West wind was softly blowing
The sky above was painted blue
The Highland cattle were gently lowing
The mountains looked a crimson hue

The silver birch its grandeur showing
Whose autumn tints are burnished gold
The mountain streams were swiftly flowing
Loch Knockie lay beneath me rolled

With rugged rocks and valleys green
With heath and birch and heather
No lovlier sight was ever seen
In bright or stormy weather.

Across the slopes of rocky bens
The deer in herds do roam
While deep in mossy shady glens
The stately monarchs make their homes.

The sun was sinking in the West
On Knockie streaked its parting rays
The thrush was singing at its best
"Oh" dreams and memories of sweet days.

(Willie Batchen, 1942.)
Picture by Ken MacPherson

THE CRAFTSMAN'S EYES TWINKLED

"He was an old hand at it, as I could see at a glance from the expert way he handled the slender bit of ash wood, dressing it and then tying the end in a graceful curve. As he straightened up from his task, the craftsman's eyes twinkled and he said, "It's coming along nicely". He produced his pipe, seated himself comfortably on a bench before his white-washed cottage and told me something about the making of a caman - or camain, if you prefer the plural.

He was old and his name known wherever shinty is played as one of the best caman makers in the West Highlands. His clubs are in demand from all the greatest teams and, as he said, he could not possibly hope to meet the demand. In his early days, he had been a famous player , many times leading his team to victory at Oban and Inveraray, at Ballachulish, fort William and Kingussie - all dour, hard fought battles. Afterwards, he turned to making the sticks and to watching and advising succeeding generations of players.

'Throughout the years, his interest in the game deepened, and his dexterity in caman-making increased prodigiously until he was the creator of some of the finest sticks to be seen anywhere in the Highlands, and made some surprisingly lovely show and presentation models.

Artist at Work

Yet, though his clubs were, and are so popular, he never made any money at it. He reckoned by the time he had searched the woods for a suitable tree, taken it home, split it, and put it through all the slow and necessary processes to make a first class caman (the old man would not produce anything else) his earnings worked out at a half-penny an hour.

"But what is money ?", the old man said, "I make camain for the love of them, I have made them all my life." There is the true artist at work, creating an article for the sheer joy of producing something beautiful, something of value.

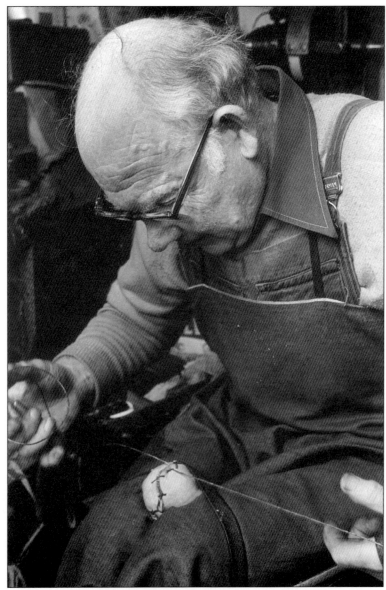

The late labour of love. A. MacKellar, Tighnabruaich, legendary maker of shinty balls.

Now, the majority of shinty clubs are mass-produced, cut out of blocks of wood by a circular saw or other means of necessity, hurriedly dressed and sent out in numbers. Their life is short, they are generally brittle in play and crack up easily, often for no apparent reason. The real caman is different. Carefully made by hand throughout, it is scrupulously and as finely made as a work of art, as indeed it is in its own way. The old man told me that in his estimation the best wood is ash and that is the wood he uses almost invariably. And, the best wood is from a tree growing in a secluded, sunless spot.

Carving the Caman

When a tree is cut it is split into four or six lenghts called 'splits'. Each split is roughly dressed and placed in a deep tin or wooden box to which steam is admitted. After twenty or thirty minutes steaming the splits are pliable and ready to be placed in a frame, and slowly bent at one end.

This bending process is critical for a good deal of the club's appeal depends on the degree of curvature - a stick is judged by its curve and bought accordingly. Some teams like the curve at approximately right angles, some prefer it slightly straighter. As the caman-maker works to order most of the time, he knows to a fraction just the right curve to give.

After the preliminary bending the split is tied with wire in its curved position and allowed to dry. In a few days it is again dressed and retied with wire. The process is repeated as many times as is necessary, each dressing reducing the split nearer and nearer the required thickness. If there is the slightest bend in the shaft or 'cas' it must be steamed over again and straightened out. Again, much depends on proper drying, as if the wood is not thoroughly dried it sometimes happens that a wetting will cause the curve to straighten out. The last prosess is to treat the caman with varnish and bind the top with thin leather or strong tape to give a good grip.

The Finished Article

All shinty clubs must conform to a sertain shape, that is the curved part- or 'bas ' as it is called in Gaelic - must be triangular in shape, both sides sloping inwards to meet the top of the 'bas ' and the bottom flat to meet both of the sloping sides at the bottom edges. No nails or metal of any kind are allowed to be used in the making of the caman, and the edges are slightly rounded to reduce the possibility of an injury to an opponent. The head of the stick must pass through a ring two and a half inches in diameter.

The old caman-maker said different teams favoured different sticks; some teams, such as those whose styles embody long hitting prefer a heavier, broader club than the team that favours short passing movements. He showed me a finished caman. The grain ran from one end through the curve. In inferior sticks, mostly hickory, the grain is often irregular, and frequently splits when the caman gets a hard knock.

When I left the old man he ws preparing to steam splits of ash wood. "Next season," he said, "you'll see these sticks in play in many parts of Argyll and Inverness-shire, and maybe even they'll have a big part in helping to win the Scottish Camanachd Cup - well, now I wouldn't be knowing who the winners will be yet!"

His eyes twinkled and he knew that I knew which team he hoped would carry off the honour."

(The Oban Times, June 15, 1946, by D.S.M.D.)

1948 Edinburgh Highland Games, at Murrayfield stadium. The famous "pots and pans" match between Newtonmore and Ballachulish. No medals for prizes - just pots and pans!

CROSSING THE SEAS AND THE CENTURIES

In 1934, the Camanachd Association and the Gaelic Athletic Association of Ireland went their separate ways. But in 1949, due to the efforts of two University students, two very junior clubs re-established the contact between the two codes of camanachd.

The connection was initially instigated by Iain MacPherson, a medical student from Skye and secretary of the Edinburgh University shinty team. His father had been connected with the previous Scotland teams which had played Ireland hurling teams in 1932 and 1933.

Colm Gallagher was a far-seeing secretary of the Queen's University hurling team and he responded favourably to the overtures for a shinty/hurling match. Finance was the one stumbling block ,but it rarely hindered enthusiastic university shinty teams and it didn't this time.

A loophole in the Queen's University Belfast financial rules provided a bigger grant for a tour than an individual match (to facilitate the University rugby teams), so Glasgow University shinty club was contacted and involved in the first shinty/hurling international tour.

In April 1949, an intrepid band from the Queen's University hurling club set sail for Scotland. They had a copy of the combined rules hammered out in 1933, but amazingly not one of them had seen or handled a shinty caman.

Glasgow University had promised to meet them off the boat. As the boat docked, they were greeted by a kilted Allan Hasson, carrying a briefcase and waving a shinty stick. The first new contact was at the Glasgow University sports ground on a Friday afternoon. No-ne, not even Jack Asher, the well-known referee and a member of that Glasgow team, can remember the score.

Queen's moved on to Edinburgh and played them on the Saturday at their new ground, East Fettes Avenue. The seas had been re-crossed, contact had been established and it led to a whole series of games. Names which still ring a bell, spanning a space of forty years, are Lachie MacPherson, Kenny Campbell, Donald Neil Nicolson and Archie MacDonald of the Edinburgh team and "Lusty" L'Estrange, Gerry Treacy, "Vinco" Kelly and Brendan McKeown of the Queens outfit.

In 1950, Edinburgh repaid the visit to Belfast. Contact was made between the two Associations but both remained seated on their pedestals. But contact between clubs had been made and the steerage of the Belfast-Glasgow boat saw many a young and not-so-young under-graduate caman wielder.

My own first experience of the composite game was on a murky November Saturday of 1951, facing a full-back pair of Archie MacDonald and D.N.Nicholson. *It was quite an experience for a beardless youth!*

Having managed to score a goal, I can still remember the vigour with which the defending camans were swung.

But the social end of things were memorable. I can recall a concert at the Usher hall, a tour of St Giles Cathedral and a late night "hoolie" in a University flat. I think it was Hamish Henderson who enquired of us - after we had sung our heads off - "did we not know any *Irish* songs?"

Edinburgh returned to Belfast in 1952. But the proximity of Finals was starting to take its toll on a very fine University squad. Glasgow University played a very strong University College, Dublin team in the same year. They played Queen's on the return journey home.

The match took place on the Monday afternoon (any excuse to miss a lecture). Allan Hasson gave an exhibition of trying to play and referee simultaneously. I bowed out of University shinty/hurling on a bright April Saturday in 1956.

A fresh team had emerged in both Edinburgh and Belfast. But the log-jam had been broken and the social contacts made. The clubs, and they were very junior clubs at the time, had been revived.

International fixtures were re-established in the 1970s and the under-21 international matches have been played in the 80s and 90s. But the Associations of both countries have not shown *full* commitment. Some of the rules still need to be looked at. Each game could no doubt learn from the other and develop. Furthermore, with the emergence of the Celtic nations, is there not a need for a regular international game which reflects a common heritage?

The University teams have continued to travel and enjoy themselves. But more importantly, the individual clubs on both sides have re-crossed the sea of Moyle. It is surely no accident that most of the Scottish clubs wend their way to Clare - *Clare of the music and the sets!*

The first crossing of the camans I witnessed this year was in early Spring bewteen a combined Scottish Universities and Ulster Universities hurling squad. In typical University fashion, the referee was notified of another venue - five miles away and with the incorrect starting time - an hour earlier!

But once the referee had discovered where and when the match was, the two teams put on a fine display of caman craft.

More importantly, the two teams mixed easily and socially afterwards - a good portent of maybe better things to come at full international level!

I have since been to Fort William to see the Camanachd Cup Semi-Final and then, to cap it all, was at Old Anniesland to see Fort William create their own bit of history, winning the Camanachd Cup for the first time.

[Brendan Harvey, Belfast, 1993.]

Fèis nan Gleann, Antrim: shinny: early 1900s. Fort William shinty club re-introduced shinty when they attended the Fèis in 1994.

GREATS

"Now whenever shinty is played
We who are left can surely relate
We knew and admired a shinty great"

(Tom MacDonald)

John Mackenzie, Newtonmore, in Donald MacKay's award-winning picture.

Newtonmore and Kyles Athletic, great rivals in the sport, marked the re-furbishment of Newtonmore's Eilan in 1979 with a special match. The teams were led out by two of the game's great legends of modern times Jock Paul MacKintosh of Newtonmore (left) and Celly Paterson of Tighnabruaich, himself a bard of some note.

THE OLD GAME

The shinty game is failing
Throughout the Northern Land
Whilst we stand here bewailing
And raise no helping hand.

Let Gaels all stand together,
As steadfast as the Bens,
To see that stick on leather
Keeps echoing in our glens.

At the drying peats I'm sitting
And back from days of yore
Come sounds of crisp, clean hitting,
The cheers, the clever score.

The jousting and the swinging,
The subtle, silken slip
From men, whose way of winning
Despised the hack and trip.

An' the great names I am minding
Flood back from yester year;
The list's too long, I'm finding,
To put them all down here.

From Oban up to Spean,
From Newtonmore to Kyles,
Come stalwarts all worth seein'
Well skilled in shinty wiles.

Strong men from far Lochaber,
All upright, broad and tall;
With strength to toss a caber,
or hit a pitch-length ball.

'PALAEOLITHIC SHINTY PLAYER'
(HOMO CAMANACHDIENSIS)
FOUND IN PEAT BOG IN SKYE.

Fleet-footed men from Furnace,
And Inveraray Town,
Went north to Ballachulish
To throw the gauntlet down.

A challenge that was taken,
In battles fierce to see,
When valiant hearts were shaken
On the famous "Jubilee".

Kingussie, cute an' cunning,
Clever, sharp an' slick ˙
Were always in the running,
Old maestros of the stick.

And cheering on the players,
The Bodachs let it rip,
Wi' no words found in prayers -
- An' "snifters" at their hip.

It wass not there for boozin',
For that was neffer done;
TO COMFORT YOU WHEN LOOSIN'
AND CHEER YOU WHEN YOU WON.

Tho' you seldom had the notion,
You sometimes made so bold,
As to swig an extra potion,
IN CASE YOU GOT THE COLD.

No man of rightful thinking
Would overdo "THE STUFF"
For he might get keen on drinking,
AN' WAN BOTTLE WASS ENOUGH.

No yelling an' no shouting,
No beer-cans on the sward;
Nor "Polis" busy clouting,
- For that we thank the Lord.

Just skill an' manly striving
In shinty's ancient arts,
That kept the old game thriving,
And gladdened Highland hearts.

All storms the Game will weather,
Both strong an' proud will stand,
If brave we fight together
Throughout this Bonnie Land.

To keep our shinty living,
With hand an' heart engage;
START WORKING AND START GIVING
TO SAVE OUR HERITAGE!

[Angus MacIntyre, Shinty Yearbook, 1971.]

RABBIE'S TRIP AROUND THE SHINTY COUNTRY
- ACCOMPANIED BY 'A LAD FRAE THE KYLE'

Last night I dreamed a pleasant dream - it thrilled me to the core,
I dreamed our National Bard had come again tae Scotia' shore,
I rubbed my eyes of sleepiness then sat upright in bed
and shouted out "Guid grief, it's Rab but lang syne ye've been dead".
But Rabbie sang in cheerful voice "Ah've just a quick trip hame
And ah've always been enraptured wi' oor grand old Highland game.

Noo, in ma day ah held the ploo amang the fields o' Ayr,
I was always keen on shinty but I'm oot o' touch yince mair,
So I've come doon frae up abune tae ask some help frae you,
Tae tak' me roon ye'r Hielan folks and introduce a few
Oor transport will be Tam's mare Meg, oor track lies up the West
So just climb up ahint me and forget the "breathing test".

"oor grand old Highland game"   Chris

I really felt quite honoured as we rode on thro' the night,
The COL-GLEN team were training at the Clachan by flood light,
And near the Creggans at Strachur Rab says "noo, who's tae blame -
There's the "Manager" and "Mister Niall" still struggling tae get hame"
But as I explained tae Rabbie shinty training's no sae silly,
Especially up at "Louis" - coached by Donald and wee Billy.

I wondered as we galloped on the road going round Loch Fyne
Aboot the INVERARAY welcome Burns received in lang lang syne
His "Hielan' pride and hunger" scrawl aboot the Ducal Town,
I telt him things are different noo - Argyll won't raise a frown.
The folks have a "Blythe-spirit" noo - MacKay aye keeps the heid,
Hamish Stewart he has used the "loaf" - Milanda's shinty "breed".

Whilst climbing up t'wards Claddich Hill poor Meg was getting slow.
We rested by the monument tae that weel kent Neil Munro.
Then heading thro' Lochawe side - to the right stands Donnchadh Bàn
We come into Dalmally where they're working on a plan,
GLENORCHY play on Market Field - Jack Kennedy keeps on raving
Tommy Gibson's taking monkey gland and MacDougall's started shaving.

Thro' the lovely Pass of Brander, doon the Bonnie Corran Brae,
We reached a shinty strong-hold there by bonnie Oban Bay.
There's CAMANACHD in red and black, the CELTIC white and green
And Cooper says "Ye'll squeeze an orange - but LORNE are tangerine!
Jock Douglas says "this is the law", Duncan Cameron says "Don't try"
But Slater says "you can't decide 'till you consult G.Y."

I introduced oor Rabbie tae some men who'd made their mark -
Some stalwarts who with caman skill had graced old Mossfield Park -
Turnbull, Currie, MacIntyre, Millar, Dougie, Mick,
MacInnes, Watt, MacCallum - hardy handlers of the stick.
Says Rab I met nae lasses here wi' a' this shinty whirl,
I says "ye widna stand a chance wi Larry and Lachie Birrell".

Then back we went tae Connel Bridge and cantered o'er free,
Next stop was BALLACHULISH and that spot - the Jubilee.
Relived memories of some battles wi' the lads who worked the slate -
The hardy boys in red and blue were very hard tae bate,
McLachlan, Dalston, Donnie Rose, as hard as their ain quarry,
Carmichael, Hugh Buchanan, and that hard man Seedy Lawrie.

The ferry's off - the Brig's no built - oor Meg could care no less,
She sprouted wings and wi' mighty leap came doon in INVERNESS.
Then galloped on up tae the FORT and MacMillan heard oor wrath,
We didn't see a shinty match but had tae tak' a bath
He says we play at Claggan noo - oor Council did the planning
Oor civic heads are a' the big shots - oor Provost is a "Canon".

Then we headed tae KILMALLIE land tae Corpach, Banavie,
And there I introduced the Bard tae oor Chief - Walter P. -
Resplendent in his Cameron kilt he's loast a lot o' weight,
His interest in Scout movement noo is surely oot a' date.
The youngsters there within his care with caman skill afire
Teenagers Derek, Fatty and the "babe" - Shep MacIntyre.

Then on we went right thro' the night and Meg wis fairly fleein,
We waved tae Donald Kennedy as we approached the SPEAN.
Tae Fort Augustus, Invergarry where oor game's been on the wane
But I think there'll be a revival here after that summer game.
We cantered o'er the hill tae Cluanie on twisted roads sae narrow
And reached the home o' KINLOCHSHIEL - a nice place Balmacara.

A late licence there in Kintail Lodge we had a dram or two,
And there I met a Fraser - a wee full back - Ian Dubh.
He said "The team's been scoring goals for that we have a "Grant",
My son is with me in the team so what more could I want.
The shinty talent's glistening right along the Ross-shire roads.
Success just breeds encouragement, well, just ask Albert Loades!

Noo time wis scarce - we left oor freens and galloped on tae Kyle,
We caught the ferry o'er tae SKYE tae blether for a while,
The shinty scene is "Taylor-made" and Hume still has his fling,
While Col. Jock MacDonald says "In Skye I'm still the King".
But in this age of Aquarius emerges one new star -
The MacDonald clan has gifted Skye a fella called D.R.

It's back tae Kyle and up the coast tae country side sae barren,
Fae Kishorn and Drumbuie tae that stronghold called LOCHCARRON,
It's there we met the Doctor - he wis fairly in a frenzy.
He wis trying tae transplant the heid of Calum of Mackenzie,
While in MacLennan's butcher's shop the folks had caused a rammy,
For Tex had sawed a sheep's heid all bedecked wi' Calum's tammy.

Now on we rode thro' the night tae Strathpeffer on the way,
At Castle Leod the call wis "Toss thine antlers CABERFEIDH".
MacMaster says the "Skye Blues" were the best you've ever seen.
By the time we got to BEAULY, Campbell says the colour's green,
For Dingwall rocks and LOVAT rocks we treat them with disdain
The only rocks that interest us, is Ronnie "Rox" MacLean.

And right on to Kiltarlity we went right to Balgate,
When Colin spied oor old freen Rab he says "ye've met yer fate",
There's Murdo here a mainstay up in Glen Affric Hotel,
Johnnie Gordon, Tommy Fraser noo are doing really well.
But this Womens' liberation noo are working oot a plan -
The Lovat team is now controlled - by one called Mary Anne.

Frae there it's up to Kerrow Brae, where Meg just proved her class,
Where Jimmac showed his colours of the Glen up at STRATHGLASS,
And over tae GLEN URQUHART Danny Shewglie's daein swell.
He has tae keep a Dolly bird, as well as Alan Bell.
For Jan and Alan's come frae Islay - they're in the SNP scene
They've even chased the "English" man a' the way tae Aberdeen.

Away doon there along Loch Ness tae the Bught Park sae weel kent,
We met up wi' MacPherson and MacKenzie - President,
Noo Willie's back in training noo since he gave up at the school
But Tommy's noo back on the rails - he's got tae work tae rule
And Duncan's taken o'er the team - it does nae gie them solace.
He's handcuffed them tae their shinty sticks - the Manager frae the Polis.

So back we rode thro' East Loch Ness - oor mare wid take some catchin,
Until we came tae Foyers toon and fell in wi' Willie Batchen,
This lad wha runs the shinty scene thro Highland climes sae braw
He's got tae watch BOLESKINE and the ither teams and a'.
Then back we rode tae Inverness and went tae the A9.
Tae this new team o'er at KINCRAIG - Donnie Ross is lookin' fine.

And then on towards KINGUSSIE where the shinty's going swell.
MacGregor had his gathering wi' the stalwarts o' the Dell,
Jimmie Murchie's noo stopped poachin' while "Rossie" had a transplant,
Kingussie noo have changed a "fuse" and Donnie's had a Grant.
But Rab says tae me "the red and blue will surely make their mark -
But I fancy their wee Secretary - Mrs Gillian Clark".

We rode on tae the Eilan tae that stronghold NEWTONMORE
We met Ally and Gaby Fraser - blue and white men tae the core.
Jack Richmond's shinty Forum, Johnnie Campbell, Kenny Smith,
Fraser, Stewart, Ralph, MacKenzie - those names are no a myth,
But I said tae Rab "here meet Jock Paul" - they had a right good blether -
Sae weel they might because we know they started the game the gether.

So o'er the Lecht we cantered thro' the countryside sae green,
Twa teams support the shinty in the toon o' Aiberdeen,
There are Englishmen and Irishmen competing for their "blues",
Even Lewismen and Sgiathanachs and Australian "Kangaroos",
A conglomerate of nations ye could ca' it a real "Hotch Potch" -
Why even Peter English has tae prove that he is Scotch.

Then we headed for ST ANDREWS tae oor exiled Heilan folks,
We were asked tae form a six-a-side by thet "Sassenach" Gerry Stokes.
Then on we went to TAYFORTH thro' country road and lane,
Tae meet up wi' that Irishman - the charming Hugh O'Kane.
And we'd have made "Auld Reekie" tae meet up wi' the creeds,
Or even tae Northallerton - but Richard Tulloch wis in Leeds.

So back we rode tae Glasgow and oor Meg fair galloped on,
It wis there we met MacInnes, Donald Skinner, Iain Cameron,
All the boys frae Glesca Uni' and the Polis Force and a'
Jack Asher even took oor names while Lachie gied a "Blaw".
There wis Beaton, Bobby Nicolson, I says "Trouble is afoot"
So with Harvey Smith salutation, we steered oor steed tae BUTE.

While on the Isle oor Rabbie says tae me, "this is nae braggin,
I couldnae noo contest the skill o' that yin Escacraggan".
John MacDonald, Jimmy Duncan and Jock Hunter - they mean Bute.
Why then even Billy Crawford has come on as substitute.
It's grand tae see oor grand old game being fostered in the Isles.
But time was really precious as we headed for the KYLES.

So it's back tae Tighnabruaich - that place I hold so dear.
I showed tae Rab the Scottish Cup that we had won last year.
We have wee Tam and Chic Jamieson and big Barney for the fray,
But noo we have the Vice Chief of the Caman - D. MacRae.
Rab says tae me "I've heard yer talk aboot yer caman wiles,
But after a' I've seen the night, I've got tae think on Kyles".

Noo after all oor travels right thro' Scotland thro' the night
I awakened in the morning in a really sorry plight,
My body pained with saddle sores - I couldnae shake a leg,
Tae think that I'd toured Scotland on the back of oor mare Meg!
The wife just shook me in the bed and said "that's Burns away".
And I realised I'd got tae rise and start another day.

THE CANINE INTRUSION THAT
CAUSED SUCH CONFUSION

Tune: Dancing in Kyle

This tale 's no invention, well it's no ma intention,
Tae project such a queer shinty game.
Oban Camanachd were riled, claimed the match had been spoiled,
And an innocent dog was to blame.

Fur it caused a sensation, a great big Alsatian,
Thought poultry had strayed off the park.
The handsome big 'cur' wis supporting Strachur,
Sunk his fangs into poor "Chookie" Clark.

Chookie let oot a howl as he yelled fur a foul,
As he hopped roond aboot like a frog.
While big shepherd Ernie shouts "surely that learns ye,
Tae watch oot fur 'One man and his Dog'."

Now the Camanachd story is covered in glory,
But thae recent events caused a blow.
G.Y.'s shinty views have been making the news,
Doon at Crufts famous old doggy show.

Then the referee 'Teak' says, "it fair makes me "seeck",
And tae book a poor dug makes nae sense,
Ah'll control any temper but nae way distemper,
Fur the Rule Book omits this offence."

Much thought has gone into the Future of Shinty,
Jack Richmond's been working like hell,
Noo this canine intrusion will cause mair confusion,
Will he consult Barbara Woodhouse as well?

Be it dogs, be it bitches, poor Chookie's in stitches,
A protest has been made, so they say.
We will just wait and see if it makes real history,
With a judgement on "Dirty dogs play".

Thae adverts on TV will a' change noo ye'll see,
Tho' each firm say their's cannot be beat.
Keep yer Pal, Bonus, Chum, Oor dog prefers "Bum",
That's a new brand called "Chookie's dog meat."

(by I.M.A. Collie, The Kennels, Barking.)
[1982 Shinty Yearbook, page 69.]

The canine intrusion   _Chris_

HOME TO THE KYLES

Will you come along with me to that haven by the sea?
Where we wandered hand in hand in days gone by.
When the summer days are here and the skies are truly clear
We'll go back to Tighnabruaich you and I.

To that place out in the west where my thoughts aye come to rest.
There's a grandeur here throughout the countryside.
Though I've travelled everywhere there's no place that can compare
With that sleepy village nestling on the Clyde.

Feast your eyes on beauties rare, free for all the world to share.
See the Kyles of Bute 'neath skies of azure blue,
Whilst the blackbird in the trees sings its haunting melodies.
How I wish that I could sing such love songs just for you.

Take the high road from Dunoon on some sunny afternoon.
At the crest the view brings life to weary eyes.
Where the islets dot the seas and the yachts glide with the breeze
Through the narrows to that sailors' paradise.

With a welcome warm and true from the good friends that we knew
In contentment we'll face life with happy smiles.
Hear the lapping of the tide by the Bonny Firth of Clyde
In our home among the hills above the Kyles.

(Celly Paterson)

Kyles Athletic, who, along with Newtonmore, dominated shinty in the 1970s.

AN T-EILEAN: THE ISLAND

Thug thu dhomh an cuibheas luachmhor	*You gave me the valuable enough*
agus beagan mheanmnachd bhuadhan,	*and some mettlesome talent,*
spàirn, cunnart agus aighear suilbhir	*struggle, danger and pleasant high spirits*
air mullaichean garbh'a' Chuilithinn,	*on the rugged tops of the Cuillin,*
agus fodham eilean leugach,	*and under me a jewel-like island,*
gaol mo chuideachd, mire 'n lèirsinn,	*love of my people, delight of their eyes;*
an seachdnar is càch am Port-righ	*the Seven and the rest in Portree,*
iomairt spioraid 's eanchainn; strì	*exercise of brain and spirit, strife*
chaman Sgitheanach air budha na h-aibhne,	*of Skye camans on the river bught,*
mire chatha, comunn aoibhneach;	*battle-joy, joyous company*
is oidhcheannan an Aodainn-Bhàin,	*and the nights of Edinbane,*
bòidhchead, òl, is annas bhàrd,	*beauty, drink and poets' novelties,*
geurad, èisgeachd, èibhneas làn,	*wit, satire, delight in full,*
an aigne Sgitheanach aig a bàrr;	*the Skye spirit at its height;*
is oidhcheannan air ruighe Lìondail,	*and nights on the slope of Lyndale,*
an t-Eilean mòr 's a mheallan lìontach	*the great Island with its many hills*
'nan laighe sìthe anns a' chiaradh,	*lying in peace in the twilight,*
glaisneulach gu bristeadh iarmailt.	*grey-faced till the breaking of the sky.*
O Eilein mhòir, Eilein mo ghaoil,	*O great Island, Island of my love,*
is iomadh oidhche dhiubh a shaoil	*many a night of them I fancied*
liom an cuan mòr fhèin bhith	*the great ocean itself restless*
luasgan le do ghaol-sa air a bhuaireadh	*agitated with love of you*
is tu 'nad laighe air an fhairge,	*as you lay on the sea,*
eòin mhòir sgiamhaich na h-Albann,	*great beautiful bird of Scotland,*
do sgiathan àlainn air an lùbadh	*your supremely beautiful wings bent*
mu Loch Bhràcadail ioma-chùilteach,	*about many-nooked Loch Bracadale,*
do sgiathan bòidheach ri muir sleuchdte	*your beautiful wings prostrate on the sea*
bho 'n Eist Fhiadhaich gu Aird Shléite,	*from the Wild Stallion to the Aird of Sleat,*
do sgiathan aoibhneach air an sgaoileadh	*your joyous wings spread*
mu Loch Shnigheasort 's mu 'n t-saoghal!	*about Loch Snizort and the world.*

O Eilein mhòir, m' eilein, mo chiall,
's iomadh oidhche shìn mi riamh
ri do thaobh-sa anns an t-suain ud
is ceò na camhanaich 'gad shuaineadh!
Is gràdhach liom gach bileag fraoich ort
bho Rudha Hùnais gu Loch Shlaopain,
agus gach bileag roid dhomh càirdeach
o Sh ròin Bhiornaill gus a' Ghàrsbheinn,
gach lochan, sruth is abhainn aoibhneach
o Ròmasdal gu Bràigh Aoineart,
agus ged a nochdainn Pàrras
dè b' fhiach a ghealach-san gun Bhlàbheinn?

Eilein Mhòir, Eilein mo dheòin,
Eilein mo chridhe is mo leòin,
chan eil dùil gum faicear pàighte
strì is allaban a' Bhràighe,
is chan eil cinnt gum faicear fiachan
Martarach Ghleann-Dal 's iad dìolte;
chan eil dòchas ri do bhailtean
èirigh àrd le gàire 's aiteas,
's chan eil fiughair ri do dhaoine
's Aimeireaga 'a an Fhraing 'gam faotainn.

Mairg an t-sùil a chì air fairge
ian mór marbh na h-Albann.

O great Island, my Island, my love
many a night I lay stretched
by your side in that slumber
when the mist of twilight swathed you.
My love every leaflet of heather on you
from Rudha Hunish to Loch Slapin,
and every leaflet of bog-myrtle
from Stron Bhiornaill to the Garsven,
every tarn, stream and burn a joy
from Romisdale to Brae Eynort,
and even if I came in sight of Paradise,
what price its moon without Blaven?

Great Island, Island of my desire,
Island of my heart and wound,
it is not likely that the strife
and suffering of Braes will be seen requited
and it is not certain that the debts
of the Glendale Martyr will be seen made good;
there is no hope of your townships
rising high with gladness and laughter,
and your men are not expected
when America and France take them

Pity the eye that sees on the ocean
the great dead bird of Scotland.

[Somhairle MacGill-Eain, O Choille gu Bearradh, 1989, pages 56-59.]

Skye Camanachd, Camanachd cup winners, 1990.

PRIDE OF THE SUMMER

I still hear the snares in the square
Colours ablaze in the evening
The air was still
Down the stormy hill
It's good to be young and daring.

I still see the blood on the knees
The camans swing without warning
The lads in white
At the speed of light
It's good to be young and daring.

Across the bay I still hear the strains
The two-step loud and blare-ing
We walked hand in hand
To the accordion band
It's good to be young and daring.

She was the pride of my summer that year
She was my sweetheart, my lady
We walked the black rock
And we stopped by the loch
It's good to be young and daring.

Beat the drum
Beat the drum
Like a heartbeat
Lonely and strong
Beat the drum.

Words by Calum and Rory MacDonald.
Courtesy of Runrig, The Cutter and the Clan

SCOTS PIP IRELAND
IRELAND 3 SCOTLAND 5

Kevin Cashman from Inverness

We heard the skirl of the pipes playing the 51st Highland Division as we approached Bught Park, Inverness, yesterday, and a Cork accent was heard to declaim, "we've no problem here, lads. 'Tis like playing them in Thurles".

He was better than right, for the sod is even more magnificent than that of Semple Stadium. And, if another stadium somewhere in the world has a more awesomely beautiful setting, I want to see it before I die.

The decision to play these internationals at U-21 level has proven well advised, giving us very satisfying contests in the past two years. This year, with the Isle of Skye having won the Camanachd Cup for the first time in the century of the Association in front of a record attendance, the Scots seemed more bouyant than they did here two years ago.

They started in precisely that mood, with Victor Smith punishing slack Irish defence with a goal inside 30 seconds.

Some terrific striking by Scotland paid off with a second goal by Ronald Ross, after a 90 yard free stroke off the ground by Alex McNicholls, when an Irish player was penalised for kicking the sliotar.

The teams lined up 14 a side: 3 at midfield, 2 full backs and 2 full forwards; otherwise as in hurling. The Irish did not respond to the "no handling" rule with the same skill and invention as they did 2 years ago. But, to be fair, the same level of preparatory work was not possible this time.

Adrian Craig, Brian Greene, Pat O'Grady and David Quirke all had shots saved or narrowly wide before a Ross Rocket from 25 yards gave Scotland their third. This caused Mick Kinsella, Ireland's coach, to switch David Quirke onto Ross with Mike Houlihan going to centre forward.

Sloppy Scottish defence allowed Sean Hughes of Armagh in for a smart goal from a narrow angle. But, similarly poor work allowed Ross in for his hat trick and Scotland's fourth, and thus it stood at half time.

The soft summer breeze freshened, and favoured Ireland in the second half. Quirke scored a direct from a 70 in the 3rd minute, but this is not allowed under the agreed rules. Houlihan bussed an open goal seconds later. And, to compound that, Ross was allowed to saunter in for Scotland's fifth almost immediately.

Ray Quigley got one back. Pat O'Grady and Damien Curley were playing at their peak and creating some clever moves at this stage, but Scotland's covering was superb. A magnificent shot by Brian McGovern from 45 yards, just under the 10 foor high cross bar, rallied the Irish and the pressure became relentless. Hughes and Adrian Craig went close with scorching shots, but, by now, with the final whistle only minutes away, Scotland's defence was growing by the second in courage and confidence.

And their breakaways were always well conceived and dangerous, and Alan Smyth from Meath was twice called ionto heroic action.

The final whistle gave Scotland a victory that might have been a goal or two greater, but, more importantly, this game was a splendid boost to a beautiful series.

Scotland: A. Borthwick, A. Robertson, A. McKechnie, E. McKinnon, J. Kirk, A. Morrison, A. Patterson, A. McNicholls, J. Clark, M. Clark, I. McDonald, V. Smith, R. Ross, and A. Borthwick. Subs.: G. Hendry, for J. Clark, E. Crawford for I. McDonald.

Ireland: A. Smyth, D. O'Neill, D. Irwin, D. Ivers, M. Houlihan, B. Whyte, D. Curley, B. McGovern, N. Delaney, B. Greene, D. Quirke, S. Hughes, A. Craig, P. O'Grady. Subs.: R. Quigley for B. Greene, R. Cuillinane for N. Delaney and S. Cross for D. O'Neill.

Referee : B. Watts

[Sunday Tribune, July 22, 1990.]

"We learned one or two tricks over there".

Chris

THE DALLAS COWBOYS

What do three men from shinty country and another from a town famous for its bridies have in common?

The answer is a passionate interest in American football - the real thing, that is, NFL-style - and all four became TV stars as a result. The Channel 4 Blitz programme featured the fearless four on a 4,000 mile car trip across the United States.

Brothers Willie and Gary Dallas, Kingussie shinty aces of the 1980s, George West, Bank of Scotland manager at Newtonmore, and a banking colleague David Taylor, from Forfar, flew from Glasgow to San Francisco on December 3rd, 1994.

Dressed in merchandise featuring Scottish Claymores - the Edinburgh-based pro grid iron team who play at Murrayfield - the gang of four watched five NFL games in a span of eight days - San Francisco v Atlanta (December 4), San Deigo v LA Raiders (December 5), Dallas v Cleveland (December 10), Atlanta v New Orleans (December 11), and Miami v Kansas City (December 12).

Their adventures included:

* Wrecking a hired car, a Buick Le Sabre, in a collision with a pick-up truck near San Diego.

* Driving 870 miles non-stop and overnight in a second hired car, another Buick Le Sabre, from Dallas in Texas to Atlanta, Georgia.

* Watching the Atlanta v New Orleans game from a luxury executive sky box in the Georgia Dome as guests of the Blitz programme staff.

They made a home video of the journey which was shown on the Blitz programme.

"We all enjoy watching American football and it was George the bank manager who told us we could all afford to make the trip," said Willie, last night.

"The whole escapade cost us about £1,000 each, which wasn't bad at all. It was a trip of a lifetime. We followed the famous Route 66 for a spell and packed a lot into the eight or nine days.

"We went to see the grand Canyon in Arizona, went over the border into Mexico and we spent one night in an old Wild West town called Williams and had a drink with a Navajo Indian there."

Would we do it again ?

"Yes, but now that I've done it once I would fly between the stops in America," said Willie.

[Shinty Yearbook, 1994-95, page 5.]

"some scepticism."

THE MONARCHS OF THE GLEN

Shinty's image as the complete macho sport of the Gael, played by hairy-legged Highlanders could be in for its stiffest examination yet, with the clash of the ash apparently causing confusion amongst the Monarchs of the Glen.

October is the rutting season and the sound of shinty players crossing camans, not to mention hitting each other, is apparently arousing more than a passing interest in Highland Glens. And the stags themselves are now becoming something of a tourist attraction far and wide with bus parties being organised to view them in all their glory.

And now a BBC film crew is standing by to try and capture the sexually challenged stags who are apparently being attracted down to pitches when matches are taking place.

Plymouth based television producer Andrew Coupar, fresh from a safari to Kenya, is the man desperately looking for a shinty field in close proximity to bellowing stags. He said: "As part of the research for a nature documentary Natural World, to be broadcast on BBC 2 next year, we are examining the relationship between people and wildlife. It is an intriguing connection to think that the stags can be attracted by the sounds of camans clashing and if we can find a venue where they are near at hand, we will do our best to get a film crew up to the Highlands to capture the action. The big problem we have is that there is just about a fortnight of the rutting season left and we need to find a venue as soon as possible. I have a film crew standing by."

The connection between the Highlanders' ancient and noble game and the Monarch of the Glen immortalised by Landseer in his painting and tourists' tea towels far and wide, is treated with some scepticism by the shinty fraternity. Kingussie's Dave Thomson, one of the game's finest sons and a gamekeeper on the Clune Estate in Tomatin Glen, described the suggestion as "weird but plausible".

Scottish Natural Heritage area manager Dick Balharry of Newtonmore, whose son David plays in defence for the local side said he felt the link between camans and the stags was "somewhat tenuous", but could no doubt be achieved by staging a match near to an area where the stags are currently in full cry.

The stags themselves are meanwhile becoming something of a tourist attraction with Forest Enterprise offices in Argyll organising tourist trips to view them in action. A series of bus trips organised to Ardgarten near Arrochar this past month has met with heavy demand and a two-hour long walk is planned this coming Wednesday into Corriebhiocair near Dalmally in Argyll. Spokesman John Spittal said: "These trips have become increasingly popular, particularly in view of the fantastic weather we are having. We send the parties into the glen, in and out of the pine forest with a Ranger and they get a magnificent view of the stags above them in full flight."

Shinty players though appear less than enamoured at the prospect of a stag charging down the side of the mountain in a fiery frenzy. One, who didn't want to be named for understandable reasons, could see some attractions though. He said: "The way our defence is playing at the moment we would probably stick a jersey on it and play it at half-back."

There is no truth in the rumour that shinty's ruling body, the Camanachd Association, is prepared to designate matches which are subject to invasion by rutting stags as "twelve-pointers". There is an added commercial advantage to all this. Newtonmore-based liqueur producers Meikles of Scotland are standing by with a possible sponsorship opportunity in connection with their appropriately named Stag's Breath.

[The Herald, October 13, 1994.]

YOUNG LOTHARIOS!

An epic bus journey to Glasgow, followed by a short flight saw Skye's shinty ambassadors step of the plane at Dublin Airport into a throng of Irish football fans. Ireland had just qualified for the second round of the World Cup and the airport was filled with those returning and some making their way out for the second round. Although obviously impressed with our kilts and Peter Beaton piping, the reason for our visit seemed unimportant to the Irish as long as we enjoyed ourselves. Burdened with this onerous task we set out to fulfil their wishes with the wise old heads and young Lotharios setting out to see the sites and sounds of Dublin. "Seventeen pints of Guinness please." It is with justifiable reason that the Irish have a reputation for their hospitality and friendliness, even the police ask if you're enjoying yourself. It is also worthy of note that it was during our first night in Dublin that we were joined by the great Irish songwriter and raconteur, Finbar Grant. Looking remarkably like our own Yogi, Finbar decided to join our tour for the duration. Being mainly a night person he added much to our social events after Yogi had gone to bed. Funny thing was, you never saw them together.

"Wise old heads and young letharios"

Friday morning dawned amid a flood of ice cream and Lucozade but morale was high as we stepped on board our bus. Destination, NEWRY, Northern Ireland. This was our first encounter with Tom the bus driver, who was to chauffeur us around night and day until our return to Dublin on Sunday. His dedication to this task was indeed impressive and nothing was too much trouble. He was so laid back it's a wonder he didn't fall over.

Skye Camanachd had been invited by Newry and Mourne District Council to take part in a three cornered tournament to celebrate the 850th anniversary of Newry Abbey. The other two teams were Newry Olympic Hockey Club and Newry Shamrocks Hurling Club.

Our first game was on Friday evening against the hockey club at their new £300,000 complex, comprising a clubhouse and artificial pitch. These facilities gave us an immediate insight to the strength of the club, and this was to be demonstrated on the field. Playing to compromise rules both teams settled in quickly but we had discovered too late that special footwear was required on the heavily sanded surface. An entertaining first half saw the teams turn round with the score even at 3 - 3. This however was the turning point with both teams swapping sticks. The Skye team did not adjust to the shorter hockey stick while the hockey players, using a shorter grip, relished the relative freedom of the caman. The final whistle saw the score 6 - 3 in Newry's favour.

After the match it was back to the task of enjoying ourselves with barbecued steaks and more "black stuff". Speeches were made and songs were sung but the highlight of the night was the first appearance of the John Finlayson Highland Dancing Formation Team. Believe me they were impressive !

Saturday morning at the Downshire Arms Hotel, Hilltown and it looks like the flight from Glasgow to Dublin has finally taken its toll: we've all got JET LAG. It is not a pleasant experience and I won't bore you with the details but in brief it is very similar to a hangover. However, we repair to breakfast and having eaten 50% of the meat and dairy produce of County Down were collected by Tom and his bus for a tour of Mourne. Pam, from the District Council acts as tour guide for the day and gives us constant information and anecdotes about all the places we couldn't see for the sea mist. We then stopped at Warren Point for lunch where again the Irish did us proud. They did however try to tempt us with some wine but our steely resolve saw us through this frightening moment and we swore to maintain our abstinence till after the hurley match. So having eaten half a bullock and a bag of potatoes each we returned to our hotel to contemplate the game that evening.

Newry Shamrocks play at the impressive Pairc an Iuir, a huge green sward with surrounding terracing and stand. The social club attached boasts a playing membership of 500. These take part in hurling, Gaelic football and athletics.

The hurlers, having already beaten the hockey club, were obviously looking forward to the challenge and certainly showed no reservations or nerves prior to the game. The Skye changing room however were only too aware that this game counted for most. Anyone from Skye watching this game could only have been proud of the way their team performed as they dominated the early exchanges giving the hurlers little of the play. Within twenty minutes Skye were two goals ahead, both scored, with casual ease, by Ali "Digg" MacDonald. By this time the hurlers were rattled and early banter turned to cries of exasperation from the sidelines. In the closing minutes Slippy Finlayson cut loose down the right wing and sent number three passed the Newry keeper, and that was the score at half-time.

The restart showed new aggression from the Shamrocks, who were about as happy as turkeys opening the last window of their advent calendar. They had found at half-time the conviction to conquer their early fear of the Skye camans. These had caused some apprehension in their first half especially in the hands of Murdo Morrison, Ewen MacKinnon and Donji MacLeod who in particular was having a superb game in the midfield. Newry then scored, with more than a hint of off-side, but the goal judge later admitted that he had closed both eyes "Just to make the game more interesting." Such is the charm of the Irish that we actually believed him, all except the aggrieved Donny Martin. Newry then scored again to draw even closer until a brilliant score from John MacRae. A neat through ball from Robbie Gordon saw John alone in front of goal. He cunningly lured the goalkeeper off his line, dummied his shot three times before dropping to his knees and scooping the ball over the advancing keeper. All the north goalies would do well to take note, we may well see this move again! With the score finishing at 4 - 2 a jubilant Skye team had shown their hosts a terrific display of shinty.

Retiring then to the clubhouse we resigned ourselves to more of this "enjoying ourselves" lark. Donnie Martin gave half a dozen speeches in English and broken-Gaelic, Slippy's dance troupe again showed their style, Stuart Jackson's version of the Galway Shawl had the rafters ringing and Murdo Morrison won the worst singer contest. Newry Shamrocks showed us the same courtesy and hospitality as everyone before them, and the band played until they could play no more.

Sunday morning and the frightening realisation that you can get jet lag twice from the one short flight. Acres of dead meat and eggs for breakfast and then back to pack our bags. It was very gratifying to see so many people turn up for our departure to Dublin. The hurley and hockey clubs were well represented as was the District Council, all now firm friends genuinely sad to see us go; the feeling was mutual. The hospitality and generosity we received was breathtaking, the concern for our well-being was genuine as was their determination that - yes you've guessed it - we enjoy ourselves. Goodness knows how we would ever be able to repay them for all that we received if these teams come to Skye.

A slow return to Dublin and another farewell to Tom and his bus, which must surely now be in a transport museum in Newry. The sights of Dublin were taken at a more leisurely pace with the flight firmly fixed in our minds and the risk once again of jet lag.

It is fair to say that everyone was impressed by the organisation and hospitality lavished on us by all concerned but special praise goes to Malcolm Scott and all the Newry and Mourne District Council for their kind invitation which made the whole trip possible.

["Anon" Jackson, Shinty Yearbook, 1994-95.]

Dublin, 1989 and the start of the modern series of shinty-hurling matches.

Allied Irish Finance

Go Bbd LNE to Britain

Esso Esso Esso Esso Esso

Irish A WINNER Irish
Press EVERYTIME Press

CROKE PARK

Inspecting the pitch

"Makes you feel very wee ...... "

PARADE OF PAST CHAMPIONS

Roll call, and players of the past parade
Sprightly, greying, smiling, waving where once they played
With honour and distinction - so much so -
That NATIONWIDE we cheer them, friend and foe.

Some household names are called and they don't come
But represented by a wife or son
They stride across the park and take their place -
A smiling wraith across their loved one's face.

If doubt there is amongst the young folk there
And wonder if those old men really were
Champions of Ireland twenty five years past -
Called to ensure our memory of them lasts.

Be they assured that mighty deeds were done
By those men there and those that could not come.
Remember friends their "far fierce hour and sweet
With shouts about their ears and palms beneath their feet."

And if one day I'm called and I can't come -
Just represented by my wife or son.
I'll be the happy halo around their face,
And pray for those who put this scheme in place.

(Joe Lennon, September 19, 1991)

"The game's not the same since they got sponsorship from the Japanese whisky manufacturer...."
This was the reaction in December, 1994, when distillers Glenmorangie announced that they were to end their eighteen-year long sponsorship arrangement with the Camanachd Association. At the time it was one of the longest-running sponsorship arrangements in sport - to many, a marriage made in Heaven.

GENNA - A FIRST COUSIN OF SHINTY

Kassu Yilala, a postgraduate student in agriculture from Ethiopia became excited when he saw a shinty match being played at the Balgownie playing fields in Aberdeen.

The more he watched, the more interested he became because of the many similarities between shinty and Genna, and ancient but popular game in his native country.

The club is shaped like a caman, and is often made of Wanza wood. The ball is also made of the same wood, although depending on availability, other woods are used.

Celebration

Like shinty, there is also a great deal of aerial play and both sides of the stick are used for striking ground shots. The game is played predominantly in the country and mainly in the Christmas season, the word genna meaning in fact "The Christmas season". Games of genna are one of the popular forms of celebration around the Christmas period and the game is played only by Christian people.

Genna is played on any available piece of suitable ground with posts or stones used to mark the goals. In organised games there are between 11 and 14 players on each side.

Often both sides come from the same village and the sides are selected by each captain having alternate choices of the available players.

Relaxation

This system will bring back pleasant memories to many through being the standard system of making up rival shinty teams in school playgrounds.

Genna has recognised rules. Each player must be seen to be playing the ball, and players cammot stop the ball with their hand, not even the goalkeeper. The game is also popular with military people in camps where it is played as a form of relaxation.

(Peter English, Shinty Yearbook, 1987-88.)

The Camanachd Association Centenary March

Willie Lawrie
Kinlochleven

CENTENARY MARCH

On April 3, 1993, the Camanachd Association began a year-long series of special events marking its first hundred years as shinty's ruling body with a reconstruction of the match between Kingussie and Cowal at the Dell, Kingussie, in 1893. The players and spectators were led to the field in a special procession with pipers at their head.

Marine Harvest joined the list of large companies sponsoring shinty in 1988. Chris Tyler's view was that "the sponsor's name on the shirt would have been adequate"!

Shinty's trophies were assembled for the special centenary travelling exhibition Shinty, the sport of the Gael.

Cruinneachadh de dh'fhaclan, gnàthasan-cainnte is eile an co-cheangal ris a chamanachd, ann an Alba agus ann an Eireann, le fiosrachadh mu dheidhinn spòrs chaman dhen aon-ghnè bho air feadh an t-saoghail.

HOW THE PUNTERS SAW IT...

A collection of vocabulary, nomenclature and terminology relating to shinty, hurling and related stick sports. (1)

jessie A jessie is an effeminate, weak, or cowardly man: *what are ye greetin for, ye big jessie?; shinty is not a game for jessies.*

[Chambers Gem, Scots Dictionary.]

FACLAIR: GLOSSARY

achadh	the field of play; often used in place-names to refer to a field, plain.
ailleog	*blow, stroke of a hurl (Sceal).*
ain/aoin/ phuill	the act of driving; old style of playing shinty, which could involve as few as two players, each equipped with a <u>caman</u> and <u>ball</u>, each attempting to drive the latter with the former into a hole dug into the ground.This may have been the precursor of golf; analogous with the English game <u>stool-ball</u>.
aisce	*free hit (Sceal).*
"at large"	a player not having designated a specific team to play for; players would have to select a side, rather than play "at large"; see also *"Clip-side ye"*.
babhta	*round of a competition (Sceal).*
bachall	variant of <u>caman</u>; also used for ashepherd's crook, crozier and, interestingly perhaps, a tennis racket.Used in Co. Clare this century to refer to a hurl. The word is also used for a bishop's crook. **(2)**
baddin	Cheshire game.
bailthe	*the two goals in cross-country hurling (Sceal).*
bàire	a game of shinty in some instances, also the word for a goal; gave way to <u>tadhal</u> for a goal; bàire, a goal - genitive bàrach; see also <u>buille-bhàrachd</u>, <u>buille-chollaid</u>, <u>leth-bhàire</u>; c.f. Inchberry (Gaelic) Innisbhàiridh in Inverness-shire, which, it is suggested in the Littlejohn Album, is derived from <u>bàire</u>, meaning "shinty-links", where the game was played; <u>leth-bhàir</u> was one goal; bàire the two goals required for a full match. According to MacBain, <u>bàire</u> meant "a game, a goal"; Irish bàire, hurling match, goal; from the Middle Irish bàire: bag-ro, root bag-, strive; see arabhaig (strife; compare the Old Irish irbag, arbag, *air-bag,; Norse, bagr, strife). In Ireland, *bàire* was the name for <u>hurling</u>, and even more widely known than <u>iomain(t)</u>, wherever the Irish language had survived down to the nineteenth century. Its precise original meaning is not clear; it seems to equate best with "contest"; the expression *buachaill bàire*, interestingly, in modern parlance, means a "playboy, trickster", with no special reference to hurling. At best, the meaning of *bàire* may be said to be obscure, its metaphorical use widespread. Other usages in Ireland include *bàire* - match, contest; *ag imirt bàire* - hurling (verbal noun); *cul bàire* - goalkeeper, mainstay; *bàireoir* - player (especially a hurler).
bàireoir	*a player, especially a hurler. (Sceal)*
ball	the ball - fungus originally, then wood, wound in twine, (or cork with horse hair), with leather outer cover in more modern times. Hair ball also common. (A. Fraser, Lochfyneside); <u>cnag</u> (a'chnag - the ball) appears to have been the original name for a

ball, then <u>ball-gaoiseid</u>, followed by <u>ball-leathair</u>; later named a "<u>nag</u>, <u>not</u>, <u>cad</u>, <u>gad</u>, <u>cor</u>, <u>coit</u> or <u>golley</u>"; the golf ball was wooden originally, its core now tensioned rubber thread; see also <u>guttie/feathery</u>. The modern shinty ball "shall be spherical - the interior cork and worsted, the outer cover shall be of leather or other approved material. The circumference of the ball shall not be more than 8 inches (20cms) and not less than 7 $\frac{1}{2}$ inches (219cms). The weight of the ball, at the start of the game, shall not be more than 3 ounces, (85gms), nor less than 2 $\frac{1}{2}$ ounces (70gms). The ball shall not be changed during the game unless authorised by the Referee". **(3)**

ball-gaoiseid	hair ball.
ball-iomanach	the ball in Scotland; see <u>ball</u> and <u>liathroit</u>.
ball leathair	leather ball.

bando — Welsh game, never established on an organised basis, although popular throughout the country. <u>Bando</u> is probably borrowed from the English <u>bandy</u>, and the earliest example of the word in Welsh occurs in the great English-Welsh dictionary published by the Glamorgan lexicographer, John Walters, in 1770-1794. Bando was common in the nineteenth century; John Elias, the famous Calvinistic Methodist preacher was a player, as was David Lloyd George in the parish of Llanystumdwy, Caerns. The "Margam Bando Boys" were immortalised in a ballad of that name. Rules were often agreed immediately before matches, which, in similar fashion to shinty, often took place between parishes, with teams of as many as 30 members each. Games were often played on sandy beaches; the aim was to send a small wooden ball between two posts at either end of the pitch which acted as goals. Teams often wore coloured ribbons to distinguish the sides. The club was known as the "<u>bando</u>". Examples of sticks survive in the Welsh Folk Museum.

bandy	English variant of <u>bando</u>.
bandy-ball	variant.
bandy-hoshoe	Norfolk and Suffolk.
bantha (ban-tha!)	*the challenge set by one team to another; anothe variant - ban tha tha (Sceal).*
barresse	barrace, barras, barres, a barrier in front of a castle, an enclosure for judicial contests in Jamieson; adopted from the Old French 'barras'.
barnagh/bàirneach	*a blow, strike (Sceal).*

bas/bois/bos — the bevelled striking end of the shinty stick; longer in some areas, usually to hip length. "<u>bas neo cas</u>" the <u>tarruing</u> - tossing the <u>caman</u> for first hit of the ball, or choice of ends in modern times; crook or straight end would hit ground, second captain had choice as club went upwards; the winner had the first hit - <u>buille-chailleag</u>.
Used to refer to the <u>bos</u> or <u>blade</u> of a hurl (the flat end); also the blade of an oar, anchor, sword. *Caman baise* would be a hurl with a wide blade.

bat	used by Jamieson to signify <u>caman</u>.
Bealtainn	Beltane, the first day of Summer (Dwelly).
berl (Eng)	*hand flourish with the stick.*
berna (bearna)	gap in wall or dyke, sometimes used as a goal.
beulag (a'bheulag)	hitting with the right hand lower on the *caman,* (ie.the forehand). See also *cùlag.*
birling	*rolling the ball along the ground (Sceal)*
bock	kick *(Sceal).*
blade	<u>*bos/bas*</u>, the blade of the hurl.
block(ing)	preventing an opponent hit from the front using the caman as a defensive implement.
bodach eadar dà cheathairne	the odd man out in games of uneven numbers, required to play on either side alternately; "the odd man", "the old fellow between two sides"; c.f. ceatharn (-airn, airne), a hero, strong robust man. **(Dwelly).**
bogha	the goal; could be stones or uprights. *Fear a bhogha* would be the goalkeeper. *(Sceal).*
bois	see bas.
borick	*ball (Sceal).*
bow	*a twig, bent with the ends stuck in the ground to form a goal. Two young sally trees pulled together to form a goal. The same size as shinty hails. (Sceal).*
bridge	*the bit of the hurl to hold.*
broc-isteach	a scrum, tussle for the ball.
buaileadh bàir	striking a goal, <u>hurling</u>.
"buaileam ort"/ "buailidh mi ort"	the <u>tarruing</u> - choice of ends - one captain threw caman to the other, who caught it and hand over hand they reached the end. The last grip had the first choice of men, usually taking the best players. "<u>Is</u> <u>leamsa</u>....", " I will take..." was the usual formula.
bualla	used for shinty clubs in Inverness, according to the *Highland News.* **(4)**

buille-bhàrach/ buille-choilleag	see also bàire; the stroke that sent the ball over the line; the goal to win the game; the first hit of a game.
bunsach	variant used for stick.
cack-handed	playing "wrong-handed", dominant hand in grip reversed.
car	knot in the wood of the <u>caman</u>.
cad	see ball. (Football in Kerry. In early days,this would have been a cover stuffed with straw - later, a pig's bladder, blown up!)
caid	*rough and tumble, i.e. football, pre-Gaelic Athletic Association, **GAA**; also a type of ball (Sceal).*
caigionn (-eann)	used for "a scrummage" **(5)**; according to Dwelly - binding together, coupling, linking.
caille	the place where the ball was driven off between the two goals; see also <u>coggie</u>.
caimin	*walking stick with hook on it (Sceal).*
Calluinn	the Old New Year - 12/13 January.
camaire	*<u>camanachd</u> (Sceal).*
camake	variant, <u>caman</u>.
camal	hurley in Omeath, Co. Louth.
caman	the single most consistently used word to refer to the curved stick used to play shinty; of various lengths - shorter in Kintyre and played with one hand; (see also <u>iomain leathlàmhach</u>); usually made of willow, hazel, oak, elm or birch; plural <u>camain</u>. Dwelly was aware of some confusion regarding the <u>caman</u>, referring to it as "not a cricket bat, as given in some dictionaries". (probably **Jamieson**). In some areas (eg Uist) lengths of "stamh" - sea-girdles, tangle, seaweed stalks were used as <u>camain</u>. The modern <u>caman</u> must conform to the following standard: (1) The head of the caman must not be of a size larger than can pass through a ring of diameter of 2 1/2 inches (6.3cms); (2) No plates, screws, or metal in any form shall be attached to, or form part of the caman. **(6)** Interestingly, perhaps, there are no similar restrictions on the size of the <u>bos</u> of a hurl.
caman a bandy	variant.
camanachd	the game of <u>shinty</u>; see also <u>iomain</u>, <u>shinty</u>. Rarely, if ever, used to refer to the game in Ireland; but *camanacht* in North Antrim.

camanaiche	a shinty player; see also <u>iomanaiche</u>.
camag	favoured in the northern districts including Badenoch **(7)**; also used for a young player's <u>caman</u>, which would be shorter; used in Canada for the crooked branch of a tree which was used to play with a stirk's dung (it being, apparently, the right size!). See also *camog*.
camake	variant.
camawg	variant.
cambaute	*a croooked stick or bat (Sceal).*
cambock/cambok	variant.
cammack	variant.
cammag	Isle of Man variant.
cammel	Breton variant.
camog	a small *hurl* (*camogie* stick)
camp	*variant; type of rugby with small ball (Sceal).*
camp-ball	football, according to Strutt; using a ball of blown bladder, driving it through goals. The blown bladder was also used in the Highlands.
camocke/camok/camoke	variants.
camog	variant.
camogie	womens' <u>hurling</u> (camoguidheacht), played in Ireland.
captain(s)	the principal players who started the game, hand to hand, in the centre of the field (the <u>tarruing</u>); see also <u>ceann-stoc</u>, head-stock.
carraigin	*a stroke with the <u>bos</u> of the <u>caman</u> (Sceal).*
carri	1589 variant in Wodrow, Life of Mr David Weems 14 in Biographical Collection II (Maitland Club, 1845); quoted in Liber Collegii Notre Domine, pxlviii).
carrick	Fifeshire game.

cas	the handle of the <u>caman</u>; "<u>Bas neo cas</u>" the caman would be thrown up between the captains before the start of a game and "<u>bas neo cas</u>" called; "*cos*" (foot) in Ireland.
cathais	*maypole or Beltaine stick (Sceal).*
ceann stoc/ ceann-stuic	captain, leader; head of the stock, family; the captain used to have to hit the ball back into play according to the Glasgow Camanachd Club rules at the end of the 19th century; also used there to refer to the goal-posts.
ceideadh (ceide)	*sandy beach, a green (Sceal).*
chamaire	a game played on ice "a mile within the sea-mark" on the Firth of Forth on 20/02/1607, according to Calderwood "History of the Kirk in Scotland".
chamie (the chamie)	name given to the game of shinty, in East Lothian, according to the *Scotsman*, December 2, 1897. Apparently <u>chamie</u> was used more often than <u>shinty</u> for the name of the game in the area.
chew	often referred to in the records of the Kirk Session of Kinneddar (Moray) for the year 1666 and thereafter, especially in relation to the profanation of the Sabbath. "The chew" appears to have been nothing more or less than shinty played with the cork float of a fishing net, instead of the more usual wooden ball.
chinnup	bent stick game.
chole	still played in Belgium; "half-way between hockey and golf."
clackans	variant.
cleek(ing)	the skill of preventing an opponent from playing the ball from behind, using the caman as a hook (8).
clip	*short, sharp stroke (Sceal).*
clippim	*to hook, catch the hurley (Sceal).*
clipping	the choosing of sides (teams).
"clip-side ye"	the player should choose the side he was to play for, rather than play "<u>at large</u>".
cludach	cover of ball (*Sceal*).
club-ball	according to **Fittis**, "the same as Lowlanders' shinty"; can be traced to the 13th/14th centuries; a straight club was used, similar to a bat.

clubby	bent stick game.
cluich' air phloc	playing shinty, used in Dornoch. The <u>shinny</u> or <u>shinty</u> was the ball in local usage. (**9**)
cluich bhall	ball-play, according to **Logan**; <u>cluidh hall</u> in Badenoch.
cluich chnèad	(Perthshire) - playing ball; (c.f. also <u>cneatag</u> for a fir cone).
cluich dhèsog	driving the ball, the game which may now be known as golf.
cluicheoir	*player (Sceal).*
cluiche mhaigh	*plain for a game (Sceal).*
cluich-sgailleag	hitting practice.
cluiche poill	"the hole game" - another possible precursor of golf?
cluidh bhall	Badenoch usage, "ball play".
cnag(an)	(a' chnag), the ball - wooden in the early days, eventually deemed too dangerous; cork was also used. Other variants - crag, raig, crig, crick, creck. (**10**)
cnapan	Welsh variant, <u>bandy</u>, <u>bando</u>.
cnèatag	the ball, Perthshire.
coggie/cogy	something to place the ball on, a little above the ground, usually a little pile of earth within the <u>den</u> or goal; the ball would be placed on it for a hit-out (**11**); the term used for golfing tee in the Lowlands; the ball was buried in the sand in Lewis.
coilleag-an	stones used for goals (in Eigg for example); in Ireland, the end of a shinty stadium (Sceal).
coimheascar	*melee, struggle (Sceal).*
coit	see <u>ball</u>
coitipeirc	guttapercha ball.
comhtharrac	*half-way line; equal; draw (Sceal).*
common(s)/(kamman)	*the ball; a caman; a bent stick; the game itself (Sceal).*

comortas	*competition; not just in hurling (Sceal).*
conabhru	*mauling, scrummage (Sceal).*
conquering goal	*(when two adjacent parishes or districts contended (instead of two small parties at an ordinary match) that was scoobeen or conquering goal - deciding goal - Sceal).*
cooley /cul	a goal.
cool-hale (cùl-thadhal)	*a hail (Sceal).*
cor	see <u>ball</u>.
corai	*wrestler (Sceal).*
cotharai	*touchline (Sceal).*
cowlee	when the ball goes beyond the goal.
cowlee man	*man in the goal (Sceal).*
crabsow/crabsowl	Lincolnshire game.
cragan	*a light blow with the <u>caman</u> (Sceal).*
crapachs	player catching ball in the air; throwing it up again and striking with the caman **(12)**; "<u>fornaird/foirnead</u>" was another term used for this, in Badenoch especially.
creatan	variant which appears in **A. Campbell's "Grampian's Desolate" (13)**.
crioch bàire	the end of the <u>barresse</u>.
criod/cneut	*soft ball, of wool/animal hair (Sceal).*
cromaiscin	*a cluster of people (Sceal) .*
cromog	*undressed hurl (Sceal).*
crook	*a rough <u>caman</u>, without a <u>bas</u> (Sceal)*
crub	*also a <u>caman</u> without a <u>bas</u> (Sceal).*

cruca	*a stick, without a* <u>*bos*</u> *(Sceal).*
cruinne	*a ball (Sceal).*
cruinneachan	*old clothes ball; rag ball (Sceal).*
cuaill	<u>caman</u> in Inverness, according to Sceal.
cuan	*bend in hurl (Sceal).*
cugail	*to "coogle" the ball, i.e. dribble (Sceal).*
cùis (-e, -ean)	the side one took in a game, according to **Dwelly**, "particularly shinty or cricket".
cùlag (a'chùlag)	hitting with the left hand lower on the <u>caman</u> (ie. the back-hand). See also <u>beulag</u>.
cùl/cùl-bàire	back or rear-guard - usually one of the team's most skilful defenders, placed near the boundary to defend the line.
cumbucam	understood to have been "a species of goff" by **Strutt** in 1801.
cuntrail	*dirty, devious, false stroke (Sceal).*
daoir	*stone in place of uprights (Sceal).*
darach	an oak caman.
deas	ground stroke, possibly referring to the right-hand side restriction which was placed on players; it was only permissible to hit on that side until the end of the 19th century; also the foot of the caman *(Sceal).*
deisigh	*pull on the right/right hand side (Sceal).*
den (English)	the goal; two heaps of stones nine or ten feet apart; the object was to get the ball through the den from which the start had been made. **(14)**
doddart	the <u>caman</u>.
doe/doe nacket	see <u>knout</u>/<u>knowt</u>.
"do luirgnean"	"watch your shins", (see also "<u>seas air do sheas</u>").
dreis imeartha	*round of competition (Sceal).*

eiteall	*wingers, players on the fringe of the play (Sceal).*
faiche	the town or village green on which the game was played.
fear-taic	sponsor, supporter. **(15)**
faithche	*"hurling green" - common in Irish topography. (Faythe Harriers - hurling team in Wexford).*
feadhnach	*team, side (Sceal).*
feathery	three-part stitched ball used in early golf; leather cover, densely packed with feathers.
fhearning	"using both hand and club in sending the ball afield and throwing the ball in the air with one hand and hitting it in its descent thus sending it much further afield than (he) would with a throw or a set blow in the ordinary way." **(16)**
fideag	the act of drawing up the ball, hitting it while still in mid-air and sending it, at a somewhat high trajectory, to the other end of the field; sourced by Dwelly to **A.Henderson**, Ardnamurchan; the word may have been confined to local usage.
fleasc iarainn	*band of metal on caman (Sceal).*
foadharan	the stroke given to the ball by the player after lifting it and throwing it in the air, which demanded "exceptional adroitness and skill in a fast game if the player was to get away with it". **(17)**
fodharlag	a hit in the air, after lifting and throwing it .
foirneid (foirneird)	aerial shot; see also <u>sgaileag-adhair</u>.
fornaird	*to lift without handling; to rise and strike on the volley (Sceal).*
fuadach	*winger raider, player on the fringe of play; also called "whip" (Sceal) .*
galus	*one of the uprights (Sceal).*
genna	ancient game in Ethiopia, caman-shaped club, often made of wanza wood; involved aerial play and ground shots, with no handling, 11-14-a-side; "Genna" means "the Christmas season"; the game was only played at Christmas.
gibireacht	*dribbling (Sceal).*
giolla	*player; inexperienced, minor role (Sceal).*
goal	or hail; Gaelic equivalents - <u>bàire</u>, <u>leth-bhàire</u>, <u>tadhal</u>.

goic	*the turn in the <u>bos</u> of the caman (Sceal).*
golf	according to **Strutt**, the "most ancient of games with a club, or bat"; the first recorded golfer appears to have been James IV of Scotland and the first lady, Mary Queen of Scots; claimed as a Scottish game, but may have come from Holland. The name probably comes from the Scots verb 'gowff', to cuff, strike hard.
golley	see <u>ball</u>.
goradh	*to incite, war, encourage (Sceal).*
gorai	*to keep goal, goal keeper (Sceal).*
grafàn	*<u>caman</u> with a narrow blade; grounder, play on the ground (Sceal).*
grounder	*ground play (Sceal).*
guttie	solid gutta percha ball introduced to golf after the feathery. (1884)
hail(s)	the goal, a goal; posts separated by measured course of (on occasion) 400 yards; see also <u>bàire</u>, <u>leth-bhàire</u>, <u>tadhal</u>. Used in football when the drivers were said to "hail the ball", to drive it beyond or to the goal. Hence "hail the dules", to reach the mark, be victorious. From Teutonic 'hael-en', 'ferre', 'ad ferre', 'accersere' - the place where the game strikes off; the act of reaching this place or driving the ball to the boundary; 'transmittere meta pila' - "to give the hail"; 'hic primus est transmissus' - "this is the first hail". (Wederb. Vocab. p.37); also:

Fresche men com and hailit the duleis
And dang thame donn in dailis.
(Chr. Kirk. st. 22. Chron S.P.R. ii 366)

The ba-spell's won,
and we the ba' hae hail'd
(Skinner's Misc. Poet. p.133) |
hail-ba	hail the dool/goal - saluting the goal (Oxford Dictionary)- described as "a ludicrous faux pas" by Ninian MacDonald (**18**); also used in Dumfries.
hail-lick	the last blow or kick of the ball, which drove it beyond the line or boundary, Kinross.
hair ball	horse hair was often used as the core of the ball, eg in Barra, boiled and covered with some other skin as a cover.
"hands"	called when the ball was driven out of bounds, by the nearest opponent of the player who had sent it out.
harpastum	Roman version of ball-game; probably derived from 'harpago' - to snatch, or take by violence!

hawkey/hawky/ hockie/hockey	variants.
head stock	see also <u>ceann-stoc</u>, captain. (**19**)
"High or low?"	the manner of returning the ball to play from out of bounds; choice was made to throw it between players "high or low".
hiley (Eng)	used in Lewis to signify a goal. The form also survived in the United States where people from Lewis played a game on the shores of Lake Superior in September, 1934. (**20**)
hook(ing)	the skill of preventing an opponent from playing the ball from behind, using the caman as a hook; also known as "<u>cleeking</u>".
horsing	*an old term for picking a girl, marriage (Sceal).* (**21**)
hummy	variant term for shinty; knotty was also used around 1840s; also Oxford-shire game.
humney	bent stick game.
hurl(ey)	the Irish <u>caman</u>; sometimes referred to as "a cross between a hockey stick and a boomerang"; there are no restrictions on the size of the hurl. As O Maolfabhail points out, the evidence from all periods of Irish history is so "occasional and intrinsically vague" that firm conclusions as to shape and substance may be drawn only with extreme caution. (**22**)
hurling	there were two versions of the Irish game; a winter game, adapted to a hard, frosty ground; and a summer variant, using a larger, softer ball, shorter and thicker clubs, and more aerial play. Both versions were homogenous and the "<u>hurling</u>" was used to describe either or both; also two versions of a game by the same name in Cornwall according to **Strutt**; a version of hand-ball, using a silver ball. According to **O Maolfabhail**, <u>hurling</u> can be traced back six hundred years in Ireland. First found in the Statutes of Kilkenny in 1366 where "the games which men call horlinges with big sticks of a ball on the ground" were forbidden. The Statutes (composed in Norman French) were aimed, not at the native Irish, but the Northern English colonies of Ireland, with the aim of deterring them from from succumbing to the Irish way of life. <u>Hurling</u> is not encountered again until proscribed in the Statutes of Galway in 1527, this time in English (the horlinge of the litill ball with hockie sticks or staves). From the seventeenth century on, <u>hurling</u> becomes the usual name in English for the summer game of south-east Ireland. Yet, at the beginning of the seventeenth century in Britain the word is used in reference to a game more in keeping with the nature of modern rugby football. Compare the Breton word "horellan", "to swing". "Horell" in Breton also signifies the small wooden ball used in the game. The word is believed to be a borrowing from either French or German sources. Its use in English is often misleading, particularly as the words *<u>caman</u>* and *<u>ioman(t)</u>* were never accepted into literary English. The term "commons" is used to signify the game in nineteenth century Ordnance Survey reports. (See also Shaw Mason, 1825.)
hurtling	Canadian variant, from which ice hockey developed.
iarraidh	*to try, attempt to hit (Sceal).*

ice hockey	possibly developed from <u>shinty</u> which was taken to Canada by emigrant Scots in the nineteenth century generally agreed to be a modern sport, although the precise origins are a matter of considerable debate. (**23**)
imleacan	*playing line/limit (Sceal).*
iomada	*challenge to play (Sceal).*
iomain (iomàint)	the older of the two Gaelic names for shinty, followed by <u>camanachd</u>, which was described by **Alex Morrison** as "an interloper" (**24**); the name for shinty in Argyll, according to **Dwelly**; played to a considerable extent all December and January. New Year's Day matches were particularly well attended, particularly when celebrating the Old New Year (January 12). Used in Badenoch for "dribbling". **Dwelly's** definition includes "driving, urging slowly, as cattle"; see also <u>camanachd</u>, <u>shinty</u>. Other usages in Ireland include iomain - hurling; iomain tGaelach -hurling; iomaint Ghallda - cricket; iomaint geata wicket.
iomaint leathlàmhach	*one-handed <u>hurling</u>.*
iomanaiche	also <u>camanaiche</u>, a shinty player; it may be noted that derivatives stem not from the name of the implement or the instrument as <u>camanachd</u> does, but from that of the *agent*.
iomartas	*playing of the game (Sceal).*
iubhar	yew shinty stick, often preferred because of its suppleness.
kamman	*impelling a wooden ball to a given point (Sceal).*
klotschiessen	Friesland game, referred to by the Marquis of Lorne in *Good Words,* January 1895.
kites	*playing with tin cans (Sceal).*
knurley	*playing with a stick and block of wood (Sceal).*
kolven	ice-golf in Holland.
knout (knowt)	the ball or bit of wood used in the game of <u>shinty</u> in Fife; synonym of "doe nacket" the piece of wood, stone or bone which boys used at shinty; (doe - a wooden ball).
knotty	or <u>hummy</u>, other designations for shinty. The game was played extensively in the fishing villages of the north and west of Scotland in the late 18th and early 19th centuries, using a simple stick (camachd?), the cork float from nets and four posts for goals. Any level field was suitable, dimensions fixed to meet the circumstances. The first rules were apparently composed by Rev Finlay Cook and the elders of the church of Lochcarron, with the object of channelling young men's energies away from "frequenting ale-houses, over-indulgence in strong liquour, the poaching of deer and salmon,the playing of the pipes, and the dangers of dancing to the fiddle with the young women in the barn or on the green". (**25**)

laisc (loisg)	*to pull, hit (Sceal).*
làr	*centre, ground, pitch (Sceal).*
Là na Bliadhn' Uire	New Year's Day - traditional date for games, still observed in Lovat and some other areas such as Heaste in Skye and Lewis once again; compare also "Là buain nan caman" in Badenoch - the day for cutting the <u>camain</u> - between Hallowe'n and Christmas.
"leag leam"	acknowledgement that sides were chosen.
leantran (leana)	*same as <u>faiche</u>; playing area (Sceal).*
leas	*metal band on <u>caman</u> (Sceal).*
leataobh	*half-backs (Sceal).*
leath-board	*broad <u>caman</u> (Sceal).*
leather	the ball.
leathimeall	wing player (Sceal).
"Leigidh mi leat"	said when allowing an opposing captain to chose a player "Let me permit you".
"Leigeam leat"	the Lewis equivalent of "Leigidh mi leat".
leth-bhàir / leath bhàire	a half-goal or goal; older than <u>tadhal</u>; <u>bàir</u> being two goals and a full match commonly used in Badenoch; In Morvern and Mull, <u>leth-bhàir</u>=1 hail; <u>bàire</u>, two hails; <u>bàire gu leth</u>, three hails (**Dwelly**) See also <u>tadhal</u>.
leth-bhàir shios/shuas	change of ends after a goal - <u>leth bhàir</u> shios on the first goal, followed by <u>leth-bhàir shuas</u> after the next goal.
leth-chluich	half-play; one score, and not enough to count; <u>cluich</u> was the full score, a hit between the stones acting as goals, at hip-height. According to **Dwelly**, leth-chluich was a hail; In Eigg, <u>leth-chluich</u> was one hail, <u>cluich</u>, two hails; <u>cluich gu leth</u>, three hails.
leth-thadhal	*as <u>leth-chluich</u> above (Sceal).*
liathrait/liathroid/ liathroit	the ball; literally the "grey circle" suggesting that, even from the time of the Irish tales, the ball was played with a covered centre, rather than a wooden block. According to **Ninian MacDonald**, (**26**) the shinty ball was "about four inches in diameter, made of some light elastic material, such as woollen yarn wound round and round and covered with leather. Sometimes a rounded piece

of wood a ball of twisted hair, cork, or even part of the vertebral bone of a sheep, or a gnarl or knob from the trunk of a tree, carefully fashioned into a globular shape (and later termed a "nag, not, cad, gad, cor, coit or golley")". The modern version is "spherical - the interior shall be cork and worsted, the outer cover shall be leather or some approved material". It has been known for cow dung blocks or packed sheep's droppings to be used as a substitute in case of emergency!

liur	*a flip of the caman (Sceal).*
"loisg e"	when the post was hit; also referred to as <u>leth-bhàir</u>; "it hit the post" (literally "it burnt").
lorc/lorg/lorg dne	variants, <u>the caman</u>; very often "made of ash, three feet in length, carefully shaped and smoothed and with the lower end flat and curved - usually called a caman", according to **Ninian MacDonald**; also used for the shaft. **(27)**
Lughnasaid	the first of August - festival day.
lurga *(lorga)*	shaft of the <u>caman</u>.
machair	Low-lying plain, usually near a beach, often used as a field for play; for example in Kintyre, Machair Ionain, which became the golf course at Machrihanish, the name probably being derived from Machair an Iomain. In Ireland, this was the traditional hurling area, eg in Lochguile, Co. Antrim - Magherahoney.
machair	a shot for goal in some areas.
machair-iomain	shinty field, see <u>machair</u>.
maide	variant for the stick.
maor	captain, umpire.
mearings	*boundaries for a game , flags, corners (Sceal).*
moltoir	*referee, adjudicator (Sceal).*
muiriocha	*field at edge of sea (Sceal).*
not	Gloucester variant, from the knotty piece of wood used as a ball.
Oidhche Chaluinn	Old New Year, traditional date for shinty matches in many areas. (January 12).
paganica	Roman game, ball stuffed with feathers, became cambuca (Latin) in Edward III's time.
pall-mall	variant of golf in reign of James I, driving the ball with a mallet.

past	*two goals or the part marked off (Sceal).*
piocadh (priocadh)	*picking teams (Sceal).*
poc	*to hit; a good strike; poc bàire a hurling stroke; poc sleasa - side-line puck; poc fada - long stroke (Sceal).*
pocog	*the last blow in a game of hurley (Sceal).*
poll	*a hole (Sceal).*
posta	*part of the goal (Sceal).*
poucher	*a short, brushing stroke which scores (Sceal).*
puck	"strike" or blow of the ball in some areas. Now the ice hockey "ball".
puck-out	hit-out *(poc cùil).*
putting-out	the equivalent of a bye-hit/goal-hit.
re	*level playing field (Sceal).*
reitire	the modern referee; *reiteoir* in Ireland.
rim	*(of hurley) small knob at end (Sceal).*
ring-ball	striking a ball with a <u>bandy</u>, through a ring fastened into the ground.
rogha bogha	*choice of goal (Sceal)*
roinn	*line on the pitch (Sceal).*
ruainnsin	*hair ball (Sceal).*
ruisceadh/ruscadh	*to bash, trounce (Sceal) .*
Samhainn	last day of summer - festival day.
saoile (taoile?)	a goal in Lewis. (**28**)

(schinnie,)/shinnie/ shiny/ shinye, *n* ,	[Obscure. Cf. Gaelic *sinteag* a skip, a pace, later Scots *shinty* (1769) the game, (1773) the stick, 18th century English shinney (1794) the stick.] A game played with a stick curved at one end like a hockey stick and used for striking a ball, also, the stick itself. [With respectt to the Kirk-yeard, that ther be no playing at golf, carrict, shinnie (Liber Coll. Glasgow, p. lxviii shinny], in the High Kirk, or Kirjk-yard, or Blackfriar Kirk-yeard, either Sunday or week day; 1589 Glasgow Kirk S. 16 Oct. in **Wodrow** Life of Mr David Weems 14 in Biog. Coll. II (Maitland Club 1845).] The bairnes of France have the exercise of the tap, the pery, the cleking, and (instead of our gouf, which they know not) they have shinyes; 1665-7 **Lauder** Journal, 125, He did transub Himself to ball, the Parliament to club, Which will him holl when right teased at ane blow Or els Sir Patrick will be the shinnie goe; c 1690 Bk. Pasquils 181. (**Dictionary of the Older Scottish Tongue, ongoing, University of Edinburgh**) (**29**)
scribin	*scratch team of four or five persons (Sceal).*
scuab	*sweep (Sceal); also scuabeen - cross-country hurling in Cork; scuab buille - a sweeping blow.*
scuaibin	*see above.*
scribin	*scrape, scratch, score in golf (Sceal).*
scrios	*destroy ; possibly "just a stout ashplant with a natural twist or just a knob at the end of it" (Sceal) .*
scrush	Dorsetshire game.
seanlamha	*veteran (Sceal).*
"seas air do sheas"	anyone touching the ball on the left was cautioned thus or "do luirgnean" -"watch your shins"; "stand your stance", with players urged to stand their ground; if a player had the ball on one side of him, it had to be carried on that side, somewhat like modern hockey (Skye); until the end of the19th Century, hitting was permitted only when the ball was on the right side of the player.
scailleag/scailleog	*wave, chop (Sceal).*
sgailleag-adhair	aerial shot.
shanty	Canadian variant, a pre-cursor of ice-hockey; <u>shinney</u> and <u>hockey</u> were also used to describe what was obviously shinty.
shindig	shinty, shindy and shindig all seem to represent the same word; in slang, a lively celebration or party; to make a disturbance.
shindy	played in England on Shrove Tuesday in some areas, according to the new English Dictionary; but compare "There's a regular **shinty** in the house" from Thackeray's Vanity Fair. (**30**)
shinney-law	variant.

shinnin/shinnock/ shinnon/sinnon	variants.
shinny (shinnie)	the commonly used name for "shinty" up to the nineteenth century; see also <u>schinnie</u> above.
shinny-club	the bat (sic) used for striking the ball. "bat" was often used by Jamieson to describe the sticks/clubs used in ball games.
shinty	probably does not derive from <u>sinteag</u> (a leap, skip, bound), although there was almost general acceptance that it did; unlikely, however, as the modern game has more to do with the driving suggested in <u>iomain</u>; modern terminology; played by teams of twelve at all ages, under the auspices of the Camanachd Association since1893.Main centres of excellence and strength are Badenoch, Argyll and Lochaber according to Dwelly; see <u>camanachd</u>.
shinty-links	where the game was played, eg in Inchberry, Kirkhill, Inverness-shire; (Gaelic, Innisbhàiridh).
shinty stick	the English equivalent of <u>caman</u> in modern usage, the stick used in play.
shon	variant, a stick, also in Ireland.
sinteag	skip, bound, hop, leap - possibly adopted, corrupted and anglicised to "<u>shinty</u>" The most credible source of the word "shinty", although <u>shinny's</u> claims cannot be totally set aside.
sippy	a rope-ball (*Sceal*) .
skinny-shanks	the camain in Campbell's "**Grampian's Desolate**". (**31**)
slathchaman	a bevelled *caman* (Sceal).
sleasog (slisog)	thin stick <u>caman</u>. (Sceal).
sliotair (slitter)	the ball used in Ireland (leather); also shlitther, slidher, slitther; liotar - hair ball. (**32**)
sliosbhuille	*cut, slice (Sceal).*
slishing	*verb from slis (Sceal).*
slogging	*a full-blooded swing (Sceal).*
smack	*a stroke (Sceal).*
smailcinn	*a small piece, knob at the end of a <u>caman,</u> to prevent it slipping from the hand.*

sniggling	*to run the ball along the ground (Sceal).*
soule	played in the north of France; half-way between hockey and golf.
speilean (iomairt air speil)	"cat and bat" - original to the Highlands and Islands, a team game, one side batting while the other fielded. (**33**)
speitire	an ill-shaped, undresed <u>caman</u> (*Sceal*).
spragging/sprigging	*sideways block of opponent's hurley (Sceal).*
sràc	strike, a shot.
sraith	*a field near a river or loch, dry in summer (Sceal).*
srann	humming sound of the ball.
stalu	*seasoning with manure or heat; compare use of linseed oil in Scotland (Sceal).*
stiall	*to cut, tear, strike (Sceal).*
stool-ball	English equivalent of <u>ain-phuill</u>; according to **Strutt**, originally play where balls were driven from stool to stool; said to be "more appropriated to the women than to the men, but occasionally it was played by the young persons of both sexes indiscriminately." (**34**)
straitnear	*straightener; a band on the blade of the caman to strengthen it, prevent it splitting (Sceal)*
stundai	*touchline (Sceal).*
tadhal (taodhal/taobhall/ taodhall)	goal, not as old as "<u>bàire/leth bhàire</u>"; became "hail".
taghadh	the process of selecting the teams (Badenoch).
taighri	*"on-side".*
taoiseach	*captain (Sceal).*
tarruing	the choice of ends, the process of selecting teams under captains; see <u>buaileam ort</u>.
teann leis	"hit it"; pull with him, shoulder to shoulder (Sceal).

"thadhail e"	on scoring a goal; "It is a goal".
thurlaich /thurlaich e	a goal was missed; past the post (Badenoch).
thush	*shouted by the man in possession; he could not be charged from the front (Sceal).*
tigh	used in Skye for a goal - "a house or home"; "chaidh i tigh" - "it went home"; see Màiri Mhòr nan Oran's poems. **(35)**
tionan/ioman (t)	*camanachd (Sceal).*
togaint	*lifting the ball (Sceal).*
tonoladh	*refreshment, at half-time (Sceal).*
toraic	*defender (Sceal).*
traidhsleach/trilseach	*cover on the ball (Sceal).*
trap-ball	14th century game; a trap was used to elevate the ball, then hit by batsmen.
treascairt	*melee, scrum (Sceal).*
tri cheile	*mixed match (Sceal).*
tuathal	*used on the island of Eigg for "past the post", compare thurlaich e above.*
turlach	*wet field in winter ("mere") - a winter lake; dry field in summer (Sceal).*
umpire	*captain or referee (Sceal).*
ur(a)chair	shot at goal; literally "a bullet".
whip	*whipsman, forward; see alsom <u>fuadach</u> (Sceal).*
yellow-belly	distinctive dress of Wexford players who played in London; the nickname is still used. **(36)**

FIOSRACHADH: NOTES

Cu chulainn òg:

The translation is based on the version of An Leabhar Laighneach found in Tàin Bo Cuailnge from the Book of Leinster, edited by Cecile O'Rahilly, Dublin Institute for Advanced Studies, (1967). See also O Maolfabhail, Caman, pages 61-63.

Like a March wind:

See also O Maolfabhail, Caman, page 74.

Mar dh'fhàg Colum Cille Eireann:

For further reading on Colum Cille, see the full text from which extract is taken and also Columba, by Ian Finlay, 1979.

Dà mhaide dhìreach:

John Morrison of Bragar, father of An Clarsair Dall (Ruaraidh Morrison, born c1656) is first to be found in the pages of Martin Martin, who describes him as "a person of unquestionable sincerity and reputation". He was known as Iain mac Mhurch' 'c Ailein, tacksman of Bragar, entered in the records of the estate as a sixteen-pennyland - the largest agricultural unit in Lewis. He was born around 1630.

In his notes accompanying this verse, William Matheson in his classic "The Blind Harper. The Songs of Roderick Morrison and his music" (Edinburgh, 1970), explains that a shinty club made from a straight stick with a head artificially bent (no doubt in a laghadair such as was used in boat-building) was stronger and lasted longer than one with a natural bend.

It is also explained that the runners of a sledge required to have "lift" at the front to ensure a smooth action. Note the form chama (; caman) taken by the attributive adjective after the noun in the dual number.

They are very nimble at it:

There are various versions of Martin Martin's description of his epic trip to the Hebrides. This one is extracted from the 1934 edition, edited by Dr D. J. MacLeod, page 461.

A sense of sin:

Extracted from the North Berwick Kirk Session Minutes. This is by no means an isolated example of "schinnie" being banned on the Sabbath. It is one of the earliest, and unusual in that it refers to Berwick, well south of the area normally associated with the game of shinty.

The extract appears as an Appendix to *The Golf Book of East Lothian* (Edinburgh, 1896). I am indebted to Gordon Gilchrist, Ayr, for bringing it to my attention. The book is a valuable source of information on the early linkages between golf and other sports, particularly throughout Europe.

FIOSRACHADH: NOTES

No resentment is to be shown:
This decription is extracted from a letter written by John Dunton in 1699. See O Caithnia for further details.

The Brigade's Hurling match:
The story embodied in this ballad was told among the people of Cork and Limerick around 1850 - how a company of the Irish Brigade in the service of France captured a town in the manner related.

The Convict of Clonmel:
This poem is believed to portray a genuine reflection of life in 18th century Ireland. Callanan is not believed to have dressed up any aspect of life here. A note accompanying the poem states that "Convicts have been peculiar objects of sympathy in Ireland. They often suffered for faith and fatherland. The air is one to which the song is wedded among the old singers of Co. Cork."

The Grampian's Desolate:
The poet added the following notes to his original work:
A cask of whisky strong, the victor's prize (p.124)

The rural sports and pastimes of the Gael are fast hastening into disuetude. Of the very few of those gymnastic excercises that still remain, wrestling, putting the stone, and shinny, or shinty (creatan) are practised ocasionally. The latter excercise, of which I have attempted a description, is by far the most active and arduous of our rural pastimes. Shinny is a game performed with a woooden ball, and sticks or clubs crooked at one of the extremities, for the purpose of hitting the ball with more address and certainty.

Alexander Campbell (1764-1824) was editor of Albyn's Anthology (1816-1818), a collection of Gaelic songs and melodies, Gaelic texts and English translations, some by Walter Scott, who took music lessons from Campbell.

See also: Claire Lamont, "A note on Gaelic proverbs in Waverly", in Notes and Queries of the Society of Highland and Island Historical research, Vol 22, 1975.

In defiance of the excise man:
Hurling has dominated in Co Antrim. Other Gaelic games such as handball and football never became established. Many attempts were made over the years to establish Gaelic football but it never really prospered.

Hurling was undoubtedly popular in Northern Antrim for many years. The Ordnance Survey Memoirs record it as having been played in Ballymoney, Carrickfergus and Loughgiel. The Shaw Mason Parochial Survey (1819) tells that "a great concourse of people assemble on the strand at Whitepark to play cammon or shinney". The name 'caman' survives in the Bushmills area - Port Caman.

FIOSRACHADH: NOTES

Lord Cushendun in his unpublished memoirs writes that his grandfather Edmund Alexander McNeill 1785-1879, was "the best wrestler and the best hurler in the Glens".

There are still many people in the Glens who have heard of the famous "shinney" matches, played around Christmas time and New Year. In each glen fields are still pointed out where shinney matches took place. However, no records survive of any games having been properly organised, or indeed, regular competitions. That was to change after the turn of the century.

The Margam Bandy Boys:

Bando, a game similar to hockey or hurley, was especially popular in the Vale of Glamorgan. (See Glossary) Villages and parishes competed against each other. The "Margam Bandy Boys" were immortalised in this ballad.

For further descriptions of the game, see Vale of Glamorgan, Charles Redwoood, (1839); G.J. Williams' article "Glamorgan Customs in the Eighteenth century", in Gwerin, (Vol 1, 1956-57); and *The Oxford Companion to the Litertaure of Wales*, edited by Meic Stephens, (OUP, 1986).

I am indebted to D. Roy Saer, Assistant Keeper, National Museum of Wales, Cardiff, for his help with this ballad.

Guth o MhacTalla:

Several interesting accounts of shinty matches were written in the nineteenth century Gaelic periodical *An Teachdaire Gàidhealach*. Some are written in the form of a letter from "Fionnladh Piobaire" (Finlay the piper) and this one is from "MacTalla" (Echo). It is allegedly an account of a match played in Glasgow in 1830 at New Year. The author recounts how three thousand people viewed the match, which was attended by "more than a thousand Highlanders with a piper at their head."

MacTalla remarks that there were several clergy in the Highlands who apparently preached against camanachd. If that was the only difficulty the clergy faced in their parish, he says, then the minister faced little to worry about!

Deil tak' the glass:

The Book of the Club of True Highlanders, a leather-bound atlas-sized volume which was a pioneer of the coffee-table books on the Highland way of life and history was compiled by Mr MacIntyre-North, of the London Branch of the Society of the True Gael. It is a grand volume of all things Gaelic, the first volume of which contained a written history, rules and an elementary coaching manual of the game of shinty. Much of its content is bogus. It does however give a fascinating insight into the way of life adopted by the urban Gael of the time. (See also Roger Hutchinson, Camanachd!, pages 75ff.)

Historian John Prebble describes the Society of True Highlanders as a "brainstorm" of Alasdair Ranaldson MacDonell. 15th Chief of Glengarry (*The King's Jaunt*, 1988, page 112.)

The Shinnie Muster Roll:

This song is believed to have been sung by Mr J. Warren, at the British Coffee House, London. David MacDonald, the author of the song, was apparently an old-world Inverness worthy. From various passages in his book, he appears to have been recognised as the laureate of the Gaels in London about the 1830s. See also Transactions of the Gaelic Society of Inverness, Volume XXX, page 43.

The drawing accompanying the poem is something of a mystery. I am indebted to Gordon Gilchrist of Ayr for bringing it to my attention. He knows little of its provenance other than that it is a tinted lithograph by "Brydone & Sons, Edinburgh", from the middle of the nineteenth century. It is one of a series of Scottish clans, this one being Drummond. Artistically, it is much removed from the quality of Mclan's portrait of Grant of Glenmoristion.

Hugh Cheape, Assistant Keeper, National Museums Scotland, describes the imagery as "very odd", with its putative tartan or perceived Highland outfit placing the subject in a context which further illustrates a Highland way of life.

O Muster My lads:

This song was also composed by David MacDonald and also allegedly sung on June 22, 1836, by Mr J. Warren on Blackheath, London. David MacDonald was pursuing his earlier calling as a baker in the great city at the time. The words are set to the Gaelic air "*ag iomain na gamhnna*." See also Transactions of the Gaelic Society of Inverness, Volume XXX, pages 39-41.

The unique silver medal known as the Thistle Club Shinnie medal is thought to have been manufactured around 1840. It surfaced at a sale organised by Christies in Edinburgh in November, 1993, but a joint bid by the Camanachd Association and Highland Regional Council to secure the medal failed. It was bought by a "mystery north collector", according to press reports.

Its history is shrouded in secrecy. It first came to the notice of shinty followers at the Camanachd Isle cup match on Islay a few years ago, when the gentleman who owned the medal, a Mr MacDonald of Glasgow, with Islay connections, showed it to Donald Woodrow of Kintyre Camanachd.

After some discussion with the Camanachd Association, the medal returned to Mr MacDonald's possession, not to be heard of again until it appeared in a catalogue of silver being sold by Christies. The best guess as to the medal's history is, according to Jack Richmond of Newtonmore, the Association's guru in these matters, that it was made as a President's match from the Highland Exiles' Office in London, and that it was presented at a game, of the kind played at Blackheath, London in the 1840's or thereabouts.

Such "one-off" medals were often not hall-marked, according to silver experts at the Royal Museums of Scotland. Its style suggests that it was moulded, rather than hand-crafted.

The medal, which Jack Richmond describes as "quite special", is just one of the fascinating links with the past which surfaced in 1993, the centenary year of the Camanachd Association.

The game of the peasantry:

"Matches are sometimes made between different town lands or parishes; sometimes barony is matched against barony, and not infrequently county against county, when the 'crack men' from the most distant parts are selected, and the interest excited is proportionately great."

"About half-a-century ago" (i.e., in the 18th century)" there was a great match played in the Phoenix Park, Dublin, between the Munster men and the men of Leinster. It was got up by the Lord-Lieutenant and other sporting noblemen, and was attended by all the nobility and gentry belonging to the Vice-regal Court,

FIOSRACHADH: NOTES

and by the beauty and fashion of the Irish capital and its environs. The victory was long contended for with varying success, till at length it was decided in favour of the Munster men by one of their number running with the ball on the point of his hurley and striking it through the open windows of the Vice-regal carriage, and thus baffling the vigilance of the Leinster goals-men and driving it in triumph through the goal. This man is still living; his name is Mat Healy, and he has been many years a resident in London. Between twenty-five and thirty years ago there were many good matches played on Kennington Common between the men of St Giles and those of the eastern part of the metropolis; the affair being got up by the then notorious Lord Barrymore and other noblemen who led the sporting circles of the time."

Sheas mi car tamull:

Little is known about this poem which is quoted in Alexander MacDonald's famous paper "Shinty : Historical and Traditional", delivered to the Gaelic Society of Inverness on December 18, 1919. The song is reproduced in Volume XXX of the Society's Transactions, pages 35-36 where it is stated that it is "the composition of a noted bard of Cowal, Argyleshire, of the name of Crawford."

Cowal was, of course, to be a name revered in shinty circles towards the end of the nineteenth century, when the game became an organised sport, and the club of that name swept virtually all before them.

To the annoyance of passengers:

I am indebted to Murdo MacDonald, Argyll and Bute District Council Archivist, Lochgilphead, for bringing this reference to my attention. This was not the first, or indeed last, time shinty was proscribed in Argyll. And nor was the proscription confined to Argyll. Shinty was often the target of official edicts, particularly in relation to play on Sundays.

The health of the sons of the north:

While the Edinburgh Camanachd Club may have claimed for a long time that they were the oldest shinty club, this reference to play in Aberdeen seems to indicate that the North of Spey Club was in fact the oldest. It is the earliest known reference to play on an organised basis and entitles North of Spey to the appellation "earliest formed club".

Hot and furious:

John Francis Campbell's overview of the game of shinty sets the game in an interesting light, when compared to the references contained in many of the tales he gathered in his collections. Most notable of these is *Popular Tales of the West Highlands* (Four Volumes, 1860-62); *Leabhar na Feinne* (1872) and *More West Highland Tales* (Two Volumes) which was published posthumously in 1940 and 1960. Much of the work collected is to be found in the National Library of Scotland and the Dewar Manuscripts at Inveraray.

Campbell is best remembered for his prodigious efforts gathering folk-lore. He has been described by Dereck Thomson in his useful *Companion to Gaelic Scotland* as an "aristocrat, courtier, lawyer, public servant and man of many talents."

FIOSRACHADH: NOTES

Enduring contributions:

For futher reading on this and related matters, see M. A. Macleod, *Red River's Festive Season*, Winnipeg, 1962; Connor, *Glengarry School Days*, 272-73; G. Redmond, *The Sporting Scots of Nineteenth Century Canada*, Toronto, 1982, 248, 266; Fischer, Albion's Seed, 739; R. Hutchinson, *Camanachd! The Story of Shinty*, Edinburgh, 1989, 92-100.

A'Chaluinn - New Year in the Highlands:

By "Finlay the Piper" from Dr Norman Macleod's Reminiscences of a Highland Parish. The unbiquitous "Finlay the Piper (Fionnlagh Piobair) was a regular vistor to the columns of the magazine An Gàidheall, where he was frequently used as the mouth-piece for old Highland tales.

Half excitement, half understood:

I am indebted to Miss Marion Campbell of Knapdale in Argyll for permission top re-produce her personal reminiscences. Her Argyll. *The Enduring Heartland* (First published 1977) remains one of the best and must readable accounts of the history of one of Scotland's most beautiful areas. Miss Campbell is the author of *The Dark Twin* and several historical studies for children.

Ball Ghlinntruim:

This song was ritten by Donald Campbell, Kingussie, son of Dòmhnall Phàil nan Oran (who was born 1830-?) the Rannoch shepherd (born at Gynack), who was quite well known in Badenoch. Donald was captain of Kingussie club at the time of their epic clashes with Cowal in the 1880's. He moved to Kingussie and began a business there after some years as a shepherd. He was "successful in this and devoted time to public work. His enthusiasm for shinty was great." (Transactions of the Gaelic Society of Inverness (TGSI), XLVIII, page 53). This macaronic appears in "Verse, story, fragments" of TGSI, Vol XLVI, page 243. It dates from about 1870 and was a great favourite for many years. Donald died in 1923, aged 89.

Lag nan cruachan:

Captain Angus Lamont was born in Lagnacruach, Cornaigmore, Tiree about the year 1844. He was the son of John Lamont, farmer, cattle dealer and merchant there. Being a lad o'pairts he entered Glasgow University as a medical student. The lure of the sea, however, was too much for him, and he soon deserted the healing profession for the romantic calling of the mariner. Having served his apprenticeship with the famous Hall Line, he rapidly rose top the position of Master. He was only about forty-one years of age at the time of his death which took place on board his ship at San Fransisco. There he was buried with masonic orders in the Ancient Order's burial ground.

He was the author of a number of songs. Unfortunately the only one we have been able to procure is the well-known "Lagnacruachan". Another song of his, was composed when the Oban and Callender Railway, as yet, only reached Dalmally, and while the author was awaiting at this place a conveyance to take him to Oban on his way to Tiree.

FIOSRACHADH: NOTES

The chorus is:
"Ho cha cheil mi, he cha cheil mi,
Ho cha cheil mi gur tu's fheàrr leam;
Cha cheil mi air sluagh an t-saoghail
Gu'n d'thug mi mo ghaol thar chàich dhut."

"Lagnacruachan" was well-known and sung during the author's lifetime. It was first circulated in semi-permanent form, hand-written and with four-part harmony, among the members of St Columba Gaelic Choir, when that choir was still in its infancy. Some of the verses are almost identical with those of another song published in Volume II of the Maclean Bards under the reputed authorship of James Maclean. Which bard was guilty of the evident plagiarism, we leave the public to judge.

Captain Lamont was, by the by, married to a sister of the famous captain Donald MacKinnon of the China Tea Clipper, "Taeping". Both Captains died in the prime of life. (Note accompanying the orginal)

Moladh a'bhàird:

"In Gairloch, on New Year's Day, a game of shinty used to be played on the Big Sand. The sides were picked from north and south of the loch. Tha ball was a large round mass of hard wood, a' chnac, rather murderous if it hit anybody, and so, called in the poem Muireardach maide, condemned to be tossed by clubs till it reached the Bràighe. Now whether Bràighe was the local designation of the goal of the game, or whether the poet in exaggeration meant Bràighe Thorasdail or Bràighe Mhiall as the final journey's end of a mighty stràc, I am not very sure. Feachd nan Tràghad means the army that turned up for the shinty match on new Year's Day on the Gainmheach Mhòr, actually on the tràigh." - A.M.

This poem also appeared in *The Highlander*, March 5, 1880. William Ross (Uilleam Ros) (21762-?91) is justly regarded as the leading Gaelic poet of love in the eighteenth century. For further reading, see Dereck S. Thomson, *The Companion to Gaelic Scotland*, pages 252-253.

Camanachd Ghlaschu:

For further reading on Màiri Mhòr nan Oran, see Donald Meek's "*Mairi Mhòr nan Oran*" which is essential reading for anyone wanting to know more about Highland history in the late nineteenth century and Martin MacDonald's excellent history of *Skye Camanachd - "A Century remembered"*.

The translation of "Camanachd Ghlaschu" is by Derick Thomson, himself a noted poet and former Professor of Celtic Studies in Glasgow University. The letter and translation first appeared first in the Shinty Yearbook, 1972-73, pages 11-12.

This song itself first appeared in the *Highlander* on January 29, 1876. The game it refers to was played on New Year's Day 1876 in Queen's Park Glasgow. It was the first game played by the Shinty Club which had been formed by the Highland Society. Mary MacPherson (Màiri Mhòr nan Oran), the famous Gaelic poetess, was one of the ladies who helped prepare the players' meals. See also the collection of her songs, *Dàin is Orain*, pages 184 -186.

A' Churachd Ruadh:

These verses appeared in the *Inverness Courier* in March, 1888 when Glenurquhart beat Strathglass 1-0 and in 1887 the same team won by the same score.

FIOSRACHADH: NOTES

(See also songs in Transactions of the Gaelic Society of Inverness, Volume XLV, page 384, and Volume XLVIII, page 342.) It was said by some after the 1888 game that Glenurquhart won because they had 24 men in the field against the 22 of Strathglass. There were complaints that Strathglass included in their team players from outwith the district. The verse were composed by one who gave his name as "PROPH".

(Transactions, Volume L, pages 428-429.)

That sense of Highland identity:

John Murdoch (1818-1903) Born in Ardclach, Nairn; brought up on Islay. Inland Revenue officer serving in Dublin, where he was involved in nationalist politics. Retired to Inverness and founded *The Highlander* newspaper (1873-81) to promote the crofters' cause during the Land Agitation. Tireless anti-landlord campaigner of major political significance and great supporter of camanachd through the columns of his newspaper. His diaries are held in the Mitchell Library, Glasgow.

For further reading see James Hunter, *For the people's cause*, Edinburgh, 1986 and I. MacPhail, *The Crofters' War*, Stornoway, 1989.

Ye never hear o' knotty noo:

The game of knotty was revived in the north of Scotland in 1992. What is believed to be the first formal set of rules was also discovered in the leaves of a Gaelic Bible.

It is believed they were promulgated by Rev. Finlay Cook and the elders of the church in Lochcarron. The stated objects were to channel the energies of young men into a healthy and competitive activity and away from habits such as frequenting ale-houses, over-indulgence in strong liquor, the poaching of deer and salmon, the playing of the pipes, and the dangers of dancing to the fiddle with the young women in the barn or on the green.

The rules were as follows:

Teams will be of seven or eleven players on either side and will consist of a goal-keeper and six or ten outplayers. The object of the game being to score more goals than their opponents. The cork must be played or hit only by the camachd (stick) by the outfield players, but the goal-keepers may use any part of their anatomy to stop the cork. Should an outfield player kick or handle the cork a foul will be given against him, which will give the opposing team a forward shot from the point at which the offence occured. In the event of a player hitting the cork over the side or back line, his opponent will take a forward shot from the point at which the cork crossed the line.

The goal posts will be four feet long and set four yards apart. The game will last as long as the teams agree, but for not more than six hours. The referee will be in complete control. He will have the powers to expel any player whose conduct he considers to be contrary to good sportsmanship or against the rules of the game. He must not be related to any member of the teams, and he must be a communicating member of the church.

I am indebted to Mr Robert I. Mowat of Lybster, Caithness for his help with the above notes.

FIOSRACHADH: NOTES

A Highlander looks back:

Angus Macpherson was a remarkable man who died in 1986, just a little over a year short of his hundredth birthday. For further reading, see Jack Richmond's obituary in the 1976-77 Shinty Yearbook, pages 42-43.

Is binne glòir:

I am indebted to Brendan Harvey for his help in tracing the source of this verse. It is frequently quoted in relation to the antiquity of shinty and hurling, eg in Alexander MacDonald's article on Shinty in the Transactions of the Gaelic Society of Inverness (TGSI, Vol XXX, page 31), an article in *The Highland Home Journal*, in Ninian MacDonald's *Shinty* (page 69) and in another article on shinty by Alexander Nicolson in *An Gàidheal*, April 1963, page 47.

Kingussie v Cowal, April 3, 1893:

The above song was sent to the *Oban Times* by a reader in response to a request from another reader who had written to the paper earlier that year, asking for the words. He pointed out that the song was well known 1893, but he had been unable to obtain a copy of the words.

Kingussie 2 Cowal 0: First Camanachd Cup Final:

The news of Kingussie's victory was received with much satisfaction in Kingussie and district, and the players were accorded an ovation on their return, pipers playing lively airs, and others carrying lighted torches, assembling at the station, and marching through the town, while bonfires were lighted above the burgh and two on the farm of Dunachton.

Needlefield, where the match was played in Inverness, was a piece of ground situated between Longman Road and Cromwell's Fort. Subsequent finals were played at Haugh Park and most often, up until the present day, at the Bught Park.

Cape Breton Reprise:

This ditty (with due apologies to the National Bard), was composed by one Anonymous Middleton, one of the stars of Canada '91, the epic journey undertaken by some of Kingussie's and Skye's finest? young? men (and women). Miss Middleton carried her flute with distinction for the whole fortnight and celebrated her birthday on tour.

Donald Campbell, The Drover:

Donald Campbell was born in 1863, the eldest of the eight children of a local fisherman, and lived in Gordon Cottage at the mouth of Leacann Water on the shore of Loch Fyne. He was about five feet and eight inches tall and of strong physique.

Most of the men in the village were employed in the stone quarry or fishing, and shinty was their great obsession. The Excelsiors were forerunners of the famous Furnace team which won the Camanachd Cup in 1923 without conceding a goal - a record which still stands.

FIOSRACHADH: NOTES

After his marriage in 1897, and a few years spent in Greenock, The Drover and his family took up residence in Plane Tree Cottage, St Catherine's on the east shore of the loch. He died in 1936 and is buried in Crarae Cemetery.

I am indebted to Gordon Gilchrist of Ayr for information about Donald the Drover. He was Gordon's grandfather.

The Kilt shall be indispensible:

The Edinburgh Camanachd Club long maintained its claim to be "the oldest organised shinty club in existence". The North of Spey Club, Aberdeen, may well have had a superior claim to that grand title however.

Tiugain a dh'iomain:

This version of the song was recorded by John Lorne Campbell from John MacKinnon, Mac Talla and Neil D. MacKinnon at Lake Ainlsie, Cape Breton, in 1937. The words were transcribed by Dr Calum MacLean.

A similar version is to be found in *Tales until Dawn* by John Shaw, page 390. Other Scottish variants are found in R.C. MacLagan's *Games of Argyleshire*, 1901, pages 31-35.

MacLagan refers to the song being used as part of a "peculiar and interesting ceremony before the commencement of the game, partaking of the character of an invitation to join in it, but used apparently as a sort of incantation".

According to Islay custom, the song was "said in dialogue before comencing play". MacLagan details two Islay versons of the song; one from Lochaweside and another from Kilninver.

The crooked ash:

While today ash still reigns as the raw material par excellence, despite the arrival of many competitors, oak, sally, hazel and furze were also used across the Irish sea. Saplings with a crook at the base were cut and shaped roughly with an axe or saw and later planed with glass, a knife or proper plane. The oak's advantage in strength was off-set by its weight while the lightness of the sally was a handicap in driving the ball a distance. Furze was generally used by young boys who could lay their hands on nothing better.

When landlords patronised inter-district hurling challenges they saw to it that their proteges had a good supply of ash. However, when landlord-tenant relationships were hostile in the nineteenth century, the ash had often to be taken by stealth from the unconsenting owner. A windy night was considered the most suitable so that the noise of the "crosscut" or axe would not be heard. Michael "Brud" White, a former Scariff and Clare hurler, who went to live in the USA, composed the poem, which the author first encountered in the Scariff Club history, on a trip to County Clare with the Skye Camanachd and Kingussie Camanachd clubs in the early 1990s.

FIOSRACHADH: NOTES

The Furnace Shinty Song:

J. Kaid MacLean, was himself a noted caman wielder for his island and a versatile entertainer in Glasgow and Highland circles, as well as one of the main proponents of links with Ireland and the international matches. Indeed he officiated at one of these games at Croke Park, Dublin on August 2, 1924, "picturesquely attired in the Highland tartan"

This song was written on the occasion of Furnace completing their record-breaking Camanachd Cup win in 1923, when they won the competition without conceeding a goal. They defeated Newtonmore in the Final. Their feat, which has never been matched, earned them a place in the Guiness Book of Records.

The New York Highlanders:

Angus MacPherson was the author of A Highlander Looks Back. (see above)

Scarcely suited to petticoats:

Although there is a reference here to the "return International match", it is not referred to in following issues of the Pictorial. Coverage of the sport in the Pictorial was uneven and irregular. Several pictures and drawings appeared over the years, but golf was the main sport covered, along with athletics, field sports, yachting and cycling.

An appropriate occupation for fallen angels:

I am indebted to Jack Richmond, Newtonmore for bringing the Blue Men to my attention. The Badenoch Record is one of the most valuable stores of historical information regarding the survival and development of shinty, particularly in the Badenoch area.

The Shinty Referee:

The February 1932 of the Camanachd Association's Council meeting heard of the death of the redoubtable Mr John Kaid MacLean, Glasgow. There was a special meeting held in Glasgow in April of the following year between representatives of the Irish National Association and the Southern Shinty League. Its purpose was to make arrangements for a fixture between an Irish hurling team and the Southern Shinty League select. An advertisement gave the details. There was an appeal: "that the Irish people in Glasgow will give them the support it would receive in Ireland by turning out in large numbers to give the Irish team a hearty welcome and show that the exiles still hold dear the National games of Ireland."

The match was fixed for May 6, 1933 in Shieldhall Park, Hardgate Road, South Govan between a picked hurling team from the constituent University colleges of Dublin, Cork and Galway and a selection from all the clubs in the Glasgow Southern Shinty League who were all of Highland birth and descent. The Irish Provisional selection was J. Flanagan (Galway), J. Hogan (Dublin), G. Gleeson (Cork), T. McCarthy (Dublin), C. Jennings (Galway), J. Lanagan (Galway), M. Cronin (Galway), J. Canning (Dublin), C. McGrath (Cork), M. O'Flaherty (Galway).

The Irish team won by the only goal of the game but: "the result was of secondary importance to the fact that this essentially Gaelic game was shown to have a large following in the West of Scotland and the possibilities for its development are attractive..."

FIOSRACHADH: NOTES

The following October Council meeting heard that report from Ex-Provost Skinner on the talks with the Irish. He remarked that Camanachd Association officials were all agreed that on no account would they agree to change their Rules which had taken forty years to perfect, and this decision he had conveyed to the Hurling representatives. At the same time the Camanachd delegates agreed that Rules on a basis of equality might be agreed on for an international match between the respective Associations.

The delegates then considered the Rules of Shinty and Hurling and agreed on a basis on which an international match might be played. These Rules were being put into 'more concrete form' by Mr Horgan, who acted as Chairman of the Conference and were sent to the Camanachd Association Secretary. He in turn was instructed to send copies of them to clubs when they came to hand.

The Rules were to be considered at the meeting of the Camanachd to be held in Glasgow in February when it was expected an invitation to play an international match in Ireland at Easter would be to hand. Ex-Provost Skinner said that it was made perfectly clear that on no account would the Camanachd Association play a match on a Sunday.

The international match was again debated at the February meeting and it was agreed to play the game under the Rules agreed at Glasgow, but that it could not be played until such time as the Camanachd matches had been completed. Financial arrangements were also discussed. It was thought that the most reasonable arrangement was to pay expenses to the visiting team and then to entertain the visitors. Any surplus would be equally divided between the Associations. However, it was decided to refer the whole affair to the AGM in April.

When it was raised there, a letter recieved from Mr Horgan of the Irish Hurling Association was read to the meeting. It contained an offer to pay the expenses of a Camanachd team to play in Dublin on April 21 or 28. The minimum to be paid was £50 and the gate was to be divided after the hurlers' expenses had been paid.At this point, the proposals began to look distinctly less attractive. Mr Paterson, the Vice-President, informed the meeting that John MacLennan, Strathconon, Vice-President had made enquiries and the information he had received was that the Association was "anti-British''. Ex-Provost Skinner said that he had the opinion of "one in high authority'' who said "Have nothing to do with such a match''.

Major Colin MacRae of Feoirlinn also spoke and was of the opinion that the whole matter had a political flavour and advised the meeting to "keep clear". The whole matter was then dropped after a vote, on the motion of Mr W. Paterson, seconded by Ex-Provost Skinner.

"With no explanation as to how it had taken the Association 50 years to learn that the GAA (hurling's ruling body) had its origins in the struggle for Irish independence... and apparently with no questioning of the right or the motivation of 'people in high authority' to dictate policy to a small sporting body in the north of Scotland, the Camanachd Association slashed the twine and let the rope bridge fall." (Roger Hutchinson, *Camanachd*).

The Association was to find, however, that it was not that easy to extinguish the moves for closer ties between the two countries and a succession of clubs and Universities continued to ply the Irish sea. In the fifties, the spectre of internationals again raised its head and died a death; in 1964 the Association again pronounced itself to be firmly against any links; its members were asked not to patronise shinty/hurling internationals. It was to be a further ten years before the enlightened few eventually convinced their peers that internationals were a worthwhile pursuit and Scotland and Ireland finally met at Inverness on August 5, 1974.

(Extracted from *Shinty!*)

Bu chridheil ar duan:

I am indebted to John Shaw, Celtic Department , Aberdeen University, from Antigonish, Nova Scotia for this verse, which also appears in *Beyond the Hebrides*, pp 56-58 and *Mac-Talla*, XI, page 112.

FIOSRACHADH: NOTES

Air machair an Dùin:

Chan eil fhios cò sgriobh na rannan seo, a th'air an tarraing bho'n leabhar a dheasaich Fred MacAmhlaigh de bhàrdachd Dhòmhnaill Ruaidh Choruna ann an 1995. Ge bith cò rinn na rannan, bha e neo i eòlach air bàrdachd Mhairi Mhòr nan Oran. (Faic Camanachd Ghlaschu mar eiseimpleir.)

Chaidh an leabhar fhoillseachadh le Comann Eachdraidh Uidhist a Tuath. Mo thaing leotha le chèile son cead a bhàrdachd a chleachdadh an seo.

An Iomain an Eige:

I am grateful to the School of Scottish Studies, Edinburgh University for permission to reproduce this article. The recording of the conversation between Donald Archie MacDonald of the School of Scottish Studies and Hugh MacKinnon (Cleadale), Eigg, is to be found in the School Archives : SA 1965/126/7-127/1. For more on Hugh MacKinnon, see *Tocher* 10.

Toss thine antlers, Caberfeidh:

The 1934 Camanachd Cup Final at Inveraray was an historic occasion for more than just the fact that it was Caberfeidh's first ever win. It was also Eric Ross Birkett's first Camanachd Cup Final as a boy. He has been composing poetry and contributing to the Shinty Yearbook faithfully since 1971 - albeit under the pen-name EROSCA.

Rabbie's trip:

Rabbie's companion on this epic journey, first published in the 1974-75 Shinty Yearbook, was anonymous - principally, it is understood, for fear of recriminations by the "polis" on various sensitive issues such as excessive loading of Old Meg, creating sacarcities of Stag's Breath at their various ports of call, overstepping the 300 mile maximum journey on a mare allowed by the Ministry of Transport etc.

Rab's companion was, however, a native of Tighnabruaich who gave outstanding and skilled service to the Kyles team over a long period - latterly as a goalkeeper after his epic journey on Meg had greatly hampered his mobility as an outfield player. The gentleman was at the time a staunch member of the Kyles committee and a Vice President of the Camanachd Association. Only Celly Paterson could have had such an epic collision with the national bard.

Home to the Kyles:

I am indebted to Mrs Mary Taylor of Tighnabruaich for providing me with a copy on one of shinty's most famous modern songs, written by one of the game's modern greats, Celly Paterson. I was fortunate enough to have been provided with a copy of the original - literally written on the back of an envelope!

The song has since been sung far and wide, and has been recorded by both the Clydesiders and Valerie Dunbar on albums.

FIOSRACHADH: NOTES - FACLAIR: GLOSSARY

(1)   Material specifically relating to Ireland has been included in the list in *italics*. I am indebted to Brendan Harvey, Belfast, for his assistance in this regard and also to Liam P. O Caithnia for his assistance and permission to quote from the invaluable glossary in his classic *Sceal na hlomana*, hereinafter *Sceal*. Entries which are <u>underlined</u> are all to be found in the glossary. References to authors and other sources should be cross-referenced to the main bibliography.

(2)   See O Maolfabhail, Caman, page 70.

(3)   Camanachd Association, Rules of Play: Rule 3. The Ball.

(4)   *Highland News*, June 16, 1928. I am indebted to Hugh Barron for bringing this reference to my attention.

(5)   Hugh Barron.

(6)   Camanachd Association, Rules of Play: Rule 4. Players' Equipment.

(7)   *Badenoch Record*, October, 10, 1937. I am indebted to Jack Richmond, Newtonmore, for this reference.

(8)   MacLagan, *Games of Argyleshire*, page 27.

(9)   D. Sage, *Memorabilia Domestica*, page 118.

(10)   O Maolfabhail, Caman, page 25.

(11)   MacLagan, *Games of Argyleshire*, page 29.

(12)   MacLagan, *Games of Argyleshire*, page 29.

(13)   Campbell, *Grampian's Desolate*, page 256.

(14)   MacLagan, *Games of Argyleshire*, page 29.

(15)   *Highlander*, May 19, 1877. The club Comunn Camanachd Fhinn had "mar fhear-taic" (as sponsor/supporter) Colonel Gardyne of Glenforsa. Hugh Barron drew this reference to my attention.

(16)   Minutes of the Camanachd Association, January 20, 1897. The word appears in relation to a protest considered by the Association, made by the Spean Bridge Shinty Club, against the Glengarry Club.

(17)   I am indebted to Jack Richmond for this reference.

(18)   Ninian MacDonald, *Shinty. A Short History*, page 59.

FIOSRACHADH: NOTES - FACLAIR: GLOSSARY

(19)   This is also referred to in a report in the *Inverness Courier*, January 3, 1844.

(20)   *Stornoway Gazette*, September 28, 1934. I am indebted to Malcolm MacDonald, Stornoway for bringing this reference to my attention.

(21)   O Maolfabhail, *Caman*, page 131.

(22)   See O Maolfabhail, *Caman*, pages 87-95 on the characteristics, shape and substance of the caman.

(23)   See for example Menke, *The New Encyclopedia of Sports*, pages 368-375 and Hutchinson, *Camanachd*, pages 92-100 for various aspects of the debate about ice hockey and its origins.

(24)   Alex. Morrison, "Shinty (Iomain)", *An Gàidheal*, 1963, page 45.

(25)   I am indebted to Mr Robert Mowatt, Lybster, Caithness for this information.

(26)   Ninian MacDonald, *Shinty. A Short History*, page 57.

(27)   Ibid.

(28)   Donald MacDonald, *Lewis. A History of the Island*, 1978, page 52.

(29)   I am indebted to Miss Lorna Pike of the Dictionary of the Older Scottish Tongue, Edinburgh University, for assistance with this entry.

(30)   I am indebted to Ronald Black, Celtic Dept., Edinburgh University, for assistance with this entry.

(31)   Campbell, *Grampian's Desolate*, page 125.

(32)   O Maolfabhail, *Caman*, pages 95-98.

(33)   I am indebted to Roger Hutchinson, Skye, for bringing this to my attention.

(34)   Strutt, Sports and Pastimes, page 97.

(35)   Martin MacDonald. *Skye Camanachd*, page 1.

(36)   The Yellow Bellies are discussed in some detail by O'Caithnia in Sceal na hIomana, pages 686-689.

Tuilleadh Leughaidh: Bibliography

"Cumaidh sinn suas an cluidh-iomain,
Cluidh is grinn' a tha fo'n ghrèin".

Chan eil a seo ach earrainn de na chaidh a sgriobhadh mu eachdraidh na Gàidhealtachd, agus na ceangalan le Astralia, Eireann is Canada. Sa chumantas, chaidh fada bharrachd a sgriobhadh ann an Eireann fhèin mar eiseimpleir mu eachdraidh na dùthcha sin, na chaidh a sgriobhadh an Alba.

Bheir an liosta seo dhuibh toiseach tòiseachaidh air eachdraidh na camanachd agus a'phàirt a th'aig sin ann an saoghal gu math nas fharsainge. Gu fortannach san latha th'ann, thathas a' cur ris fad na h-ùine.

The following represents an introductory list of reading on shinty, hurling and related matters - historical, literary and to some extent socio-economic. It is by no means an exhaustive list of everything written about both sporting codes and the links with Australia, Ireland and Canada. It is, however, thankfully a list which is being expanded on a regular basis, as a result of ongoing research and a more enlightened approach to the study of Scottish history in particular.

Abraham, J. W. and Wilton, M. J., (eds) "Report on the Evaluation of the Continuing Supply of Camans and Balls for Shinty". (*Highlands and Islands Development Board, Inverness, 1981*).

Adams, Ian, and Meredyth Somerville, *Cargoes of Despair and Hope. Scottish Emigration to North America, 1603-1803.* (Edinburgh, 1993).

Aithris is Oideas. Traditional Gaelic Rhymes And Games. (London, 1964).

Arlott, John, *Oxford Companion to Games and Sports*. (OUP, 1975).

Barron, Hugh. The First Hundred Years. *A short history of Inverness shinty club, 1887-1987*. (Inverness, 1987).

Barron, Hugh (ed) *The Third Statistical Account of Scotland. Vol XVI. The County of Inverness*. (Edinburgh, 1985).

Barron, Hugh and Campbell, J.W., *A History of Comunn Camanachd Strathghlais, Strathglass Shinty Club*. (Inverness, 1980).

Barron, Hugh, Campbell J.W., and MacLennan, H.D., *Lochcarron Camanachd 1883-1983*. (Inverness, 1983).

Blackie, J. S., *The language and literature of the Scottish Highlands*. (Edinburgh, 1876).

Bumstead, J. M., *The People's Clearance. Highland Emigration to North America, 170-1815*. (Edinburgh, 1982).

Caberfeidh Shinty Club, Centenary. 1886-1986. (Dingwall, 1986).

Cameron, A. D., *Go Listen to the Crofters*. (Stornoway, 1986).

Cameron, Iain, "The "terrible parochialism" that is stifling shinty - and what needs to be done". (*North 7, Highlands and Islands Development Board, Inverness, November/December, 1979*)

Campbell, John Francis, *Popular Tales of The West Highlands*. Four Volumes. (Edinburgh, 1861).

Campbell, J. L., *Collection of Highland Rites and Customs; copied by Edward Lhuyd.* (Folk-lore Society, 1975).

Campbell, J. L., *Songs Remembered in Exile.* (Aberdeen, 1990).

Campbell, Marion, *Argyll. The Enduring Heartland*. (Bath, 1977).

Cardell, Kerry, and Cumming, Cliff, "Scotland's three tongues in Australia : Colonial Hamilton in the 1860s and 1870s", *Scottish Studies*, 31, pages 40-62.

Carola, Leslie C., *The Irish. A Treasury of Art and Literature*. (1993)

Canny (O Caithnia), Liam, "The Irish game of Hurling", (*Folklife: A Journal of Ethnological Studies, Society of Folk Life Studies, 19, 1981*).

Cox, Allan, *A History of Sports in Canada*, 1860-1900 (nd).

Dagg, T. S. C., *Hockey in Ireland*, (The Kerryman, 1944).

Darwin, Bernard, *A History of Golf in Britain*. (London, 1952).

de Burca, Marcus, *The GAA. A History of the Gaelic Athletic Association.* (Dublin, 1980).

Devine, Tom M., *The Great Highland Famine*. (Edinburgh, 1988).

Devine, Tom M., *Clanship to Crofters' War*. (Manchester, 1994).

Devine, Tom M., and Mitchison, Rosalind, (eds), *People and Society in Scotland, I, 1760-1830*. (Edinburgh, 1988).

Devine, Tom M., *Improvement and Enlightenment*. (Edinburgh, 1989).

Devine, Tom M. (ed), *Irish Immigrants and Scottish Society in the Nineteenth and Twentieth Centuries*. (Edinburgh, 1991).

Devine, Tom M., (ed), *Scottish Emigration and Scottish Society*. (Edinburgh, 1992).

Devine, Tom D., *Scottish Elites*. (Edinburgh, 1994).

Devine, Tom M., *Exploring the Scottish Past.* (East Linton, 1995).

Dewar, John, *The Dewar Manuscripts*. (Glasgow, 1964).

Dunn, Charles W., *Highland Settler: A Portrait of the Scottish Gael in Nova Scotia.* (Toronto, 1953).

English, Dr Peter R., *Glen Urquhart. Its places, people, neighbours and its shinty in the last 100 years and more. (Aberdeen, 1985)*.

Finlay, Ian, *Columba.* (London, 1979).

Fittis, Robert, *Sports and pastimes of Scotland.* (Paisley, 1891).

Fullam, Brendan, *Giants of the Ash*. (Dublin, 1991).

Geddes, Olive, *A Swing through Time. Golf in Scotland, 1457-1743*. (Edinburgh, 1992).

Gray, Malcom, *The Highland Economy, 1750-1850*. (London, 1957).

Gray, Malcom, *The Fishing Industries of Scotland, 1790-1914*. (Oxford, 1978).

Henderson, Ian T., and Stirk, David, *Golf in the Making*. (London, 1979).

Hunter, James, *Scottish Highlanders. A People and their Places*. (Edinburgh and London, 1992).

Hunter, James, *A Dance Called America*. (Edinburgh, 1994).

Hunter, James and MacLean, Cailean, *Skye: The Island*. (Edinburgh, 1986).

Hutchinson, Roger, *Camanachd: The Story of Shinty*. (Edinburgh, 1989).

Hutchinson, Roger, *All the sweets of being. A Life of James Boswell*. (Edinburgh, 1995).

Jarvie, Grant and Walker, Graham, *Scottish Sport in the making of the Nation*. (Leicester, 1994).

Keltie, John S., (ed), *History of the Scottish Highlands, Highland Clans and Highland Regiments*. Two Volumes. (Edinburgh, 1879).

Kissane, Noel, *Treasures from the National Library of Ireland*. (Dublin, 1994).

Lang, Andrew, *History of Golf*. (London, 1890).

Lang, Andrew, *A Batch of Golfing Papers*. (London, 1892).

Lang, Andrew, *The Poetry of Sport*. (London, 1896).
Littlejohn Album. (1905). (Held in Aberdeen University Library).

Lovat Shinty Club. Centenary 1888-1988. (Inverness, 1988).

Lucas, A. T., "Hair Hurling Balls", *Journal of the Cork Historical and Archaelogical Society*, 57, (1952).

Lucas, A. T. "Two Recent Finds : Hair Hurling Balls from Co. Limerick". *Journal of the Cork Historical and Archeological Society 59, (1954).*

Lucas, A. T., "Hair Hurling Balls from Limerick and Tipperaray". *Journal of the Cork Historical and Archaeological Society*, 76, (1971).

Lucas, A. T., "Hair Hurling Ball from Knockmore, Co. Clare". *Journal of the Cork Historical and Arcaeological Society*, 77, (1972).

MacDonagh, Oliver, and Mandle, W.F., *Ireland and Irish Australia: Studies in Cultural and Political History*. (Kent, 1986).

MacDonald, Alexander, *Shinty, Historical and Traditional*. TGSI , XXX, pages 27-56. (Inverness, 1932).

MacDonald, David, *The Mountain Heath*. (London, 1838).

MacDonald, Donald, *Lewis: A History of the Island*. (Edinburgh, 1978).

MacDonald, J.A., *The Burgh of Kingussie*. (Kingussie, 1966).

MacDonald, Rev. J. Ninian, OSB, *Shinty. A Short History of The Ancient Highland Game*. (Inverness, 1932).

MacDonald, Martin, *Skye Camanachd. A Century Remembered*. (Portree, Skye, 1992).

MacDonald, William, *The Glencoe Collection of Bagpipe Music. Book 1*. (Inverness, 1993).

MacDonnell, J. A., *Sketches of Glengarry in Canada*. (Montreal, 1893).

MacFarland, Elaine W., *Ireland and Scotland in the Age of Revolution*. (Edinburgh, 1994).

MacIntyre-North, C. N., *Leabhar Comunn nam Fior Ghael*. (London, 1881).

Mackay, Donald, Scotland Farewell: *The People of the Hector*. (Toronto, 1980).

MacKay, Donald, *Flight From Famine*. (Toronto, 1992).

MacKay, W., *Urquhart and Glenmoriston*. (Inverness, 1914).

MacKay W., *Sidelights on Highland History*. (Inverness, 1925).

Mackinnon, Roddy, *Beauly Camanachd Centenary*. (Inverness, 1992).

MacLagan, Robert Craig, *The Games and Diversions of Argyleshire*. (London, 1901).

MacLean, Calum, *The Highlands*. (Edinburgh, 1990).

MacLean, Malcolm and Carrell, C., *As an Fhearann: From the Land*. (Edinburgh, Glasgow, Stornoway, 1986).

MacLean, Marianne, *The People of Glengarry*: Highlanders in Transition, 1745-1820. (Montreal, 1991).

MacLennan, A. B., "A Spectre Arbiter: A New Year Shinty Story", in *Celtic Review*, Vol 1, 1893, pp 62-63.

MacLennan, Hugh D., *Shinty! Celebrating Scotland's game*. (Inverness, 1993).

MacLennan, Hugh D., *An Gearasdan: Fort William Shinty Club's first hundred years*. (Inverness, 1994).

MacLennan, Hugh D., *Not an Orchid*. (Inverness, 1995).

Maclugan, P. D., (Carbery), *Hurling. Ireland's National Game*. (Tralee, 1940).

MacPherson, Angus, *A Highlander looks back*. (Oban, no date).

MacPherson, Margaret, *The Shinty Boys*. (London, 1963).

Mandle, W. F., "The GAA and Popular Culture, 1884-1894", in MacDonagh O., W. Mandle, P.Travers, (eds), *Irish Culture and Nationalism*. (London, 1983).

Mandle, W. F., "The IRB and the beginnings of the GAA", in *Irish Historical Studies*, 20, (1977).

Mandle, W. F., *The Gaelic Athletic Association & Irish Nationalist Politics*, 1884-1924. (London, Dublin, 1987).

McKenzie, Lorraine, *Voyage & Mutiny of the "Georgina"*, 1852. (Geelong, 1994).

Meek, Donald, *Mairi Mhòr nan Oran*. (Glasgow, 1977).

Metcalfe, Allan, *Canada Learns to Play. The Emergence of Organised Sport , 1807-1914*. (Toronto, 1987).

Mokyr, J., *Why Ireland Starved : A Quantative and Analytical History of the Irish Economy*, 1800-1850. (London, 1983)

Morrison, A. "Uist Games", in *Celtic Review*, Vol IV, 1908, pages 361 - 371.

Nicolson, Alex, *History of Skye* .(Glasgow, 1930; revised and enlarged, Portree, 1994).

O Caithnia, Liam P., *Sceal na hlomana*. (Dundalgan Press, 1980).

O'Grada, C., *The Great Irish Famine*. (Basingstoke, 1989).

O'Kelleher, A., and Schoepperle, G., *Betha Colaim Chille. Life of Columcille*. (Illinois, 1918).

O Maolfabhail, Art, Caman: *2,000 Years of Hurling in Ireland*. (Dundalk, 1973).

O'Riain, Seamas, *Maurice Davin* (1842-1927). *First President of the GAA*. (Dublin, 1995).

O'Sullivan, T. F., *Story of the G.A.A.* (Dublin, 1916).

O'Tuathaigh, G., *Ireland before the Famine*. (Dublin, 1972).

Poirteir, Cathal, *The Great Irish Famine*. (Dublin, 1995).

Prebble, John, *The Lion in the North*. (London, 1971).

Prebble, John, *The King's Jaunt. George IV in Scotland, 1822*. (London, 1988).

Prentis, Malcolm D., *The Scots in Australia: A Study of New South Wales, Victoria and Queensland, 1788-1900*. (Sydney, 1983).

Redmond, Gerald, *The Caledonian games in northern America*. (Rutherford, 1971).

Redmond, Gerald, *The Sporting Scots of Nineteenth Century Canada*. (Toronto, 1982).

Richards, Eric, *The Leviathan of Wealth*. (London, 1973).

Richards, Eric, *A History of the Highland Clearances*. Two Volumes. (London, 1982, 1985).

Richards E., and Clough, M., *Cromartie: A Highland Life, 1650-1914*. (Aberdeen, 1989).

Richmond, Jack, (ed), *Shinty Forum Report*. (The Camanachd Association, 1974).

Richmond, Jack, (ed), *Future of Shinty Report* . (The Camanachd Association, 1981).

Robertson, John, *Kingussie and the Caman*. (Inverness, 1994).

Ross, A., *The Pagan Celts*. (London, 1986).

Ross, R. J., and Hendry, J., (eds) *Sorley MacLean : Critical Essays*. (Edinburgh, 1986).

Sage, Donald, *Memorabilia Domestica: Or Parish Life in the North of Scotland*. (Second edition, Wick, 1899).

Shairp, J. C., *Glen Dessary and other Poems*. (London, 1888).

Sheehy-skeffington, F. *Michael Davitt*. (London, 1908).

"Shinty in Eigg", (Transcript of a conversation with Hugh MacKinnon) *Tocher*, 36-37, (School of Scottish Studies, Edinburgh, 1982).

Shinty Yearbook Annually since 1971, various editors.

Sinton, Rev. Thomas, *The Poetry of Badenoch*. (Inverness, 1906).

Sinton, Rev. Thomas, *By Loch and River*. (Inverness, 1910).

Skene, W. F., *The History of Scotland*. (London, 1837).

Skene, W. F., *Celtic Scotland*. (Edinburgh, 1880).

Skene, W. F., *The Highlanders of Scotland*. Two Volumes. (London, 1887).

Snell, D. K. M., (ed) *Letters from Ireland during the famine of 1847 - Alexander Sommerville*. (Dublin, 1994).

Somers, Robert, *Letters from the Highlands on the Famine of 1846*. (Inverness, 1877).

Speedy, T., *Sport in the Highlands and Lowlands of Scotland*. (Edinburgh, 1886).

Stewart, Culin, *Games of the North American Indians*. Two Volumes. (Washington, 1907).

Strutt, Joseph, *Sports and Pastimes of the People of England*. (London, 1801 and 1830).

The Land of Exiles. Scots in Australia: (Edinburgh HMSO, 1988).

The Highlands Committee (Empire Exhibition), *The Highlands and The Highlanders*. (Glasgow, 1938).

Thomson, Derick, *An Introduction to Gaelic Poetry*. (London, 1974).

Thomson, Derick, (ed), *The Companion to Gaelic Scotland*. (Oxford, 1983).

Walsh, Maurice, *And No Quarter*. (Chambers, 1980 edition).

West, Trevor, *The Bold Collegians. The development of sport in Trinity College, Dublin*. (Dublin, 1991).

Wilson, Brian, *Celtic. A Century with Honour*. (London, 1988).

Wood, Ian S., (ed), *Scotland and Ulster*. (Edinburgh, 1994).

Woodham-Smith, C., *The Great Hunger*: Ireland, 1845-9. (London, 1962).

"We shall keep up the shinty play, the finest game under the sun".